"This Is America"

Critical Perspectives on Music and Society

Series Editor: David Arditi, University of Texas at Arlington

This book series produces books that present a critical perspective on popular music and the music industry. Two dominant strains of thought exist for the study of popular music. First, many texts in the popular culture tradition celebrate the artists, fans, and cultures that arise from popular music. Second, Music Industry Studies texts give students a "how-to" perspective on making it in the music industry. In both cases, texts rarely address the way that the music industry produces and reproduces power. The purpose of this book series is to provide a platform for authors who explore the social production of music; as such it is broadly interdisciplinary.

The series invites submissions by scholars from the fields of cultural studies, American studies, history, sociology, literature, communication, media studies, music, women's studies, ethnic studies, popular culture, music industry studies, political science, economics, and history.

Specific topics addressed:

- Musicians as Labor
- Identity (Sex, Gender, Race, Ethnicity, Disability, and Sexuality)
- Critical Representations
- Music Industry Studies
- Music in the Global South
- Production of Genres
- New/Old Technologies
- Sound Studies
- Access Inequalities to Music Production and Consumption
- Spaces of Music Production, Creation, and Consumption

iTake-Over: The Recording Industry in the Streaming Era, Second Edition by David Arditi

Cruisicology: The Music Culture of Cruise Ships by David Cashman and Philip Hayward

"This Is America": Race, Gender, and Politics in America's Musical Landscape by Katie Rios

"This Is America"

Race, Gender, and Politics in America's Musical Landscape

Katie Rios

LEXINGTON BOOKS
Lanham • Boulder • New York • London

Published by Lexington Books
An imprint of The Rowman & Littlefield Publishing Group, Inc.
4501 Forbes Boulevard, Suite 200, Lanham, Maryland 20706
www.rowman.com

6 Tinworth Street, London SE11 5AL, United Kingdom

Copyright © 2021 Katie Rios

All rights reserved. No part of this book may be reproduced in any form or by any electronic or mechanical means, including information storage and retrieval systems, without written permission from the publisher, except by a reviewer who may quote passages in a review.

British Library Cataloguing in Publication Information Available

Library of Congress Cataloging-in-Publication Data Available

ISBN 978-1-7936-1916-7 (cloth)
ISBN 978-1-7936-1918-1 (pbk)
ISBN 978-1-7936-1917-4 (electronic)

To Erik, Trinley, and Tucker

Contents

Acknowledgments ix

Introduction 1

1 "We're Drowning in Our Own Stories": Laurie Anderson's Call to Artists and Her Performance Art as a Commentary on Current American Democracy 15

2 "At the Intersection of Racism and Sexism": The Encoded Resistance and Social Activism of Beyoncé, Rhiannon Giddens, and Janelle Monáe 45

3 "We the People?" Hip-Hop as Resistance in the Trump Era 81

4 "Look Around," "History Is Happening": Heterogenous Topics in Lin-Manuel Miranda's *Hamilton* 123

Conclusion 153

Bibliography 155

Index 173

About the Author 183

Acknowledgments

Writing a book is a difficult activity under any set of circumstances but pales in comparison to completing a book in the midst of a global pandemic. At the same time I am fortunate to be employed and to be able to work from home on a topic that has called to me. I am indebted to many people who have supported and inspired me and who continue to support and inspire me throughout this period.

Thank you, essential workers. If I knew all of your names I would list the names here. Thank you for bringing groceries, for delivering mail, for delivering food, and for doing everything you can to help keep us safe in a pandemic in the turbulent year of 2020. Thank you to the Instacart shopper Annie who left our groceries a with personal card and handwritten note, adorned with gold around the edges and bright yellow lemons on the front, a card that was so cheerful and so needed at the time it arrived that it stayed on the refrigerator. Thank you as well to doctors, nurses, and first responders.

I am grateful for the artists and agents who granted me copyright permission to feature their brilliant material in this book. Thank you to Touba Alipour, Joel Tretin, Laurie Anderson, and Jason Stern. I had wonderful conversations with Touba and Joel over the phone when I first reached out for copyright permission, and they willingly and thoughtfully answered questions that I had about their works. They have regularly kept in touch to check in about my progress with the book and to ask how everything is going for me. Jason Stern and Laurie Anderson replied quickly and helpfully to my copyright request. Knowing such people who are willing to engage in these ways is energizing and motivating. I am honored that all of these artists let me share their work, beginning right on the book's cover with Touba's provocative neon design.

Thank you to my friends who are especially active on social media and who have posted meaningful readings, videos, and blogs that have helped me as I reckon with difficult material. There are too many such friends to name individually here, but a few stand out. For example, I thank Andrew Dell'Antonio for sharing a thoughtful Facebook post that included a strategy for talking to people who might not agree with #BlackLivesMatter.[1] I send the same thanks to Mark Katz, who in a post on May 27, 2020, articulated the importance of asking "How can I be a better person?" instead of defensively stating that "I am not a racist."[2] Felicia Miyakawa has supported and inspired me since our days together in graduate school at Indiana University, and she is tireless in her effort to spread voter awareness. Thank you, Felicia. Kennedi Johnson not only regularly and vulnerably shares relevant and useful information about her experiences as a Black woman but also created a blog to document it.[3] Thank you, Kennedi.

I owe my friends and colleagues heartfelt thanks for reading drafts of my material, for talking about it with me whether in person, on the phone, over email, via Zoom meetings, by text, or by sharing coffee and ideas at academic conferences. Those types of exchanges profoundly shaped this book. Thank you to Chris Schmitz, Liz Pridgen Killion, Kristen Strandberg, John McCluskey, Chris Schmitz, Kristen Strandberg, John McCluskey, Nathan Clevenger, Annie Stephens, and Samantha Murfree. Kristen Turner, Chris Schmitz, Kristen Strandberg, John McCluskey, and Nate Myrick pored over substantial portions of drafts and revisions of this book and offered their insights and observations, and I am utterly grateful for their help. Kristen Bailey and Naz Pantaloni answered several questions that I had about research and copyright, and I thank both of you for your expertise and for your help. I am grateful for the anonymous peer reviewers whose comments helped to sharpen the focus of my book. My friend and mentor Peter Burkholder spent much time with me to talk about the concept for this book and has been, as always, tremendously helpful and supportive. Thank you to Mercer University for being an outstanding institution that supports teaching, learning, and research, and thank you in particular to Dean David Keith in the Townsend School of Music for the extraordinary leadership that you have demonstrated, especially when it has been most needed after the global pandemic began in 2020.

In some of my undergraduate classes and graduate seminars at Mercer University, students read assigned portions of the book as I was writing it and often commented on the topicality of the chapters, at times speaking personally about how the sensitive issues affected their lives. I am grateful for their vulnerability to share these kinds of experiences, and I am also thankful for their keen insights and suggested edits. These students include Chelsea Cline, Allyson Cohen, Myles Gonzalez, Constantine Janello, Kunal Kumat, Sara Scanlon, Augusta Schubert, Beautiful Sherriff, Lichi Acosta, Luke Baker, Anna Black, Caleb Esmond, Noah Grant, Joycelyn Jackson, Collin LaHood, Madeline Londa, Peyton Magalhaes, Faith Parker, Luis Parra, Rachel

Pearson, Dylan Reckner, Emily Roher, Cameron Rolling, Reagan Sanders, Olivia Scott, Sarah Kate Sellars, Johnathan Alvarado, Samantha Friedman, Ben Gessner, Zach Golden, Lyman Hinson, Sarah Vermazen, and Dillon Watkins. I am grateful for lunches with Sophie Leveille and Victoria Yrizarry and for their enthusiasm, exchange of ideas, and support as I developed the content of this book.

My heartfelt thanks to the publishers and editors at Lexington Books who have been so supportive of this project since the first phone call when I pitched the book idea. They have spent so much time reading material that I have sent to them, answering dozens of questions that I have emailed, and simply being there for me. Thank you especially to Courtney Morales, Shelby Russell, and David Arditi.

My last "thank yous" are the easiest to remember and the most difficult to articulate. Mom and Dad, thank you for your unending support and love. Thank you for reading umpteen texts and Word files that I sent to you as I worked through material and for all of our phone calls. Tucker and Trinley, thank you for supporting me in every way. Thank you for welcoming me into your family as your stepmom in 2020 and for treating me like a member of the family since I first met you. Thank you for listening to me regularly talk to you at the dinner table about such things as systemic racism; redlining; the problem of calling that Monday in October "Columbus Day"; what White privilege means; why Black lives matter, when your twelve- and nine-year-old imaginations might prefer to wander instead to Fortnite and Roblox (I know your minds do wander there sometimes, and that's okay. But you always listen to me). To the love of my life, Erik, thank you for being there no matter what. You listen to me. You hear me. You support me, always. I love living life with you by my side.

NOTES

1. Andrew Dell'Antonio, 2020, "I doubt there are many—any?—folks in the bubble of my FB feed who don't understand why it's important to assert that #BlackLivesMatter—but maybe some of you do, and I think this is a good explanation which points to the central role generational wealth plays in success in the US, and clarifies why Black folks have been structurally hampered by the systemic racism on which the USian nation was built, politically and economically, even after they ostensibly gained equal legal standing," Facebook, September 14, 2020, https://www.facebook.com/andrew.dellantonio/posts/10116217303580500.

2. Mark Katz, 2020, "Fellow white people," Facebook, May 27, 2020, https://www.facebook.com/mark.katz.3766/posts/10158636251895962.

3. *Rage Fueled Rants of a Tired Black Girl Found Here*, https://kennediajohnson.com/blog-2/.

Introduction

When Donald Glover (b. 1983), whose performance name is Childish Gambino, released his trap Afrobeat single "This Is America" in 2018, I received dozens of emails and messages from students wanting to talk to me about the content of the music video. Even though our spring semester had drawn to a close and there were no pressing assignments to turn in, grades to worry about, or presentations to prepare, my students wanted to talk as though they were in the midst of an intense classroom discussion or final project about the urgency of Gambino's musical message. The conversations all had a similar tone: "Have you heard 'This is America'?" "You've heard the song, but have you seen the video?" "I'm in shock after watching the video; it is difficult to watch, but it is important to watch." The shift from joy to terror in the video is swift.

    The video begins with an innocent tone, showing a guitar placed on a lone chair in what appears to be an empty factory as the musician Calvin Winbush (b. 1984), known as Calvin the Second, walks barefoot and picks up the guitar to play a joyful accompaniment to upbeat lyrics: "We just wanna party / Party just for you."[1] Calvin the Second is seemingly alone, until we see the camera pan to Gambino, who is turned away from our view and who until this point has been hidden by one of the warehouse pillars. Gambino stands calmly and shirtless with his arms at his side, moving very subtly, first with his head, and then turning around to face us. Calvin the Second is now out of sight for the time being. Gambino begins to move his body to groove with the music, but there is a sense that something is off: his facial contortions suggest discomfort. He walks toward Calvin the Second, back in sight, who has stopped playing the guitar and has a white cloth wrapped around his whole head. Forty-nine seconds into the video, Gambino pulls out a gun, striking a deliberate posture that evokes Jim Crow, with his right leg bent and his head cocked to the right as he aims the gun with his right hand, at the same time that his left leg is straightened out in front of him, and his left elbow is angled out wide with his left hand placed on his left thigh, an effect that I will discuss in more detail in the fuller analysis of the video in chapter 3.[2] Four seconds later, he shoots Calvin the Second in the head before calmly looking directly in the camera and stating: "This is America." When he looks directly at the camera, he is in effect turning his gaze directly toward his audience, challenging the notion of who is watching whom.

The concept of the watcher and the one being watched in the video of "This Is America" becomes increasingly complicated given that many people have recorded YouTube videos of themselves or others watching the video for the first time. One *Atlantic* article describes the process of watching videos of people who are themselves watching a video:

> Many of these viewers sway along with Glover at first, rolling their own shoulders, nodding to the Afro folk-inspired melody as the musician twists his bare torso, revealing his own musculature and contorting his body in ways both alluring and disturbing. But the benign nature of that contagion is shattered when the first gunshot rings out fifty-three seconds in, and with the jarring transition of melody to dark, pulsing trap. In the reaction videos, mouths fall open, and people are stunned into paralysis. The shooting itself is shocking, but so is that fact that Glover carries on dancing as if nothing happened.[3]

The shock that these viewers experience echoes the questions that I received from my students. The jolt is not only in seeing the violence and experiencing it over and over again throughout the video but also in the juxtaposition of that violence with what would otherwise be innocent and joyful moments. The experience of watching the horror unfold becomes even more shocking because the video begins so happily in its tone. The relentless and merciless violence becomes normalized throughout the video, a grim reality that the video's title underscores. Gambino's example is one among countless others that draws attention to splintering fractures in American society.

Gambino's gestures, including symbolic components such as how he moves his body, how he uses his voice, and how he engages his audience directly relate to current political and social issues. Throughout this text, I explore the ways in which artists are relating to and representing underrepresented groups—especially groups that are not traditionally perceived as having a majority voice—using a variety of symbols and gestures that are repeated over time. All of the artists use encoded elements of resistance that recur across performances and video recordings so that these elements begin to become recognizable as repeated acts of resistance directed at injustices based on a number of categories, including race, gender, class, religion, and politics. At times these categories overlap; at other times the artist focuses the audience's attention more toward one of the categories than the others. With the repetitions of resistance and the ability to attract an audience of supporters, enhanced by the digital proximity of their platforms, these artists in turn create a larger community of people who want to enact change. Examples of encoded resistance that I evaluate can include any or all of the following elements: dress/clothing; props; accessories; hairstyles; dance styles; body movements such as marching; the absence of body movement in an attention to stillness, often paired with another gesture such as kneeling or holding a fist in the air; playing with the concept of the one watching versus the one being watched; lighting effects in both visual art and in stage lighting; visual distortion such as dissimilar elements that appear simultaneously or glitches on a screen; sonic distortion such as grumbling, screaming, or fuzzy bass lines, mistuned or bent pitches; and word play, particularly playing with the meaning of words, including techniques such as call-and-response that can draw attention to the repetition and meaning of certain words.

The source material for my evaluation of these encoded gestures of resistance appears in a variety of media formats, and the role of digital media and the high likelihood of the repetition of these gestures are central in how all of the works have been promoted. With increased visibility, these gestures transform from encoded resistance to overt and normalized sociological dissonance, signs that something must change in American society. They are a direct challenge to the status quo. The normalization and regular presence of these gestures turn them into tropes that we see over and over again in music and art. These gestural and symbolic tropes offer both an interpretation and a critique of what "This is America" means for the artists who speak to America's social injustices. The musical and artistic selections that I have chosen to highlight in this book contain symbols that deepen the meaning of the words or the sentiment that is being expressed based on the way that the performer or artist communicates with and provides visual cues for the audience. All of the examples are also deliberately confrontational in some way; they are meant to provoke and to elicit a reaction. They are inherently political in this manner.

My interpretation that encoded gestures of resistance can be political draws upon recent work by the sociologist Nick Crossley, who has applied similar arguments to the field of popular music. Specifically, Crossley notes that "musical gestures can raise consciousness about and stimulate debate in relation to an issue, encouraging people to discuss and think about it, rather than necessarily persuading them of a view in and of itself."[4] Describing how the inherent political nature of music could be applied to the concept of race as an example, Crossley argues that

> If the content of songs is political, provokes a political response and engages political views and identities, moreover, then the interaction is political too: artist and audience are co-creating a political public sphere. Furthermore, if the music, for example, speaks to racial identities and draws listeners with a shared racial identity together . . . then it contributes to the "doing" of race and racial division.[5]

As another example of how Crossley examines how gestures of resistance can be encoded and repeated in such a way that pertains to race, he points to African American musical traditions that developed during slavery. Crossley argues that "music . . . became an important vehicle through which coded expressions of dissent could be shared and collective sentiment and identities created."[6] In Crossley's example, enslaved persons as encoders function as both performers and audience; they build the musical codes of dissent into the works that they create, and the repetition of these codes becomes recognizable and increasingly meaningful. All of these kinds of interactions result in a profound relationship between performer and audience. The artist's engagement with or representation of the audience is central to delivering the political message of dissent. According to Crossley, the symbiotic relationship between the artist and the audience can, in turn, have the potential to reach even broader audiences in that "Music may serve to publicize views and voices already existing and refined by way of debate and argument within particular communities, which would not otherwise be heard outside of those communities; voices of politically underrepresented groups."[7]

Crossley speaks specifically about popular music's unique abilities to channel outside support because of the accessibility of popular music that appeals to many listeners. He turns to a variety of examples of popular songs as containing "conventional formal devices" that "serve to deliver [the] content in a way which many of us find both forceful and persuasive."[8] The examples that he names include Edwin Starr's "War" (1970), with Crossley citing the rhetorical power of the lyrics "What is good for / Absolutely nothing!"; Aretha Franklin's "Respect" (1967); and Lady Gaga's "Born This Way" (2011). He does not go into much more detail about what the "conventional formal devices" are in these examples, but presumably he is including the songs for their powerful lyrical content, the individuated delivery of the content, and the resulting appeal for the audience. It is curious that he includes Lady Gaga in the mix as contrasted to the other examples that are from decades before, especially given the contrast in the lyrics of "Born This Way" that focus on acceptance of nonbinary gender and sexual identity, such as one verse that opens with the phrase "No matter gay, straight, or bi/ Lesbian, transgender life" and concludes with the refrain repeated throughout the song that affirms self-positivity: "I'm on the right track, baby."[9] All of the songs do share the commonality that they are about rejections of stereotypes, from the notion that war does not solve America's problems, to the idea that Black women deserve respect, to the statement that gender is not binary. All of the songs are also popular and relatively well known. In the context of his discussion about popular music, he contrasts these types of examples with what he believes to be the lesser appeal of avant-garde music, because that music is not as accessible to groups outside of the "elite" who understands or seeks to understand it.[10]

In this book I broaden Crossley's argument to include a wide range of styles of art and music—both mainstream and outside the fray—that, while appealing in the respect that there is an element or combination of elements that attracts the audience's attention in the form of the encoded gestures that I listed, is at the same time deeply unsettling. We are meant to feel disturbed. We are meant to feel uncomfortable. And we are meant at the same time to feel impelled to engage. The feeling of discomfort amidst something that is also accessible aurally, visually, and often available in a wide variety of platforms suggests that something must change after the performance has been received, similar to the state of paralysis captured in the videos of people watching the video for "This Is America." It is unideal to remain in stasis, and the implication is that change must occur. The material that I include in this book is not for the deliberate purpose of entertainment but rather for the purpose of initiating action and change, something that we can recognize in the repetition of symbols.

As an example of a forceful statement that is intended to initiate change and enhanced in its delivery through encoded gestures that relate to current affairs in America, Gambino pointedly declares that "This *Is* America" (my emphasis) and shows what he believes to be America's current infractions through elements including choreographic depictions of the nineteenth-century minstrel character Jim Crow and onscreen simulations of random shootings that relate to current events in America. Perhaps one might think of Jim Crow racism as a thing of the past, but Glover suggests that it is present and alive in his use of the present tense in the song's title. At the same time that Gambino invokes Jim Crow, he simultaneously calls to mind the minstrel character Zip Coon, the more stylish and refined stereotype as contrasted to the unsophisticated Jim Crow. For example, Gambino's clothing suggests an homage to Black culture, specifically to the distinct style of the Nigerian musician Fela Kuti (1938–1997), who often dressed shirtless and in stylish pants, with gold chains around his neck.[11] The symbols of the clothing alongside the distorted movements are thus both an honoring of Black culture and a reckoning with nineteenth-century stereotypes of that culture. This symbolic negotiation of chronological space for Black people becomes further problematized in the title of the song itself. The title is not "This Was

America." There is no past America that he seeks to "make great again." In an article entitled "Donald Glover's 'This Is America' Holds Ugly Truths to Be Self-Evident," the NPR reporters Audie Cornish and Monika Evstatieva refer both to the title of the song and to words in the Declaration of Independence, with the twist that these truths are ugly and not what Americans want.[12] The trap beat begins at the moment of the first shooting, and the use of trap as a distorted sonic reference here symbolizes that America is in a state of entrapment. Opening the video and interspersed throughout are purely joyful musical moments that dissolve in the context of violence, repeated throughout in a sort of twisted feedback loop in which it seems as though the violence never happened, reinforced by the careful removing of the weapon from Gambino's hands that we see after each violent event.[13] At another moment in the video, as the popular culture historian Joel Stice points out, a "cloaked figure" on a white horse receives a full police escort; this is a "Biblical reference to the end times."[14] As the video relates to current topics in America, the discussion surrounding the repeated cycle of—and the literal protection of—gun violence in America is one example of how topical the video is.

As another example of a current event depicted in the video, Gambino includes a Black gospel choir singing that he guns down with an assault rifle, but not before first throwing his hands up in the air—the weapon not yet visible—as though he is going to join in the participatory singing and celebrating. This inclusion of the gospel choir is most likely a reference to the shooting that took place at Emanuel African Methodist Episcopal Church in Charleston, South Carolina on June 27, 2015. The NPR Music hip-hop journalist Rodney Carmichael discussed the video with Cornish and Evstatieva on *All Things Considered*, explaining how "the South African melodies suddenly give way to this really dark Southern American trap music," with the rest of the video a "barrage of symbolism and chaos," including "Jim Crow imagery, dancing schoolchildren toting firearms and [the] Black gospel choir" that Glover guns down.[15] When the choir first appears and sings, the range of the material is higher than Gambino's rapping timbre and the low-bass trap accompaniment that precedes that choir's entrance. The timbral contrast of the harmonious and lively choir—singing joyfully, hands raised, hips swaying—for about sixteen seconds in what begins as sounding each pitch of a bright first-inversion diatonic chord in F major is further symbolic as a stark contrast to the violence framing the choir's appearance.[16]

The repeated symbols heighten the meaning of the art, the words, or the actions of the artist. Gambino's title, for example, might implicitly change in meaning from "This is America" to "This can not be America," because it is unimaginable and at the same time very real that atrocities disproportionately affecting disadvantaged groups continue to occur and to play out in real time in America, not just in the digital space of Gambino's video. The meaning is made more distinct and powerful through a multiplicity of encoded gestures. When Gambino says "This is America / guns in my area" and represents it by including lighthearted and popular dances interspersed with horrific violence, he means just that: "This is America" means that America is in a staggering state of disarray. The visual markers that he includes highlight the words that he sings and raps; while they do not change the meaning, they intensify it.

In many cases, the role of social media platforms and digital media is central for these artists as they are promoting social justice while sharing content with their audience. The digital aspect broadens audience engagement in that it changes the interaction from an in-person, human-to-human experience to a human-via-machine performance seen by a human that then might share the performance with a new audience (i.e., the repetition of the trope that is being performed). In addition, while it is key to consider the persuasive role of live performance, the digital component that I include adds another layer.

With the multiple ways for artists to communicate with their audiences, the concept of audience engagement thus has several layers. Crossley describes these layers as "multivalent" given the variety of people that comprise an audience:

> I will be suggesting that musical action is *multivalent*; that is to say, in doing music we often, simultaneously and by the very same actions, do much else besides. For example, musical interactions are also often economic interactions, political interactions, bonding rituals etc. In addition, participants in musical interaction are *highly embedded*. In taking up the role of the musician or audience member they do not thereby cease to be, for example, a mother, tax payer, citizen and neighbor, and their performance of their musical roles will both influence and be influenced by these other roles.[17]

Further, Crossley's concept of multivalence takes on a new meaning when the means of social media and digital distribution are included; it is possible for an audience to consist of only one person who may in turn build another audience by sharing content or opinions of the work. As I have already argued, audience engagement can also consist of coded elements of the performance that can be interpreted by the viewers, such as items of clothing that the performer is wearing or colors that the performer chooses to highlight in the performance. As one example of how this has been applied in recent scholarship pertaining to specific musical examples, the American studies and art historian scholar Nicole Fleetwood applied the work of the French literary theorist Roland Barthes (1915–1980) in order to explore how fashion could function as a semiotic indicator of identity in the 1960s, and she used this theory to explore how hip-hop artists—particularly Black and male—identify with hip-hop culture.[18] Other work featured in a collection by Toija

Cinque, Christopher Moore, and Sean Redmond has focused on a specific artist, David Bowie (1947–2016), whose images across multimedia formats spanning theater, film, television, the internet, and performance art pieces provide a fluid context in which to evaluate his art.[19] In addition to the way the role of dress and fashion as an encoded element of performance and as a means to engage the audience, certain props and accessories that the audience sees also affect the performance in a meaningful way, especially when the artist refers to the item and iterates its meaning. Audience engagement also has overlaps with the way that we see how the performers are moving their bodies. It becomes retrospectively haunting when Gambino slowly turns around to face us in the beginning of the video for "This Is America," when upon the first viewing the audience had no idea of the violence that was to unfold. In many of the videos and performances, the artists are moving their bodies in a way to elicit reactions from their audience, whether by emphasizing words or by demonstrating the visceral effects of the words they are rapping, speaking, or singing. There is also a distinction between choreographed movements as on-the-spot and improvisational (or seemingly improvisational) movements to emphasize words in a song or in a rap. All of these kinds of details can be both telling in what they represent to the artists and, in turn, what they might represent for the audience.

In many of the examples that I discuss, I also include discussion about how the timing of the absence of movement is just as important to consider as the presence of movement. The absence of movement is a deliberate nonaction that can add emphasis to the words that we are hearing, because there is little else for our eyes to see. In the performances and videos that I discuss, "absence of movement" often translates to performers standing still, often with a defiant expression, such as putting hands on the hips, crossing the arms in front of the body, holding a fist in the air, or kneeling. Another trope is the absence of movement of a particular person or group of people on the stage amidst a flurry of activity from the other performers, creating a stark contrast that adds dramatic effect.

Throughout this book I explore the innovative ways in which artists use encoded gestures in order to engage with underrepresented groups in a similar manner to the way in which Gambino so powerfully delivers his message in the video for "This Is America." The featured works and artists speak to injustices against nonmajority groups and how the artist is engaging with those groups and the audience. Within that framework, recurring signals are particular to the artwork or composition that I discuss. The works have come to symbolize a divided America. Laurie Anderson sets the stage in chapter 1, drawing our attention as she has always been keen to do toward questions about who is in charge and how that relates to current American politics, especially her frequent articulation of her discomfort in the Trump era. She is ever aware of the marginalization of women and often plays with gender stereotypes in her works, including a vocal distortion that alters her voice to sound like a man's so that people will understand it to be more authoritative than if it came from a woman. In addition to a discussion of two of Anderson's performance art pieces and, in particular, the ways in which she perceives Donald Trump (b. 1946) to reinforce borders based on gender, race, and religion, chapter 1 also includes visual artwork from a gallery that Anderson helped to inspire. Although the artwork is not Anderson's, it powerfully reflects the same messages of resistance that I explore throughout the book, and the art can be seen both as a visual representation of resistance and as a connection to Anderson, who frequently comments on the marginalization of women and minorities. Curiously, she does so without explicit reference to many of the current social justice movements, such as #MeToo, #TimesUp, and #BlackLivesMatter, whose aim is to draw attention to this kind of marginalization. In chapter 2 I extend Anderson's questions about power and authority to include representative examples of Black feminism from Beyoncé, Rhiannon Giddens, and Janelle Monáe, specifically calling attention to how their encoded gestures of resistance are also sonic markers for the #MeToo, #TimesUp, and #BlackLivesMatter movements. The encoded challenges to authority highlighted in chapter 3, in which I examine hip-hop as resistance in the Trump era, are particularly ironic given that many artists in the hip-hop world praised Trump as a businessman before condemning Trump as a president. Finally, chapter 4 features the musical *Hamilton*, in which hip-hop-styled numbers outweigh numbers with more traditional features of a musical. The encoded gestures in *Hamilton* have become a way for many Americans to articulate their politics by measure of how closely they identify with the issues. As with all of the examples in this book, the signs and symbols that fill *Hamilton* have created political rifts, including a Twitter reaction from Trump himself, who criticized the politicization of the theater after the cast made a statement about equality addressed to Vice President Mike Pence (b. 1959), who was in the audience. All of the artists featured in this book, like Gambino, are making a statement about what America is today by demonstrating the meaning of the statement "This Is America" in symbolic and powerful ways that call to mind Crossley's aforementioned description of a song's ability to "provoke a political response" and "engage political views and identities" that I am extending to be a multidisciplinary effect.[20] The accompanying musical examples that I reference throughout the book are available on a playlist that I have created—and will continue to update—on Spotify.[21]

Although Gambino's "This Is America" has been received with much acclaim, including both record and song of the year at the 2019 Grammys, it has also been criticized, such as in one example by the *Washington Post* critic Chris Richards, who finds it to be one of many examples of "contemporary protest pop" that is "deeply unimaginative and embarrassingly insufficient."²² Richards points out that the song shows all of the racism and violence in contemporary society and ends in apathy and stasis. Others have critiqued Gambino's artistic representations of this concept of stasis and his portrayal of violence as creating a voyeuristic opportunity for his audience. For example, Gambino's video "This Is America" has been criticized by the Africana Studies scholar Greg Carr and others as "trauma porn," or the act of a creating an artistic product that allows for viewer to take twisted pleasure in watching something violent unfold.²³ In a similar criticism, in her "Black Girl in Maine" blog, Tiffany Foster condemns the video as another example of "Black trauma porn made for White folks" and is disgusted by the number of "articles and videos dedicated to breaking down every little facial expression and every single dance movement."²⁴ My entire book is based upon breaking down gestures that include facial expressions and dance movements (and the absence of facial expressions and movements), not only in this video but in the way that they are repeated in and have resonances with other examples. Foster further blasts Gambino as using the video purely for violence-as-entertainment—she does not mention Gambino's collaboration with the director and filmmaker Hiro Murai (b. 1983)—especially for White women. I am a White woman, and Foster's words are not lost on me. I must negotiate my own Whiteness and the privilege that that allows when confronting these topics. As the philosopher George Yancy has also argued, my (and other White people's) Whiteness has also allowed me to "reap comfort from being White," at the same time that minorities "suffer for being Black and people of color," and that such White "comfort is linked to [BIPOC] pain and suffering."²⁵ With these points in mind and with respect to Gambino's video, I am arguing that Gambino is juxtaposing violence with what might otherwise be entertainment, making the lasting effect sickening rather than entertaining, in such a way that commands attention and reflection. What these types of critiques miss is the very stasis that Gambino is capturing not merely for eliciting shock but also for enacting change. This is not a video that solves a problem, but that is not the point. Gambino and Murai are showing that we are in a state of inaction, of inertness, and of stasis. We are stuck. That is part of what is so brilliant about the video, that we are stuck in the violence and rhetoric of a Jim Crow past-as-present.²⁶ To that end, I am unconvinced by Richards's argument that protest music is stuck in the past, because that is a key point of what the video represents: we are stuck, and we are in a feedback loop of horrible patterns that keep repeating. Richards does point out a couple of examples that he believes to be more progressive, notably Kendrick Lamar's "Alright" (2015) and the gospel song and what would become the Civil Rights anthem "We Shall Overcome" (originally published in 1947), seemingly because they imply hope, movement, and direction, rather than the static message of "Resist."[27] But it is also an important form of resistance for Gambino to hold his metaphorical mirror to America. The reflection is terrifying, and it also demands actionable change. There are many Americans right now who might feel as though we are not going to be alright. There are many Americans who might feel as though it is difficult, if not impossible, to overcome.

Gambino's provocative gestures are similar to many other contemporary examples, and these resonances are the basis for this text. Some highlights: Anderson's regular call to audiences to join in a collective scream to protest the policies of President Trump during his four years of presidency (2016–2020). Beyoncé's statement of Black female pride in "Formation." A Tribe Called Quest's incendiary condemnation of Trump as "Agent Orange" in their 2017 Grammy performance of "We the People." Lin-Manuel Miranda's ability to tie together twenty-first-century themes with eighteenth-century Revolutionary ideals in *Hamilton*. In these examples and the many others that I discuss throughout the book, there is also the accompanying digital proximity that listeners have not only to the content itself but also to the mercurial, unpredictable, and often virulent world of current American politics. This proximity heightens the sense of urgency and puts a hyper-focus on the problems being addressed. What we see becomes just as profoundly important as what we hear, and vice versa. The selected musical and artistic examples in this text and their accompanying references to contemporary movements are interwoven with politics, gender, and race in the digital age. The works that I have chosen to highlight here are merely a sample, and there is plenty of room for additional chapters and updated playlist selections. The result is an overt and urgent message that America is in trouble for its continued dismissal by people in power of minorities, particularly in BIPOC communities, and even more particularly the women in those communities.[28] As the scholar Matthew D. Morrison has recently argued in an article entitled "Race, Blacksound, and the (Re)Making of Musicological Discourse," misguided assumptions abound regarding America's progress when it comes to human rights: "The current political moment—in which the lives and basic rights of Black and Brown Americans and many other marginalized groups are under constant threat—cautions us against assuming we have already made significant advancement toward racial justice, equity, or inclusion."[29] Along with Morrison's statement, Gambino's gestures and actions in "This Is America" and in the parallel examples in this book remind us that we are nowhere near where we need to be in the social advancement of American society.

As I am completing this book in 2020, in the midst of a global pandemic that is disproportionately affecting the lives and livelihoods of minorities, simultaneously marked by protests amidst increasing police brutality against minorities, including a spate of recent shootings, the questions about power and control that recur throughout the book are deeply underscored. Throughout this period, new example after example has continued to pour from the hearts of the artists that I discuss (and, invariably, important examples that I am missing). For example, Run the Jewels released an entire album on June 2, 2020, entitled *RTJ4*, that was not only prescient in its material but wholly relevant in the midst of the violence, destruction, and chaos that the pandemic only intensifies. As one *Rolling Stone* article title put it, "Run the Jewels Wish Their New Album Didn't Make So Much Sense Right Now."[30] Naming the controversies and the relevance of the controversies is a key step toward change. In my own teaching and research, I regularly try to engage in controversial topics so that my students and I will continue to have a better understanding of the ramifications of structural racism. At the same time, I will always remain a student, and subsequently there is always more for me to learn, to practice, and to incorporate into my research and into the classroom. All of the underpinnings that have been built into our system that "is America" make this pandemic especially terrifying in America for the underrepresented groups that are the subject of my book. It is nonetheless my hope that these case studies provoke difficult but necessary conversations that might begin to have reparative effects.

NOTES

1. Donald Glover, "Childish Gambino – This Is America (Official Video)," YouTube Video, 4:04, May 5, 2018, https://www.youtube.com/watch?v=VYOjWnS4cMY. I discuss the video in additional detail in Chapter 3.

2. For a comprehensive guide to imagery and objects associated with Jim Crow, visit the following website: Ferris State University, "Jim Crow Museum of Racist Memorabilia," https://www.ferris.edu/jimcrow/.

3. Aida Amoako, "Why the Dancing Makes 'This Is America' So Uncomfortable to Watch," *The Atlantic*, May 8, 2018, https://www.theatlantic.com/entertainment/archive/2018/05/this-is-america-childish-gambino-donald-glover-kinesthetic-empathy-dance/559928/.

4. Nick Crossley, *Connecting Sounds: The Social Life of Music* (Manchester: Manchester University Press, 2019), 180.

5. Ibid., 9–10.

6. Ibid., 178.

7. Ibid., 180.

8. Ibid., 177.

9. Lady Gaga, "Born This Way," track 2 of *Born This Way (Special Edition)*, May 23, 2011 2014 Interscope Records, Apple Music.

10. Nick Crossley, *Connecting Sounds*, 177.

11. Hayley Miller, "Childish Gambino's 'This Is America' Video, Explained," *Huffpost*, May 7, 2018, https://www.huffpost.com/entry/childish-gambino-this-is-america_n_5af05c12e4b041fd2d28d8e9.

12. Audie Cornish and Monika Evstatieva, "Donald Glover's 'This Is America' Holds Ugly Truths to Be Self-Evident," *NPR*, May 7, 2018, https://www.npr.org/2018/05/07/609150167/donald-glovers-this-is-america-holds-ugly-truths-to-be-self-evident?fbclid=IwAR0lenULK-4-2sAcBrM9aUJn0wKDFHIXcKR-NULrRJ-kNFbeoZ1ieFMyc4g.

13. I thank my Mercer University colleague Nate Myrick for pointing out this detail in a discussion that we had about the video.

14. Joel Stice, "10 Symbols You Missed in Childish Gambino's 'This Is America', Explained," *Buzzworthy*, 2018, https://www.buzzworthy.com/references-from-childish-gambino-this-is-america/.

15. Ibid.

16. In a similarly titled song that Public Enemy released in June 2020 as an explicit protest to President Trump's politics, "State of the Union: STFU," the groove that they use sounds very close to a distorted sample transposed by a whole step of the first three notes of Gambino's gospel choir, with the third pitch as the most altered and dissonant. "STFU" stands for "Shut the fuck up," which William Jonathan Drayton, Jr. (b. 1959), AKA Flavor Flav, repeats throughout the chorus. The title also refers to the president's annual state of the union address that takes place at the beginning of the year, so the request to "STFU" is aimed directly at the president. Public Enemy, "State of the Union: STFU," track 3 on *What You Gonna Do When the Grid Goes Down?* September 25, 2020, 2020 Enemy Records, LLC, under Exclusive License to Def Jam Recordings, a Division of UMG Recordings, Inc., Apple Music. The connection of the now-dissonant material in "State of the Union" that was first used as a consonant and timbral contrast to trap in "This Is America" is another way in which Gambino's depiction of violence has continued to resonate with his audiences and fellow musicians.

17. Crossley, *Connecting Sounds*, 4–5.

18. Nicole R. Fleetwood, "Hip-Hop Fashion, Masculine Anxiety, and the Discourse of Americana," in *Black Cultural Traffic: Crossroads in Global Performance and Popular Culture*, edited by Harry J. Elam, Jr. and Kennell Jackson (Ann Arbor, University of Michigan Press, 2005), 326–45.

19. Toija Cinque, Christopher Moore, and Sean Redmond, eds, *Enchanting David Bowie: Space/Time/Body/Memory*, 1st ed. (New York: Bloomsbury Academic & Professional, 2015).

20. Crossley, *Connecting Sounds*, 9–10.

21. "This Is America," Spotify Playlist, 2020, https://open.spotify.com/playlist/38rkXZt2CMSiC82S7RWumw.

22. Chris Richards, "It's a Brave New World. Why Is Our Protest Music Stuck in the Past?," *The Washington Post* (September 4, 2019), available online at https://www.washingtonpost.com/lifestyle/style/its-a-brave-new-world-why-is-our-protest-music-stuck-in-the-past/2019/09/03/7d9c1056-ca97-11e9-a4f3-c081a126de70_story.html.

23. Zaynab, "Childish Gambino's 'This Is America' Criticized as 'House Slave' Trauma Porn," *Hot New Hip Hop*, February 12, 2019, https://www.hotnewhiphop.com/childish-gambinos-this-is-america-criticized-as-house-slave-trauma-porn-news.71790.html.

24. Tiffany Foster, "'This Is America' Really IS America, and That's a Shame," *Black Girl in Maine Media*, May 17, 2018, https://blackgirlinmaine.com/current-events/this-is-america-really-is-america-and-thats-a-shame/ (accessed August 28, 2020).

25. George Yancy, *Backlash: What Happens When We Talk Honestly about Racism in America* (Lanham, MD: Rowman & Littlefield, 2018), 22.

26. As Patrisse Khan-Cullors and Asha Bandele summarize a living Jim Crow set of conditions in America as it relates to the founding of #BlackLivesMatter, the social movement that I consider in more detail in chapter 2, "America—the world—knew it owed us for centuries of slavery and Jim Crow. And instead of doubling down on how to repair the harm, it made *us* the harm. After removing a debilitating number of jobs and the funding to ensure quality schools, after instituting laws that disrupted families' possibility to thrive . . . our mothers and fathers and daughters and sons were criminalized for choices made often out of absolute desperation and lack of any other real options." Patrisse Khan-Cullors and Asha Bandele, *When They Call You a Terrorist: A Black Lives Matter Memoir* (New York: St. Martin's Griffin, 2018), 144.

27. Zaynab, "Childish Gambino's 'This Is America' Criticized."

28. The acronym BIPOC stands for Black, Indigenous, and people of color. For further reading on the origins of the term and frequent references to it in the context of the pandemic that began to affect Americans in 2020, see Sandra Garcia, "Where Did BIPOC Come From?" *The New York Times*, June 17, 2020, https://www.nytimes.com/article/what-is-bipoc.html.

29. Matthew D. Morrison, "Race, Blacksound, and the (Re)Making of Musicological Discourse," *Journal of the American Musicological Society* 72, no. 3 (Fall 2019): 787–88.

30. David Fear, "Run the Jewels Wish Their New Album Didn't Make So Much Sense Right Now," *Rolling Stone*, June 18, 2020, https://www.rollingstone.com/music/music-features/run-the-jewels-rtj-4-interview-el-p-killer-mike-1015466/. Run the Jewels has had a longstanding cynicism with American politics, and despite the album's timing during a period in which many have been critical of Trump, the album is not explicitly anti-Trump. In the Rolling Stone interview, Killer Mike explained: "I'm not saying Trump isn't horrible. I'm just saying that the Black community is used to politicians failing them." The album is Run the Jewels, *RTJ4*, June 3, 2020, 2020 Jewel Runners LLC under Exclusive License to BMG Rights Management (US) LLC, Apple Music.

Chapter 1

"We're Drowning in Our Own Stories"

Laurie Anderson's Call to Artists and Her Performance Art as a Commentary on Current American Democracy

As someone who likely does not identify as a popular mainstream artist, the performance artist Laurie Anderson might be surprised to find an entire chapter devoted to her in this book.[1] Yet, as is true for the other artists whose work that I explore in this book, who provide keen insights into the cyclic loop that victimizes marginalized groups in American news, mass media, and politics, Anderson fits right in, especially in the age of the Trump presidency of which she has been explicitly critical.[2] While Anderson has been critical of many presidential administrations, and she has regularized distortion and gender play in her works for decades, she has been especially outspoken about Trump's threats to defund the arts and to close borders, making some of her most recent works timely and relevant for the context of this book. While the topic of issues such as border control is not limited to Trump or to the Republican Party, Trump's outspokenness about such divisive issues has particularly aggrieved Anderson.[3] Many of Anderson's works challenge authority, particularly authority by those perceived to be in power, and, in turn, how that authority affects marginalized groups. In one interview, Anderson asked the following series of questions: "What is suffering? What is justice? What is language? What's a story? Whose story are you going to believe? Who's in charge?"[4] These questions have arguably never been more urgent for Americans to ask than now, in a time marked by a one-term president reluctant to condemn White supremacy and eager to threaten marginalized groups. The foundational questions about power that Anderson asks are implicit not only in all of the works in chapter 1 but also throughout the rest of the book. The implicit answers to these questions are what turn out to be many similar interpretations of "This Is America." Throughout this chapter I will highlight many ways in which Anderson has both inspired and created artistic works that speak to underrepresented voices, all of which rely on some combination of the encoded visual and sonic tropes of resistance that I outlined in the Introduction. The first part of this chapter, subtitled "Call: *Art Action Day*" and "Response: *One Year of Resistance*," includes a discussion of an exhibition of nonmusical works inspired by a project that Anderson co-led called "Art Action Day" in 2018 as a protest against the one-year anniversary of the inauguration of President Trump. In the second part of the chapter, subtitled "Laurie Anderson's Art as Action," I consider how Anderson has recently offered perspectives on questioning authority; first in repeated calls to her audiences to join in a collective scream to protest Trump; second in her 2016 performance *The Art of Falling* that includes a comparison of Aristophanes's parable *The Birds* (originally performed in 414 BC) to Trump's proposed border wall between the United States and Mexico; and third in a 2015 work entitled *Habeas Corpus* that, although composed before Trump took office, has newfound relevance in the Trump administration. Anderson has stated that "the bodies that I relate to the most are the No Bodies. I've written many songs and stories for these 'people.' They have no names, no histories. They're outside of time and place and they are the ones that truly speak for me."[5] Her reference to marginalized "No Bodies" implicitly questions authority, and it is an ongoing theme in many of her works. Her "No Bodies" are this chapter's—and this book's—"Every Bodies."

When asked in a 2018 *New York Times* interview how she feels about revisiting past works that she has created, Anderson recalled one of her songs from 1981: "O Superman." Although she wrote the song about the failed operation during President Jimmy Carter's administration to rescue American hostages in Iran in 1980, she noted that it "always seems to have been written yesterday. It's because the world hasn't moved ahead; we're still caught in the same loop of war."[6] Many of Anderson's admirers have often been struck by her clairvoyance, especially when it comes to making political statements that seem relevant in today's America, regardless of the date of composition. Her comment about the "loop of war" can be extended to the themes explored throughout this book that highlight many Americans' tendencies to react to something ostensibly horrible, unfair, or unjust that happens, then seemingly move on with day-to-day life, and then watch it replay again in pernicious ways. As much as it was true for Gambino, who used the present tense in "This Is America" and who portrayed a similar "loop of war" in the video, the artistic and musical examples that follow are about what is happening today, examples that reveal Americans to be stuck in a chaotic loop.

PART I

Call: *Art Action Day*

Anderson frequently makes clear that she is no fan of Donald Trump. She recently said in a panel with the writer Margaret Atwood (b. 1939) that she finds "no comfort" in having him as a president.[7] As a means of using her voice to challenge authority, she co-led a moment called "Art Action Day" to protest policies that he introduced that were anti-art and anti-immigration. In 2017 Trump pledged to close borders and to defund the arts, including funding for the National Endowment for the Arts and the National Endowment for the Humanities.[8] In response, Anderson and two other women turned to social media to make a call to artists, all of whom were invited to protest the specific policies. Anderson was among many who vehemently objected to these proposals. Timed to coincide with the one-year anniversary of the inauguration of President Trump on January 20, 2017, Anderson, along with the writer and producer Taynya Selvaratnam (b. 1971), and the media executive Laura Michalchysyn (b. ?) organized a nationwide event entitled "Art Action Day" that officially began on January 20, 2018.[9] According to the official website for the event, Art Action Day was a larger part of a group known as "The Federation," a group that desires to "send positive messages about the power of the arts for uniting peoples, cultures, cities, the world."[10] The Federation's original website provided details about Art Action Day and not only encouraged those willing to participate to promote the event through social media outlets—they encourage supporters to "share/tweet/post"—but also provided hashtags so that interested participants could help to spread the message. For example, some of the suggested hashtags that reinforced this message were #ArtIsEssentialtoDemocracy, #SingScreamDanceLaugh, #ArtUnitesUs, and #CultureKeepsBordersOpen, revealing one of many examples in this book that shows the close interconnections between digital activism and calls for social justice.[11] The message of Art Action Day was clear: Art heals. Art unites. Art incites. Art creates action. The Federation urged performers and artists who wanted to participate to be as digitally inclusive as possible about the process that would in turn allow for the possibility of the artwork to be reposted on social media and then, perhaps, sent to a person with political clout, such as a senator. Art Action Day represented a call for change and for social justice in a time of American strife, particularly echoed in excerpts of prominent social reformers whose words appeared on the site's page. The suggestions for excerpted works were chosen because of their ability to embody "ideas of democracy, civic dialogue, and open cultural borders."[12] Some of the recommended resources included Chimamda Ngozi Adichi's *We Should All Be Feminists* (2015); Wajahat Ali's *My Resistance*

Movement (2017); Gloria Anzaldúa's *Borderlands/La Frontera: The New Mestiza* (2012); and James Baldwin's *The Fire Next Time* (1963). The call to create change as part of its mission was both urgent and participatory given the digital shareability that would result in repeated performances of a message of resistance. In total, Art Action Day attracted over 100 participants. Anderson's close involvement with Art Action Day provides a critical foundation, not only for this chapter exploring her role in using performance art as political commentary, but also for this book given the role of Art Action Day as a digital conception and as a call for social justice. Because Anderson was a key player in the very existence of *One Year of Resistance*, these works, in part, reflect her interpretation of what it means to live in America today.

Response: *One Year of Resistance*

One of the responses to the Federation's call to artists at large in the Art Action Day project came to life in a gallery entitled *One Year of Resistance*. A complete listing of the works appearing in the exhibit is available online.[13] The artwork featured in this gallery protests many of the injustices covered in this text such as the gun violence and systemic racism that the "This Is America" video portrayed, along with policies aimed at the exclusion of women and minorities. *One Year of Resistance* was sponsored by a Manhattan gallery named Untitled Space, and the exhibit ran from January 16, 2018, to February 4, 2018.[14] A portion of the money earned in the show went to the American Civil Liberties Union (ACLU), which also served as the legal representation for The Federation. As CNN contributor Aileen Kwun commented, the exhibit was part of "a nationwide initiative" that was "the brainchild of The Federation, a volunteer-run arts organization spearheaded by artist Laurie Anderson and producers Tanya Selvaratnam and Laura Michalchyshyn."[15] Kwum went on to comment about the far-reaching impact of Anderson's project, noting that it "began as a series of informal monthly meet-ups," but that it "quickly mobilized into an organized network of creatives."[16] All of the resources mentioned above that were listed on The Federation's site were a means for artists to protest loudly rather than silently, as had happened on the day of Trump's first inauguration, when many museums and galleries closed in protest.[17] The accompanying website for *One Year of Resistance* described it as a celebration of "art as activism, giving voices to contemporary artists from all backgrounds, ages, and genders."[18]

Many of the works in *One Year of Resistance* are about entrapment and the feeling of representing what it feels like to be disadvantaged and part of someone else's agenda, revealing a generic form of violence that disadvantaged groups experience regularly in America, with the implied question: What will you do to enact change? In a podcast that was recorded in front a live audience, Selvaratnam put it this way: "We're going to build this network outward, so that it's not just about moving toward [the anniversary of Trump's inauguration on] January 20th, [2018] . . . Art has the power to transform consciousness in ways that speeches don't. Culture and art are very scary to those who want to have tight political control."[19] Speaking after Selvaratnam's remarks and drawing laughter from the audience, Anderson added that she was hoping that Art Action Day would be "really chaotic. . . I'm an artist because I want to be free. . . I don't like being part of an agenda."[20] Similarly, the artists involved in *One Year of Resistance* flipped the script so that art and culture become the means of control—that is, the threat—to those in power, rather than the reverse.

The reversal of power for culture and art among artists and the people in power whom they resist is a powerful trope for what it means, as Anderson described, for the artist to be truly free. If we can apply analysis of symbolic elements in musical examples that include performance art, by which what we see becomes just as important as what we hear in the intersections among these works, the very experience of viewing the art in Art Action Day can also become a powerful tool of resistance. Similar to the cyclic violence that we see without reprieve in Gambino's video "This Is America," given the recorded reactions of people watching the video for the first time, along with Gambino's facial contortions that suggest that he is in pain, Art Action Day is another visual reminder of a chaos loop. As was true for the video, the art is simultaneously a display of violence while also a criticism of that very violence. Again, the focus turns to us, demanding us to examine what our next steps will be. As a call to action, the art transforms in such a way that it turns the lens to us as a society. The tropes in the visual and sonic artwork are markers of resistance, calls to potential ensuing actions to combat social injustices and to include Anderson's "No Bodies" as part of the "Every Bodies" in America.

Over the phone, I interviewed two artists whose works were featured in the exhibit: Joel Tretin (b. 1953) and Touba Alipour (b. 1992). I am grateful to both of them for allowing their thought-provoking work to be reprinted in this book and for discussing the art with me. Both emphasized the sense of community present among all of the artists featured in the exhibit. Specifically, I wondered whether the artists worked directly with Anderson. Tretin and Alipour explained that while they did not work directly with her, they were moved by the call to action begun in The Federation project. Commenting on Anderson's role as an activist and as an artist, Tretin specifically remarked that "I love Laurie Anderson. In the artist's community, Trump was a seismic shift in the democracy. In turn, the curator put together a great show [with *One Year of Resistance*], making an entirely positive experience."[21]

Figure 1.1 Joel Tretin, "Donald Trump's First Snowman." Image reprinted with permission from Joel Tretin.

The images that Tretin and Alipour shared with me that I include in this section are deliberately provocative. Referring back to the list of questions that I quoted from Anderson at the beginning of the chapter, these images question who is in charge, and they question whose story you are going to believe. In the first photograph pictured in figure 1.1, Tretin replaces a snowman with a diabolical image of a caped and hooded Ku Klux Klan member whose arms have morphed into the snowman's twig arms, whose eyes and mouth are coal.

In the original depiction of the image on the Untitled Space's website, it is captioned as "Bannon's First Snowman." The work's title refers to Steve Bannon (b. 1953), who served as Senior Counselor to President Trump from January 20, 2017, until August 18, 2017, and who in 2020 became the subject of investigation on charges of a criminal fraud case in which he allegedly used money originally intended for Trump's border wall with Mexico.[22] Bannon's initial appointment caused alarm for many individuals and groups because of Bannon's previous involvement with the right-wing website *Breitbart News*. According to *Time* reporters Philip Elliott and Zeke J. Miller, the site often includes "racist, sexist, xenophobic, and antisemitic material" couched in the language of the "alternative right."[23] Evidence supports Elliott's and Miller's description. For example, here is a sampling of some recent *Breitbart* headlines: "The Solution to Online 'Harassment' Is Simple: Women Should Log

Off." "Steyn: 'In the Space of about Twenty Minutes, We've Gone from "The Confederate Flag is Racist" to "The Star-Spangled Banner is Racist.'" "Gay Rights Have Made Us Dumber: It's Time to Get back in the Closet." "Bill Kristol: Republican Spoiler, Renegade Jew."[24] The vitriolic nature of headlines such as these is what led so many people to critique Bannon as the president's top choice for counsel in 2017. If someone like Bannon was in charge of an organization such as *Breitbart* that in turn was capable of reinforcing messages promoting social injustices and reinforcing negative and harmful stereotypes to its millions of readers, what then would Bannon's influence be as senior counselor to the president?[25] Tretin's original title of the photograph is one interpretation.

But when I spoke with Tretin, I learned that he changed the title of the photograph to "Donald Trump's First Snowman," adding an implicit layer of urgency to the photograph's message, because of course Trump was the president at the time of the creation of the photograph and perceived to be the one wielding power. Tretin also articulated one of the most important messages of Art Action Day: Art becomes the means of control over the politicians and those in charge rather than the reverse. I asked Tretin why he changed the title of the photograph, and he responded with the following comments:

> At first it was "Bannon's," then "Trump's"; I was just playing around with the context of the image. The thing I really wanted to say was [that] there is a cultural perspective that never really gets illuminated. I think racism is something that happens and is discussed over the kitchen table and is a thing that gets normalized. If that's the family you grew up in, that would be the visual representation of that, and that's how I got to the snowman.[26]

Tretin's choice to bring to light the normalization of racism is what makes this photograph particularly shocking. Something as ordinary, innocent, and joyful as a snowman in front of a family home transmogrifies into an emblem of racism, similar to the way in which the video for "This Is America" opens: joy morphs into horror. What happens behind closed doors is now on the front lawn for all to see, because the racism represented in the photograph and the title is in plain sight. The message that we must take action becomes more urgent.

Tretin was not the only artist to include images of the KKK in his works at the show, recreating the perpetual cycle of violence against Black Americans. The 2018 timing of the *One Year of Resistance* exhibit coincided with several recent incidents of violence caused by racist hatred in America. One such incident occurred in Charlottesville, North Carolina on August 11–12, 2017. A Unite the Right rally brought together neo-Nazis and White supremacists in order to protest the recent removal of Confederate monuments memorializing the Civil War. The protestors saw this removal as an attempt to erase history and also an extreme reaction to another brutally violent act: the actions of [redacted] (b. 1994), the White supremacist who shot and killed Reverend Clementa Pinckney (1973–2015), Tywanza Sanders (1988–2015), Cynthia Hurd (1960–2015), Reverend Sharonda Coleman-Singleton (1969–2015), Reverend Myra Thompson (1955–2015), Ethel Lee Lance (1944–2015), Reverend Daniel Simmons (1940–2015), Reverend DePayne Middleton-Doctor (1965–2015), and Susie Jackson (1928–2015) at the Emanuel African Methodist Episcopal Church in Charleston, South Carolina, on June 17, 2015, an event that Gambino also alluded to in "This Is America" when he gunned down the Black gospel choir, as I discussed in the Introduction. Many of the protestors at the Unite the Right rally argued that symbols such as the Confederate flag and statues commemorating Civil War figures were an intrinsic component of identifying with Southern culture. Counter-protestors used this very argument against them, saying that the glorification of such symbols was itself an erasure of the violence and brutality against Blacks that defined not only the Civil War but the hundreds of years of injustice brought against them since African Americans first arrived in America in 1619. As counter-protestors yelled "Black Lives Matter!" to the neo-Nazis and White supremacists, the White supremacist [redacted] (b. 1997) rammed his car into them, killing the paralegal Heather Heyer (1985–2017), who had in her profession worked tirelessly to aid those at risk of repossessions and evictions.[27] Trump's initial Twitter reaction was to "condemn hatred, bigotry, and violence on many sides," which many people interpreted to be sympathetic to the ideals of White supremacists, something that Trump managed to exacerbate by stating that he knew "very fine people on both sides."[28] Trump had already convinced several people that he was racist. This tweet was another strong piece of evidence to suggest that he was trivializing the experience of racism for minorities by equalizing "both sides" in such a manner. The philosopher George Yancy in response to the tweet asked

> How many sides were there? The White supremacists are those who hate. Their agenda, their racist philosophy, is predicated on hate. Their very identities are founded upon self-avowed White racist beliefs and practices . . . I fail to see the "many sides" of violence when only one side is the embodiment of White supremacist hatred and violence.[29]

Not only had the cycle of violence continued to repeat and to play out in real time at the Unite the Right rally, the president implied that because "both sides" were equal, he thus condoned the violence even as he purported to explicitly "condemn" it.

A similar representation of the destructive perpetuality of violence in America, including the very possibility of violence, occurs in the second of Tretin's two photographs included at the Untitled Space's gallery. Entitled "Selling Guns Like Gumballs," the photograph depicts a vending machine that is visible in the aisle of a convenience store where items like magazines, gum, and candy would normally be sold. A White woman peers at the machine, as though contemplating the purchase of one of the guns. In the photograph, Tretin plays on the spelling of the word "gun" by changing it to "gum," creating a similar effect to the one discussed for figure 1.1, in which he morphed a snowman into a KKK figure. In other words, he retains familiar elements by juxtaposing them with shocking and seemingly displaced elements that one would not normally see together. But something has to happen behind the scenes for these kinds of things to appear together. As an analogy, in the song "This Is America," Gambino's lyrics offer one explanation: guns are a quotidian part of American culture. He raps "This is America, guns in my area."[30] Tretin's image captures this same type of sentiment. In Tretin's photograph, guns can sell as quickly as candy does because of their placement by the check-out line in a grocery store, a place where customers often make impulse purchases or purchases of convenience, such as the gift cards that are displayed on the left and right sides of the machine. The photograph depicts that guns are available for easy sale in the grocery store, which is in turn a visual reminder of violent cyclic loops causing chaos in America. Guns are commercialized and made for easy sale. Thus, one interpretation of figure 1.2 is that it could be an example of a visual representation of Gambino's lyrics.

Figure 1.2 Joel Tretin, "Selling Guns Like Gumballs." Image reprinted with permission from Joel Tretin.

The second artist with whom I spoke, Touba Alipour, created a captivating image of what America is to her in a neon sculpture with mixed media signage entitled "America," the image of the contiguous United States that also appears on the cover of this book. The vividness of the neon is immediately striking and creates a sense of urgency. Human eyes tend to move toward light. Alipour's use of neon, she explained, "automatically attracts" the attention of the viewer, offering a "powerful message to look closer."[31] Alipour vividly captures the closure of borders that resulted from a series of President Trump's travel bans in 2017. He signed an executive order on January 27, 2017, that disallowed entry of refugees into America, along with a temporary barring of people from seven countries: Syria, Iraq, Iran, Libya, Sudan, Yemen, and Somalia. Even those holding green cards—documents that are specifically designed to allow people to live and work in the United States—were initially banned from entering America. The ensuing confusion and chaos surrounding this travel ban affected many lives, and that was something Alipour wanted to represent with her work "America." When I spoke with Alipour in a phone interview, she told me that she "came up with the piece when Trump proposed the travel ban . . . It was something personal for me. I was in the process of getting my green card and I didn't see my parents [who were stuck in Iran] for four and a half years."[32] An Iranian, Alipour mentioned to me that she moved to America in 2013 because it "was a big dream in my eyes."[33] But the America she discovered was very different than the one that she had hoped for: "I was hearing people that had green cards—that were permanent residents—that could not return to the country."[34] In her eyes, America was closed and remains closed. Figure 1.3 is her visual representation of that closure.

Figures 1.4 and 1.5 appeared below the bottom right area of the installation of "America" in the *One Year of Resistance* exhibit, the usual place where an explanatory placard would often appear for an exhibit work. The explanations here resemble instructions similar to those one might read upon boarding an airplane, but since America is "closed," the possibility of flying to it is eliminated, as the instructions help to explain. In figure 1.5, for example, the sentences "Keep in mind your gender, race, color and religion may be used against you" and "We would like to thank you for your _____ as we make America great again" are a blistering critique of Trump's campaign slogan to "make America great again." Coincidentally, Anderson also composed a song, "From the Air" (1982), that includes a message from an airplane's captain who is preparing his passengers for a crash landing that has very similar language to Alipour's warning on one of the signs that notes: "In the event of sudden turmoil, thinking caps will automatically drop from above. If this happens, put your cap on and proceed to the nearest exist around you. Please secure your own thinking cap before assisting others." It is an uncanny

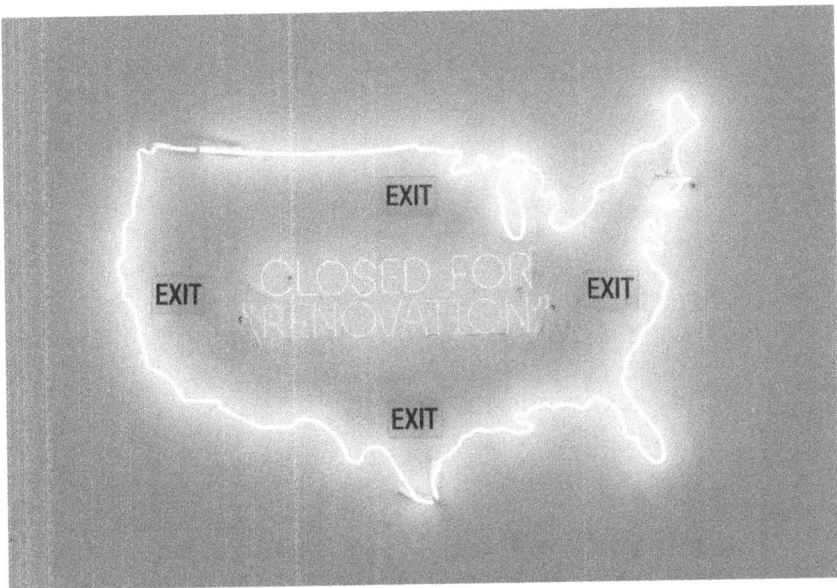

Figure 1.3 Touba Alipour, "America." Image reprinted with permission from Touba Alipour.

coincidence that Alipour's parodic use of the flight instructions have strong parallels with Anderson's "From the Air," a song that incorporates phases, looping, and dissonance to add to the chaos of the lyrics depicting a captain instructing the passengers on how to prepare for a crash landing before declaring that "There is no pilot." "I've got this funny feeling I've seen this all before," the captain says in the song.[35] Alipour did not know the song but was eager to hear about the artistic parallels. "From the Air" is out of the chronological scope for this book, but the representation of subjugation is similar to Alipour's message in "America": the captain allegedly in control is, in reality, out of control.

In addition to the continued relevance of Alipour's artwork in the era of the Trump presidency, Alipour and I spoke about how her work "America" has now shifted in meaning in the context of the current COVID-19 crisis, resulting in a global pandemic and the shutting down of countries worldwide. The bitter irony of the pandemic that is disproportionately affecting disadvantaged groups is that much of America actually is closed and that many other countries have closed their border to America because of the global health threat that America represents.[36] Rather than interpret the image and its continued relevance to the dire state of America as a literal stopping point, one can see it as an opportunity to create change. When I asked Alipour about her thoughts on how art can combat social injustice and impel others to act, she

Figure 1.4 Touba Alipour, "America." Image reprinted with permission from Touba Alipour.

responded with incisive and inspiring wisdom. Like Tretin, she talked about the election of Trump as a "shift" in America. Her emphasis on wanting to create works that are about "what is happening right now" are another take on "This is America":

> Generally my body of work is that people look at it as activism. I usually want to make art pieces that are relevant to what is happening right now. People are so used to looking at art in museums, but it doesn't have the same social message. It's the goal to make people question or ask why what they believe is true.

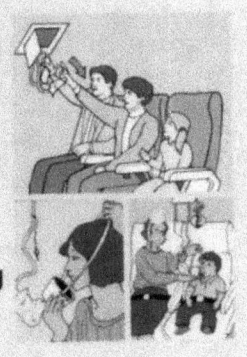

Figure 1.5 Touba Alipour, "America." Image reprinted with permission from Touba Alipour.

I think it's very important to create work that has a meaning and makes the audience think twice. It sparks a question and becomes a discussion between the viewer and themselves. It might change the outcome of what they believed before and what they think now or spark a conversation with someone else. Conceptual art has been a perfect platform for this. It's important to use any platform we have to make a change for the better. You have the freedom of speech. You invite the audience to see if they agree with you. We've been so immune not to talk about politics. I don't even consider myself a political person. Politics were part of my daily life [in Iran]. There was no conversation here around politics when I came to America. I moved here when Obama was president. Social activism was looked at in a different way. When Trump got elected the conversation shifted. We have the right to talk about politics. We have the right to talk about it and state our opinion. I want to spark a conversation that will lead to change. Change doesn't just happen overnight. You have to talk about it. Not "everyone should be a Democrat" or "everyone should be a Republican." You need to be able to talk.[37]

Alipour's "America" invites the possibility for that very conversation to take place, first between the viewer and self and, second, between the viewer and other(s) to whom the initial viewer might speak.

The messages in Tretin's and Alipour's pieces—along with the dozens of others that I have not discussed here—that are featured in *One Year of Resistance* as a response to Anderson's key involvement in a call to action in Art Action Day capture a sense of urgency and recall many of the same sentiments in Gambino's video: We are in trouble. Props, symbols, and messages repeatedly appear as meaningful symbols and gestures. In the video for "This Is America," the silences in the video are when the violence happens. As the musicologist Sarah Lindmark has argued, they also create an opportunity to form a brief relationship with the victim.[38] The built-in silence of a noiseless image is also at the same time deafening in its call to action. These works do not exist in a vacuum, and the stasis that they imply suggests that it is up to us—the viewers, the receivers of the art—to decide what the next steps should be.

PART II

Laurie Anderson's Art as Action

We have seen in the creation of The Federation and its associated projects that messages spread via technology and social media played an essential role in promoting the notion that art can enact change, illustrating the critical role of technology and social media in Anderson's collaborations. Words that began on a website and on social media platforms led to tremendous artistic creations. The power of such language is clear. At the same time, Anderson is simultaneously fascinated by the very imprecision of language. She frequently quotes the American writer and visual artist William Burroughs (1914–1997) and even titled one of her songs after a Burroughs quote: "Language Is a Virus from Outer Space."[39] A recurring trope in her works is the rhetoric of language and how the way that something is said or how the text appears can impact the meaning of the words themselves. For example, in her 2015 film *Heart of a Dog*, she discusses the linguistic imprecision of the "If you see something, say something" phrase invoked by the Department of Homeland Security after the terrorist attacks in America on September 11, 2001. Then a quote from the philosopher Ludwig Wittgenstein (1889–1951) silently scrolls across the screen: "Language has the power to change the world."[40] As a visual example of how she has incorporated this into her own works, figure 1.6 contains text that is translated into "ERST," a software program that Anderson helped to develop specifically for the composition of her 2018 work *Landfall*. The acronym stands for "Electronic Representation

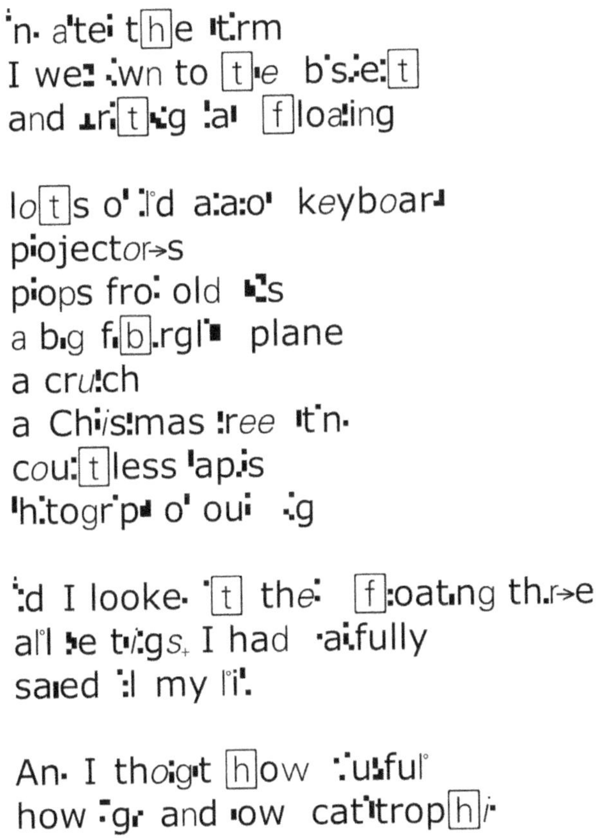

```
'n· a'tei t[h]e 't:rm
I wer :wn to [t]'e b's:e:[t]
and ir[t]:g 'a' [f]loa'ing

lo[t]s o' :'d a:a:o'  keyboar
p'ojector→s
p'ops fro: old  's
a b·g f:[b].rgl  plane
a cru:ch
a Chi/s:mas 'ree  't'n·
cou:[t]less 'ap·s
'h:togr'p  o' oui  ·g

:d I looke· '[t] the:  [f]:oat·ng th·r→e
al'l :e ti:gs,  I had  ·a:fully
sa·ed ·l my 'i'.

An· I tho:g·t [h]ow :u:ful°
how :g· and ·ow cat'trop[h]·
```

Figure 1.6 ERST Rendering of Text from Laurie Anderson's "Everything Is Floating." The text for this image is: "And after the storm, I went down to the basement and everything was floating. Lots of my old keyboards. Thirty projectors. Props from old performances. A fiberglass plane. A motorcycle. Countless papers, and books. And I looked at them floating there on the shiny dark water. Dissolving. All the things I'd carefully saved all my life becoming nothing but junk. And I thought: How beautiful. How magic. And how catastrophic." Image reprinted with permission from Laurie Anderson.

of Spoken Text," but the literal meaning of "erst" is also "long ago" or "formerly," suggesting the loss of something that once was. According to Anderson's description, "ERST uses many fonts and symbols which I often combine to express and play with the many ambiguities of language. I designed it to remind myself that all the art forms I work in—including language—are about representation of life and that they often fall short of expressing its mystery and complexity."[41] The original text before rendered into ERST in figure 1.6 appears below the image; in this case, an itemization of things that Anderson lost after Hurricane Sandy flooded her basement in 2012 that she incorporated into her 2018 composition *Landfall*. The ambiguities of language in figure 1.6 are immediately visible.

For Anderson, language is not only ambiguous but also has the potential to be destructive. Similar to the way in which the artists' images, titles, and descriptions of the images from Art Action Day expressed implicit violence, harms, and injustices in America, particularly in the age of the Trump administration, Anderson is troubled by the explicitly violent rhetoric of much of what Trump says. This echoes the disturbing rhetoric of the news content that I explored earlier by offering a sampling of some of the recent headlines in *Breitbart*. In an interview for *The Atlantic*, Anderson spoke of the visceral effects on her resulting from comments that Trump has made, stating that "I feel socked in the body when I hear the things Trump says. Language can hurt you physically."[42] Anderson consistently refers to him as "Don Trump" rather than using his full name "Donald," perhaps because the clipped, one-syllable names might give the impression of sounding more authoritative and decisive. She invokes Burroughs as a way of explaining why Trump appeals to his followers:

> So William Burroughs for example invented a very good way of using the word "you." The word "you" meant you people in the audience, you Americans, you ... He would speak to those people. And you would know who "you" was. Not many people are skilled at that. Don Trump is very skilled at that. That's why he's doing so well [as of the pre-2016 election]. He speaks right to those people. He's not in the kind of third-person thing that Hillary [Clinton], and Bernie [Sanders] too, are doing. They're not going for the gut response. Don is.[43]

The tremendous power of being able to elicit such a gut response, as Anderson explains, is that it broadens his support base. In the *Atlantic* interview, she invoked the language of his promise to "make America great again" as an example of demagoguery: "'I will make *you* great.' It's very personal. 'You're going to be great again.' You're like, this is such horseshit, you know? But he's got a whole messianic thing going on. He's good."[44] Not only does this type of language strengthen the rhetoric of what "Don Trump" might say, she explained in another interview, but it also incites a general level of panic from everyone that "this is America" as such is insufficient, regardless of whether the people hearing Trump speak support him or not. Put more simply, he implies that America is in a state of disrepair by claiming that it needs to be "great again," as vague and retrogressive as that sounds. And with that, Anderson claims that he has the power to keep Americans in a constant state of panic: she admits that she is glued to her phone to see "what Don Trump said today" because she's "in media panic mode" (similar to the depiction of children being glued to their cellphones in Gambino's "This Is America" video).[45] In the brief interview in which she speaks about being glued to her phone, she refers specifically to the proposed policy to keep borders closed rather than open and emphasizes the importance of opening borders. She does not name Trump explicitly until just before the last minute of the short three-minute interview, but the implication throughout is a critique of his proposals to close borders with many countries. On the topic of opening borders, she urges Americans to "try to see these great surges [of immigrants] and changes in another mode that's not panic. What positive ways could we make this work? Fighting is a disaster, and being angry is a disaster."[46] The content of her response is framed within an evaluation of the power of Trump's rhetoric, particularly for its power to incite anger from supporters and non-supporters alike.

Frequently Trump spoke through his tweets (Twitter permanently suspended his account in January 2021), and with his nearly seventy-seven million followers on Twitter, the language of his digital platform reached many listeners. Journalist Meghan Keneally provided some of the examples of Trump's tweets that could be interpreted as violent, including the following passages: "Any guy who can do a body slam, he is my type!"; and, referring to a protestor at one of his rallies, "Get him out. Try not to hurt him. If you do, I'll defend you in court. Don't worry about it."[47] Twitter flagged multiple examples of Trump's tweets as glorifying violence and of violating their policies against abusive behavior.[48] In an article describing the move, *New York Times* reporters Peter Baker, Raymond Zhhong, and Russell Goldman explained that Trump had "violated [Twitter's] rules against glorifying violence," leading Twitter to "prevent users from viewing the tweet without reading a brief notice, the first time it has restricted one of the president's messages in this way."[49] In addition to the digital violence contained in many of his words, Trump frequently expressed outright anger at press conferences, often berating reporters if they asked questions that he did not like. For example, in response to NBC reporter Peter Alexander, who asked what Trump should say to the millions of Americans feeling scared during the 2020 global health pandemic, Trump responded by stating "I say that you're a terrible reporter. That's what I say."[50] Such examples demonstrate the power of language that Anderson interprets as dangerous. Words can become weapons.

So, too, can art become a weapon as a tool of resistance, and Anderson organized one shocking response originally conceived by the multimedia performer Yoko Ono (b. 1933) as a demonstration of the awful effects that Trump's rhetoric had on so many people. On November 11, 2016, just after Trump was declared to be the president, Ono released a Twitter video that consisted of nothing but a long, nineteen-second scream, captioned "Dear friends, I would like to share this message with you as my response to @realdonaldtrump," tagging the president by using his own Twitter handle.[51] The video is captured as a still image of Ono clutching a microphone with both hands, with her mouth wide open, and as the video plays, the sound of the scream varies in pitch and intensity. The beginning sounds very similar to a wailing baby, and midway through, Ono stops to catch her breath with four pronounced exhales before continuing the scream. Screaming is a regular part of Ono's feminist repertoire, and she uses it as timbral resistance. As the musicologist Shelina Brown has argued, the roots of the scream occurred "in [Ono's] 1972 feminist album, 'Sisters, O Sisters,'" in which "Ono calls upon women to stand up and vocalize their resistance against patriarchal oppression, declaring, emphatically: 'it's never too late/to shout from the heart'."[52] Ono's use of the scream as protest has become regularized in her performances, and this in turn affected Anderson, particularly given her shared feelings toward Trump.

On November 8, 2017, the one-year anniversary of Trump's election, Anderson took a cue from Ono. As Anderson described timbral effects of Ono's scream, she used words such as "no-holds-barred, bloody murder, hara-kiri," and "disemboweling."[53] At a Performa benefit in New York City in November 2017, she again expressed her desire to be free, something that she repeated on the podcast a month later: "I, like many people in this room, became an artist and joined this community in New York City because I wanted to be free."[54] She then expressed her desire to do a trial run of an idea that she developed with the visual artist Marilyn Minter (b. 1948) for as many people to scream out their windows on the first anniversary of election day 2016. Anderson hit a gong and the room went wild, and she spoke with Minter about adding the scream to existing Facebook events that had a similar agenda. Anderson's orchestrated scream and its impact reveals her important role not only as a performance artist but also as a human who struggles. In the absence of language, a scream is one of the most visceral responses to trauma and to grief. So the scream itself becomes a new kind of language. It is Anderson's and Minter's response to something that is too much for words. The shocking rhetoric of the scream becomes an agent of change. And Anderson has regularized the scream in recent performances by making it a part of the performance itself, using it as a tool for resistance in repeated scenarios.

For example, in a recent performance with the pianist, organist, composer, and arranger Tammy Hall (b. ?) at the San Francisco Jazz Fest in 2019, Anderson mused aloud about stereotypes against women while Hall improvised on the piano:

> I guess your ideas about who men are and who women are . . . are sometimes kinda sketchy and start with the ideas that you have about your own parents. . . . My first impression was that men didn't have a care in the world. They were these lighthearted beings and the women were the serious ones, the driven ones [Hall adds a crescendo to add emphasis to the text]. And because tonight is centered on women I want to start with a tribute to one of my favorite artists.[55]

Anderson then explained the origin story for the collective scream she was about to request from her audience. As Hall improvised on the piano and Anderson played her electric violin, Anderson talked about how women are traditionally perceived at the beginning of the video before transitioning to a section in which she would begin the tribute to Ono, something that she started doing regularly two years ago. Her setup is dramatically charged with Hall's musical accompaniment:

> It started on a gray November day the morning after the election. It was really quiet that morning, and most of the people that I knew could barely drag themselves out of the house or out of bed. And reality had started to be something that we just didn't recognize anymore. And I'm thinking, "Why isn't anyone saying anything?" And the next thing I hear is this blood-curdling scream. Yoko Ono had posted her reaction to the election, and she had screamed for one minute [At this point, Hall interjects with three loud dissonant chords on the piano]. This was not an avant-garde scream with all sorts of metaphorical hidden meanings, no, this was a straight-up, no-holds-barred, bloody murder, death scream from hell. And since then, I have to say that it's Yoko's scream that I hear almost every morning. And I'm so grateful that someone is going way out there. Anyway, in honor of Yoko Ono I'm going to ask you to scream. Not for a minute, but just for ten seconds, and I want you to prepare for this by thinking about, I don't know, nuclear arsenals, North Korea, the melting of the ice caps, the masks everyone had to wear here last week for the smoke from the fires [this was on December 31, 2019, just before the pandemic would unfold and upend life as we know it], Margaret Atwood's new edition of *The Handmaid's Tale* . . . or really any of today's presidential tweets—take your pick, or you could just think about all the things in your own life that are really screwed up right now. And I'm gonna time this. And I want you to give it all you've got. Don't

hold back. Are you ready? Yes? Are you ready? Okay. 1, 2 . . . [music stops, video stops].[56]

Her emphasis that the scream "was not an avant-garde scream" brings to mind Nick Crossley's perspective that I outlined briefly in the Introduction and speaks to Anderson's broad appeal. She is not being weird for the sake of being weird as a performance artist. She has a substantial following—her Facebook page has nearly 132,000 followers—supporting her ability to cross boundaries between performance art, popular music, language, and visual art that makes her an ideal starting point for this book. Her reference to Margaret Atwood was significant both in the timing of an interview that Anderson did with Atwood at the MacDowell Colony that took place around the same time of Anderson's performance with Hall in December 2019 and in her specific reference to Atwood's dystopian novels *The Handmaid's Tale* (1986) and its sequel *The Testaments* (2019). Both of Atwood's novels are centered upon the mistreatment, neglect, and abuse of women in patriarchal societies, and Anderson's reference to the works circles back to her opening statements about notions of "who men are and who women are." The connections between dystopian visions, gender stereotypes, bad weather, and the election of Trump could not have served as a better backdrop for inviting the crowd to become part of the performance and engage in a collective scream, and as her 2017 Performa appearance showed, this was not the first time that Anderson would incorporate an opportunity for the audience to scream with her as a message of timbral resistance.

Like so many of the works that I discuss throughout the book, Anderson frequently uses distortion to emphasize resistance. In a performance of a continually changing set entitled *The Language of the Future* at the music and technology festival known as Moogfest in 2016 in Durham, North Carolina, she included a number of performances centered around how people tell stories. One of the stories that she told involved a comparison of Aristophanes's parable *The Birds* to Trump's proposed border wall, and distortion appeared in several guises.[57] First, she created dissonant chordal patterns on her electric violin that were looped into overlapping repetitions. Second, the dark blue lighting behind her appeared next to a dark gray panel, with what seemed to be blurred and enlarged condensation droplets that drizzled down in slow motion on a screen behind her.[58] At points, it seemed as though Anderson was bathed in the bright blue light, which gradually shifted to red, suggesting the colors of the American flag, a trope seen in many of the videos and performances that I discuss in this book. The atmosphere was ominous. As the lighting shifted back to a gray-black background, the droplets that gathered appeared to start moving in reverse, as though they were moving back toward the sky. The effect in the video is quite disorienting. Anderson moves to the microphone after about two minutes of playing the live music and switches to synthesizer before calmly greeting her audience—"Hello, everybody," to enthusiastic applause—and stating that she wanted to talk about stories and particularly about "technology, and stuff breaking down."[59] In the video she goes through various stories about different presidents, beginning with John Kennedy, whom Anderson refers to as Jack. The Kennedy story is positive in its tone and is about a letter that Anderson received from him when she was a child, but her discussion of other presidents becomes more critical. As the performance progressed, the *Atlantic* article summarized, Anderson

> dissected Americans' love of military jargon, mocked the 'If you see something, say something' campaign, and delivered an extended analogy between Donald Trump's plan for a border wall with Mexico and Aristophanes's *The Birds*, in which a philosopher tries to convince avians to construct a sky barrier.[60]

Her retelling of *The Birds* is not only an analogy but also a kind of distortion, since it is a reinterpretation of an original story. The sky barrier in *The Birds* serves the purpose of giving higher power to the birds than to Zeus, the ruler of all the gods, because they would be on the ideal side of the border by physically being higher than Zeus. The analogy that Anderson makes in her performance is twofold: first in her comparison of a wall that Trump refers to as a means of making America safe from immigrants; and second in her implication that Trump is a demagogue in thinking that immigrants wanting to come to America are inherently dangerous. His desire to create more borders in America is a threat to American democracy, and Anderson expresses her resistance in the visual, sonic, and literary distortions during this component of *The Language of the Future*.

Similar distortions used for alienating effects occur in her 2015 work *Habeas Corpus*, another work about the injustice of imposed borders. Although she composed *Habeas Corpus* one year before Trump took office, his policies have had an effect in shaping the work's meaning, especially as it pertains to Anderson's inclusion of the "no bodies" in so many of her works. In *Habeas Corpus*, the focus is on the social injustice and lawlessness that has occurred at Guantánamo Bay detention camp. Since its inception in 2002 as part of George W. Bush's "War on Terror," the presence of the camp has faced intense scrutiny and criticism. Due to concerns of indefinite detention without trial, insistence that its detainees are "non-persons," and perceived violations of the U.S. Constitution, President Barack Obama (b. 1961) and many others wanted to shut the prison down.[61] Unable to bypass Congress in getting approval to shut it down completely, Obama instead made efforts to reduce the number of men in prison. He was successfully able to reduce the number from 245 to 41. According to a description of Guantánamo detention camp on the website for the ACLU, almost all of the remaining forty-one men in prison are being "held without charge or trial."[62] The term "habeas corpus" refers to an arrested person's right to a trial, but none of the detainees at Guantánamo is ever brought to trial, so Anderson's title is deliberately ironic. It also speaks to the ACLU's point that

> federal courts are well equipped to prosecute terrorism suspects and handle sensitive national security evidence while protecting defendants' rights... The ACLU fights in courts and advocates with Congress and the executive branch to secure the release of detainees who have never been charged with a crime; to close the prison at Guantánamo Bay; and to end Guantánamo's flawed military commissions.[63]

Habeas Corpus reflects these sentiments and is another example of Anderson's awareness of the tiring cycle of American politics and policies. There is a call for much-needed change, a call that is unanswered, allowing discrimination to persist. On January 30, 2018, President Trump signed an executive order to allow Guantánamo to remain open, with no indicated date of closure.

Habeas Corpus features the former Guantánamo detainee Mohammed el Gharani (b. 1986), whom Anderson digitally brought from Africa to the United States via a projected image onto a huge chair sculpture. Anderson's conception was not voyeuristic in the sense that the audience would be peering into el Gharani's world, that the audience would be seeing him and watching him at whim. In fact, her design was humanistic. Just as the audience could see el Gharani, he could also see them. He shared his story with them. As he explained, as was the case for many Guantánamo men in prison, el Gharani was captured and subsequently tortured—in his experience, for seven and a half years—without a single charge brought against him. Before his imprisonment, he traveled from Saudi Arabia to Pakistan to study computers. While in Pakistan, he was captured in a mosque after a Northern Alliance raid, whereupon he was taken to the United States-led Bagram detention base in Pakistan before being sold to Americans in order to be transferred to Guantánamo. For six months, el Gharani did not know where he was or why he had been captured. Since no charges were filed against el Gharani, there were none that could be released. One of the rules at Guantánamo is that if someone is imprisoned there, that person is barred from ever returning to the United States, should that person be released. Thus, upon el Gharani's release, he was banned from returning to the United States, leading to Anderson's idea for the projection of the satellite image of him in order to view him seated in the chair at The Armory.

In an interview with the English broadcast journalist Laura Flanders about the indoctrination process for the guards there and the difficulties faced by the men in prison there, Anderson asked several questions that I listed at the beginning of the chapter, questions repeated over and over again throughout this book: "What is suffering? What is justice? What is language? What's a story? Whose story are you going to believe? Who's in charge?"[64] Because so many of Anderson's works are about "words and stories and how they're told," as she explained to Flanders, the legal stopping points in *Habeas Corpus* were fascinating and deeply concerning.[65] For example, she explained that there was the story from el Gharani himself, there was the story from the United States government, and there was also a "bigger story of borders."[66] Much in the same way as she used authority as its own type of border that deserved questioning in the creation of Art Action Day, Anderson focused on the liminality of borders in *Habeas Corpus*. These borders are not merely geographical. They are political. They are religious. They are gender- and color-based. The unjust crossing of these borders can lead to unimaginable violence and horror. Anderson questions that horror—the torture, the uncertainty, the placelessness and personlessness that are a representation of her "No Bodies"—who are stuck at Guantánamo: "Why is this combination of pornography and violence happening? Why are we doing this? What right do we have to do this?"[67] el Gharani interprets the horror as a comparison to slavery, something that he believes has never ended in America: As was the case for many of his ancestors before him, he was taken in shackles from Africa, without explanation, and he landed in the Caribbean. Thanks to Anderson's activism and el Gharani's willingness to share his experience, we can hear el Gharani's story and hear how much it matters. He was imprisoned without explanation in America and will be forever affected by the experience. Who is really in charge?

Anderson's interview with Flanders also features several video excerpts with music from the premiere of *Habeas Corpus* at The Park Avenue Armory in New York in October 2015, including projections of stars filling the room and of the text of el Gharani's words scrolling across the walls in a large font. At one point, el Gharani breaks down when he speaks of one of his closest friends, Shaker Aamer (b. 1966), whom he met there, whom often resisted commands not to pray, and whom was endlessly tortured before eventually being released in October 2015. el Gharani is unable to keep talking as he speaks of the integrity of Aamer. He removes his glasses and lowers his head into his hands. During the silence, Anderson zooms the focus away from el Gharani and back to the stars and the projected words on the walls, reflecting her preternatural ability to invoke the cosmos and the universal complexities of language in so many of her works. She also adds music to accompany the moment that el Gharani stops talking.

The music that Anderson uses is a sample that also appears in other works that she has composed as a signification of grief. Pregnant pauses of silence alongside sustained notes and occasional glassy harmonics accentuate the feelings of incomprehensibility. A long-short pattern of two notes on the same pitch is repeated: first with E-flat, then with A-flat, then with B natural, then back to E-flat. Then the pattern repeats, shifted down a half step to D with a G pedal, implying a submediant to dominant nondirectional oscillation in a C minor tonality. Throughout the music, there is an alternation between stable consonance, a perfect fifth, and unstable dissonance, a tritone, depending on the single note that is being sustained. One moment there is a kind of stability, albeit fragile given the hushed dynamics and harmonics; at another moment that stability has disappeared. The players use different speeds of vibrato while sustaining the C to create this effect before the track ends with the outline of a minor third ascent, from C up to E-flat. At the moment that this music begins in *Habeas Corpus*, el Gharani experiences a breakdown, not only of language as he was at a loss for words but also in his attempt to try to understand what had happened to him at Guantánamo. In *Habeas Corpus*, the musical motive that accompanies el Gharani's experience represents a lament. It accompanies feelings of grief and inexplicable pain. The person watching the performance of *Habeas Corpus*—more of an experience than a performance, because el Gharani is not reading from a script; he is speaking of his own experience—has the opportunity to contemplate how to respond to ongoing tragedies in America, in this case the uncertainty, the loss of humanity, and the questions that arise about authority when one considers the human experience of the men in prison at Guantánamo.

Whether indirectly inspired by Anderson or created by Anderson herself, the works in this chapter create a space and a voice for marginalized groups, interweaving elements of current politics and rhetoric in the United States and challenging the creation of borders that intend to separate people in power from people who are not in power. Tropes that represent prejudices against race, class, gender, and religion are all actively at play. The artists are delivering subtly different interpretations of what "This Is America" means while simultaneously using similar symbols as a means of transmission. All of them in some way represent Anderson's series of questions that I listed at the beginning of the chapter about suffering, justice, language, storytelling, and truth. These are all hallmarks of many social justice movements. The specific links and references to social movements that Anderson might call to mind for the reader, movements such as #MeToo, #TimesUp, and #BlackLivesMatter, are often absent in these powerful works, although the proactive tweets that Art Action Day promoted have strong parallels, as do Anderson's repeated questions about power and authority. In the next chapter I explore how musical examples from Beyoncé, Rhiannon Giddens, and Janelle Monáe have more specifically addressed the calls for social justice on their digital platforms—particularly for Black girls and women—in the intersectionalities of the #MeToo, #TimesUp, and #BlackLivesMatter movements. The following words from Anderson offer an apt transition: "I've always thought that women make excellent social critics. We can look at situations, especially those involving power, and size them up fairly well: since we don't have much authority ourselves, we don't have that much to lose."[68] In the realm of performance, too, Anderson has commented on the unique role of women with a tongue-in-cheek reference to performing: "Women have rarely been composers. But we do have one advantage. We're used to performing."[69] And in a fitting reference to one of her own works as it pertains to the role of women who have the potential to create change, she asks in the song "Transitory Life" (2010): "When the doctor says: Congratulations! It's a boy! Where do all the dream baby girls, those possible pearls, go?"[70] The following chapter contains several musical answers to that question, specifically as they pertain to current social justice movements with the aim of advancing the rights of Black women and girls.

NOTES

1. Besides, the concept of "mainstream" is relative, because the art or music that might align with popular tastes is constantly changing.

2. In addition to occasionally dressing androgynously or as a man in her performances, she frequently alters her voice to what she has labeled "The Voice of Authority," also known as "Fenway Bergamot" after her late husband and *The Velvet Underground* lead singer Lou Reed (1942–2013) suggested the name. The voice distortion lowers the range of her natural voice in order to create the illusion of sounding authoritative.

3. As the cultural anthropologist Damien Sojoyner has argued, "To get beyond the grandiose statements that [Trump] makes, the actual policies that have been put in place by previous administrations have been just as structurally detrimental." Damien Sojoyner, interview with Gene Demby and Shereen Marisol Meraji, *Code Switch*, podcast audio, October 21, 2020, https://www.npr.org/transcripts/925385389.

4. The Laura Flanders Show, "Laurie Anderson & Mohammed el Gharani: Habeas Corpus," YouTube Video, 26:01, November 3, 2015, https://www.youtube.com/watch?v=WfuvAG_gXUM.

5. Laurie Anderson, "Stories from the Nerve Bible: A Retrospective, 1972–1992," interview by Nicholas Zurbrugg (1994), 137, in Jon McKenzie, "Laurie Anderson for Dummies:" 34.

6. Matt Weinstock, "Six Artists Revisit Their Works from the Early '80s," *New York Times*, April 26, 2018, https://www.nytimes.com/2018/04/26/t-magazine/larry-clark-laurie-anderson-bill-t-jones-80s-work.html?fbclid=IwAR0F0zodTA3Ym1wZhjzDINBi9_pq_5q03ykb0Jo8EGMmpHxRLOFknT5hpHs.

7. MacDowell, "Margaret Atwood & Laurie Anderson with Michael Chabon for 2019 Chairman's Evening," *YouTube Video*, 1:00:07, December 12, 2019, https://www.youtube.com/watch?v=ud9hjJ1b1zQ.

40   *Chapter 1*

8. Peggy McGlone, "For the Third Year in a Row, Trump's Budget Plan Eliminates Arts, Public TV and Library Funding," *The Washington Post*, March 18, 2019, https://www.washingtonpost.com/lifestyle/style/for-third-year-in-a-row-trumps-budget-plan-eliminates-arts-public-tv-and-library-funding/2019/03/18/e946db9a-49a2-11e9-9663-00ac73f49662_story.html.

9. Aileen Kwun, "Artists Mark Trump's Inauguration Anniversary with Day of Protest Art," *CNN Style*, January 9, 2018, https://www.cnn.com/style/article/trump-one-year-art-action-day/index.html.

10. The original link for The Federation's website is no longer active as of December 2020 (https://wearethefederation.org/events/art-action-day/), likely because the event has already occurred, but there are many descriptions of the project. See "The Federation," *StoryCorps Archives*, https://archive.storycorps.org/communities/the-federation/; The Federation's Facebook page, "The Federation," https://www.facebook.com/WeFederation/; "The Federation," *State of the Arts NYC*, https://stateoftheartsnyc.net/2018/02/21/the-force-behind-the-federation/; and Tanya Selvaratnam, "Art Is Essential to Democracy," *Howlround Theatre Commons*, January 18, 2018, https://howlround.com/art-essential-democracy. Another website describes the significance of the group's logo—an "F" that has a slash through it—as a mark of resistance: "The Federation," *Pentagram*, https://www.pentagram.com/work/the-federation/story.

11. "The Federation," *StoryCorps Archives*.

12. Tanya Selvaratnam, "Art Is Essential to Democracy."

13. The Untitled Space, "One Year of Resistance: Group Exhibition Curated by Indira Cesarine," January–February, 2018, https://untitled-space.com/wp-content/uploads/2018/03/ONE-YEAR-OF-RESISTANCE-CATALOGUE.pdf

14. Untitled Space, "One Year of Resistance: Group Exhibition January 2018," http://untitled-space.com/one-year-of-resistance-group-show/.

15. Kwun, "Artists Mark Trump's Inauguration Anniversary."

16. Ibid.

17. Ibid.

18. Untitled Space, "One Year of Resistance."

19. Eugene Hernandez, moderator, "Laurie Anderson & Special Guests," *Film at Lincoln Center*, Podcast Audio, December 6, 2017, https://soundcloud.com/filmlinc/159-laurie-anderson-special-guests.

20. Ibid. At that very point, a gospel choir entitled The Resistance Revival Chorus broke into singing "Woke Up This Morning (with My Mind on Freedom)," completely surprising Anderson, the audience, and the rest of the panel. Their timing could not have been more effective or symbolic, as she was speaking about freedom and also about the importance of being surprised by art. The song is a reworking of a gospel song from the 1960s entitled "I Woke up This Morning with My Mind Stayed on Jesus." (The choir begins singing around 37:52.)

21. Joel Tretin (http://www.joeltretinphotography.com), interviewed by Katie Rios via telephone, December 2019.

22. Benjamin Weiser and William K. Rashbaum, "In Steve Bannon Case, Prosecutors Have 'Voluminous' Emails," *The New York Times*, August 31, 2020,

https://www.nytimes.com/2020/08/31/nyregion/steve-bannon-build-the-wall-fraud.html.

23. Philip Elliott and Zeke J. Miller, "Inside Donald Trump's Chaotic Transition," *Time*, November 21, 2016, https://time.com/4574493/donald-trump-chaotic-transition/.

24. Milo, "The Solution to Online 'Harrassment' Is Simple: Women Should Log off," *Breitbart*, July 5, 2016, https://www.breitbart.com/social-justice/2016/07/05/solution-online-harassment-simple-women-log-off/; Jeff Poor, "Steyn: 'In the Space of about Twenty Minutes, We've Gone from "The Confederate Flag is Racist" to "The Star Spangled Banner is Racist"'," *Breitbart*, September 29, 2017, https://www.breitbart.com/clips/2017/09/29/steyn-space-20-minutes-weve-gone-confederate-flag-racist-star-spangled-banner-racist/; Milo, "Gay Rights Have Made Us Dumber, It's Time to Get back into the Closet," *Breitbart*, June 17, 2015, https://www.breitbart.com/politics/2015/06/17/gay-rights-have-made-us-dumber-its-time-to-get-back-in-the-closet/; David Horowitz, "Bill Kristol: Republican Spoiler, Renegade Jew," *Breitbart*, May 15, 2016, https://www.breitbart.com/politics/2016/05/15/bill-kristol-republican-spoiler-renegade-jew/.

25. Bannon has since been arrested for fraud. Matt Zapotsky, Josh Dawsey, Rosalind S. Helderman, and Shayna Jacobs, "Steve Bannon Charged with Defrauding Donors in Private Effort to Raise Money for Trump's Border Wall," *The Washington Post*, August 20, 2020, https://www.washingtonpost.com/national-security/stephen-bannon-arrested-charged/2020/08/20/6d46847c-e2ea-11ea-b69b-64f7b0477ed4_story.html.

26. Joel Tretin, interviewed by Katie Rios.

27. At least thirty-three others were injured, and two state troopers lost their lives in a helicopter crash while attempting to respond to the unrest. Benjamin Hart and Chas Dunner, "3 Dead and Dozens Injured after Violent White-Nationalist Rally in Virginia," *New York Intelligencer*, August 13, 2017, https://nymag.com/intelligencer/2017/08/state-of-emergency-in-va-after-white-nationalist-rally.html.

28. Katie Reilly, "President Trump Again Blames 'Both Sides' for Charlottesville Violence," *TIME*, August 15, 2017, https://time.com/4902129/president-donald-trump-both-sides-charlottesville/.

29. Yancy, *Backlash*, 9.

30. Glover, "Childish Gambino – This Is America."

31. Joel Tretin, interviewed by Katie Rios.

32. Touba Alipour (http://www.toubaalipour.com), interviewed by Katie Rios via telephone, April 2020.

33. Ibid.

34. Ibid.

35. Laurie Anderson, "From the Air," track 1 on *Big Science*, April 19, 1982, 2007 Nonesuch Records, Inc., Apple Music.

36. Andrea Salcedo, Sanam Yar, and Gina Cherelus, "Coronavirus Travel Restrictions, Across the Globe," *The New York Times*, July 16, 2020, https://www.nytimes.com/article/coronavirus-travel-restrictions.html.

37. Touba Alipour, interviewed by Katie Rios.

38. I thank Sarah Lindmark for her incisive observations of the role of silence in Gambino's video. Sara Lindmark, "'Hip Hop Causes Violence': Arguments and Analyses Concerning Childish Gambino's 'This Is America,'" paper presented at the American Musicological Society, Boston, MA, November 2019.

39. The phrase emerged as a concept in Burrough's novel *The Ticket That Exploded* (Paris: Olympia Press, 1962), and Anderson popularized the concept in her 1986 song "Language Is a Virus from Outer Space."

40. Laurie Anderson, *Heart of a Dog*, directed by Laurie Anderson (Burbank: Nonesuch Records, 2015), video.

41. Laurie Anderson, *All the Things I Lost in the Flood: Essays on Pictures, Language and Code* (New York: RozzoliElecta, 2018), 13.

42. Nadja Sayej, "Language, Politics, and Performance with Laurie Anderson," *i-D*, March 7, 2017, https://i-d.vice.com/en_uk/article/gyvxg7/language-politics-and-performance-with-laurie-anderson.

43. David Graham, "Making Art in the Age of Trump," *The Atlantic*, June 1, 2016, https://www.theatlantic.com/entertainment/archive/2016/06/laurie-anderson-qa-hamilton-trump-hillary/485054/.

44. Ibid.

45. Louisiana Channel, "Laurie Anderson Interview: We Are in Constant Panic Mode," *YouTube Video*, 3:22, February 25, 2019, https://www.youtube.com/watch?v=hpec93exiHI&feature=emb_logo.

46. Ibid.

47. Meghan Keneally, "A Look back at Trump Comments Perceived by Some as Encouraging Violence," *abc News*, October 19, 2018, https://abcnews.go.com/Politics/back-trump-comments-perceived-encouraging-violence/story?id=48415766.

48. Lauren Feiner, "Twitter Flagged Another Trump Tweet for Violating Its Policies," *CNBC*, June 23, 2020, https://www.cnbc.com/2020/06/23/twitter-labeled-another-trump-tweet-for-violating-its-policies.html.

49. Peter Baker, Raymond Zhong, and Russell Goldman, "Twitter Places Warning on a Trump Tweet, Saying It Glorified Violence," *The New York Times*, May 29, 2020, https://www.nytimes.com/2020/05/29/technology/trump-twitter-minneapolis-george-floyd.html?action=click&module=Top%20Stories&pgtype=Homepage.

50. Bess Levin, "Trump Uses Coronavirus Press Conference to Confirm He's an Actual Sociopath," *Vanity Fair*, March 20, 2020, https://www.vanityfair.com/news/2020/03/donald-trump-peter-alexander-coronavirus-press-conference.

51. Yoko Ono (@yokoono), 2016, "Dear Friends, I would like to share this message with you as my response to @realDonaldTrump love, yoko," Twitter, November 11, 2016, 4:21 PM, https://twitter.com/yokoono/status/797187458505080834.

52. Shelina Brown, "Scream from the Heart: Yoko d's Rock and Roll Revolution," Chapter 10 in *Countercultures and Popular Music*, ed. Sheila Whitely and Jedediah Sklower (Burlington, VT: Ashgate), 171–86.

53. Carl Swanson, "Laurie Anderson and Marilyn Minter Want Us All to Scream Bloody Murder on the Anniversary of Trump's Election," *New York Vulture*, November 2, 2017, https://www.vulture.com/2017/11/laurie-anderson-marilyn-minter-scream-about-2016-election.html.

54. Ibid.

55. SFJAZZ, "Laurie Anderson – Songs for Women [Excerpt] (Live at SFJAZZ)," *YouTube Video*, 3:39, December 31, 2019, https://www.youtube.com/watch?v=W5sOpqoDLKE&feature=emb_logo.

56. Ibid.

57. Stories about birds are a recurring trope in many of Anderson's works, suggesting liminality in the undefined borders between the ground and the sky.

58. The liminality of water is another theme in many of the works in this book, perhaps most so for Beyoncé (see chapter 2). Zulal Kalkendelen, "Laurie Anderson Performing @ Moogfest," *YouTube Video*, 4:18, May 23, 2016, https://www.youtube.com/watch?v=uoxvAzmXwPQ&feature=emb_logo.

59. Ibid.

60. Graham, "Making Art in the Age of Trump."

61. Arun Rath, "Trump Inherits Guantanamo's Remaining Detainees," *NPR News*, January 19, 2017, https://www.npr.org/2017/01/19/510448989/trump-inherits-guantanamos-remaining-detainees.

62. https://www.aclu.org/issues/national-security/detention/guantanamo-bay-detention-camp

63. Ibid.

64. The Laura Flanders Show, "Laurie Anderson & Mohammed el Gharani."

65. Ibid.

66. Ibid.

67. Ibid. Her reference to pornography is similar in its tone to the "trauma porn" criticisms leveled against Gambino for his video for "This Is America" in that she suggests that the Guantánamo guards might take some kind of pleasure in the horrific and repeated acts of violence experienced by the men in prison there.

68. Laurie Anderson, interview by Nicholas Zurbrugg, 261.

69. Quoted in Susan McClary, *Feminine Endings: Music, Gender, and Sexuality* (Minneapolis: University of Minnesota Press, 1991), 139.

70. Laurie Anderson, "Transitory Life," track 1 of *Homeland*, 2010 Nonesuch Records, Inc., Apple Music.

Chapter 2

"At the Intersection of Racism and Sexism"

The Encoded Resistance and Social Activism of Beyoncé, Rhiannon Giddens, and Janelle Monáe

In the liner notes to the album *Songs of Our Native Daughters* (2019), whose title is likely a reference to James Baldwin's work *Notes of a Native Son* (1955), the artist Rhiannon Giddens (b. 1977) spoke of the complexity of articulating identity for Black women in America because of the powerful intersecting forces of racism and sexism, as reflected in part of this chapter's title.[1] Her work is one example among many of how Black female musicians have raised their voices to speak out against social injustices, particularly within the context of the bitterly divisive politics that have come to the fore during the single-term Trump presidency between 2016 and 2020. In this chapter I evaluate how the encoded tropes of protest that I labeled in the Introduction come to life in powerful examples of resistance by Black women: Beyoncé's performance of "Formation" (live and video, 2016) along with brief mentions of similar tropes in her documentary *Homecoming* (2019) and in her visual album *Black Is King* (2020); Rhiannon Giddens's concept and development of *Songs of Our Native Daughters*, in addition to a video for another song, "At the Purchaser's Option" (2017); and Janelle Monáe's performance of "Americans" (2018) on The Late Show with Stephen Colbert.

Added to the complexity of these performances is the undercurrent of the #BlackLivesMatter, #MeToo, and #TimesUp movements that have gained momentum in recent years, including the all-too-frequent marginalization of women of color within these very movements whose proponents seek to provide equal opportunities for women. To that end, there are also hashtags such as #SayHerName, #BlackGirlsMatter, and #BlackWomenMatter that, as Elaine Richardson and Alice Ragland point out, "illuminate intersectionality within the Black Lives Matter movement" and point to some of the discrepancies in the other movements.[2] Even more generally, the very concept of intersectionality and its shared oppressions has been an important factor shaping Black feminism and has the potential to be applied to other groups of people. For example, the sociologist Patricia Hill Collins argues that "not only do intersectional paradigms prove useful in explaining U.S. Black women's experiences, such paradigms suggest that intersecting oppressions also shape the experiences of other groups as well."[3] In a roundtable on the topic of the overlap of the forces behind the social justice movements that addressed the urgency of naming these kinds of overlaps and intersections, the participating panelists concluded in their work that:

> The Black American struggle for civil rights and the struggle for women's empowerment in the twentieth century—and continuing into the twenty-first century—are two of the most important stories in American history. Though these have not been, and are not now, two separate stories, they are all too often told as such. . . . We are still faced with ongoing struggles for women's and Black rights. We still grapple for how to make manifest the real promise of freedom through the lens of gender, race, and other identity markers. We continue.[4]

I will first provide a brief account of the movements, their focus, and their interrelationships to each other. After I do that, I will turn to the specific musical examples, meant not as an exhaustive list but rather as a powerful symbol of the tropes throughout this text, most compellingly in the transformation of how the person being viewed regains power and becomes the social commentator and the metaphorical mirror revealing the message to the audience. In the second section of this chapter in which I discuss the selected examples, the performers' use of body and voice along with engagement with the audience both implicitly and explicitly relates to current political and social issues. The examples that I discuss in this chapter address violations against women—and, in particular, Black women—in an era charged with ongoing debates about women's rights and responsibilities.[5] Since part of the premise of this book is that what we see is just as important as what we hear, I highlight videographic elements in addition to sonic ones. In all cases, the songs have become more popular through social media sources and other internet promotions, rendering the songs' messages even more urgent through their digital proximity. Beyoncé, Giddens, and Monáe are a few among many women suggesting that it is time—well past time—to have important conversations and to enact change. As Monáe has argued, "We . . . have the power to undo the culture that does not serve us well."[6] Speaking to that culture, it is critical to acknowledge the overlaps in these three movements, particularly the role of the African American woman. While it is not my goal in this chapter to come up with a hashtag that might represent the intersection of the three social movements, it is my goal to evaluate examples that represent some of the women of color who are too often overlooked in these movements as the intersection's focal point and to interpret the meaningful ways in which they connect with their audiences.

#METOO

#MeToo originated as a movement that Tarana Burke (b. 1973) began in 2006 in order to address violence against women of color in impoverished communities. The hashtag became well known after numerous accounts of sexual harassment and sexual assaults by the film producer Harvey Weinstein drew national attention in 2017, specifically when the actress Alyssa Milano (b. 1972) tweeted: "If you've been sexually harassed or assaulted write 'me too' as a reply to this tweet."[7] Milano's 2017 tweet caused the original #MeToo movement to reemerge with new momentum. Milano was at first unaware that she was using a phrase that Burke had coined, but upon learning this she was quick to give Burke credit.[8] The organization's website provides several useful features to describe the movement and the type of protection that it seeks for victims; there is even a "safety exit" link that remains fixed on the top center of the screen that, when clicked, takes the user directly to a blank Google search page.[9] The site also includes a glossary of terms and the citation source for each term, including "consent," "gender," "gender stereotypes," "healing," "intersectionality," "misogynoir" (a combination of the words "misogyny" and "noir" in order to, as the site explains, "describe the anti-Black sexism and misogyny that Black women face"), "sex," "sexual assault," and "sexual coercion."[10] With its wealth of information, including toolkits and resources for both healing and advocacy, the website is an invaluable resource for victims of sexual violence. In the "About" section of the website, the first sentence makes clear that #MeToo is a movement that originated to support women of color, stating that "The 'me too' Movement was founded in 2006 to help survivors of sexual violence, particularly Black women and girls, and other women of color from low wealth communities, find pathways to healing."[11]

To this end, Burke has made efforts to ensure that women of color are not forgotten in this movement, even as it has become more widespread. In a discussion with the reporter Hari Sreenivasan on PBS News Hour, she talked about working with a friend in an organization they established called "Just Be Inc." that allowed them to work with women who had experienced sexual violence.[12] According to Burke, they soon realized that they "needed to shift and start dealing with the issue of sexual violence in the community we were in." At that point, she had still not used the "#MeToo" reference. Burke explained that she became a part of the widespread national conversation that took place in 2017, stating that she wanted

> to make sure that the marginalized voices I represent weren't erased, but also to provide people some context for the use of Me Too. We have a theory called empowerment through empathy, which is the basis for how we do the work. And I felt like it was necessary to ground the conversation in a body of work.[13]

She also noted the difficulty that women of color have had simply having their voices heard, and more importantly, centered, as an all-too-often occasion. For that matter, the movement that she began drew more widespread national attention only after a prominent, non-Black Hollywood actress promoted it. Burke described the problem of including the minority voice in more detail in the interview after Sreenivasan asked: "You've said before that sexual violence doesn't see race or class, but the response to it does. Tell me what that means." She replied

> That means that when we see things like Harvey Weinstein having dozens and dozens of accusers, and the only person he responds to is Lupita Nyong'o and to the Black woman, that means something. It also means that when you have all of these powerful, rich, wealthy men who are White and attacking or victimizing White women, it gets all of this attention. But you have somebody like R. Kelly, who has been a known sexual predator for two decades, but his victims are all Black girls . . . The reality is that [all of these] people operate within systems that allow them to flourish. When we look at patriarchy, when we look at capitalism, these are systems that are in place that allow men [like this] to exist because people are more invested in those systems than they are in human dignity.[14]

The tremendous attention that the #MeToo movement has received needs to be considered within the context of its origins in order to better understand the connections to the systems that are driving injustices against women. Ultimately, Burke's goal was to create a platform for victims' voices to be heard in a nontraditional way. In another interview, she asked

> What does "justice" look like for a survivor? . . . We've got to get a clearer understanding of what justice is and what people need to feel whole. If we're ever going to heal in our community, we have to heal the perpetrators and heal the survivors, or else it's just a continuous cycle.[15]

The questions about authority, justice, and control are ongoing themes throughout this book. As those words pertain to the #MeToo movement, the direction of the movement is critical for confronting another cyclic loop of injustices in America, particularly as those injustices affect Black women.

#TIMESUP

The #TimesUp movement began in 2018 to bring focus to sexual harassment and assault in the workplace. Specifically, it began with a letter published on the website, as a full-page advertisement in *The New York Times*, and in another advertisement in the Spanish-language newspaper *La Opinion* on January 1, 2018, signed by "over 300 women who work in film, television, and theater."[16] An accompanying article by the reporter Cara Buckley, published the same day in *The New York Times*, summarized some of the initiatives in the letter, naming it as "an impassioned pledge of support to working-class women."[17] Buckley goes on to explain that the timing of the development of #TimesUp was important for addressing criticism that arose after many #MeToo cases focused on high-profile celebrities, once again bringing to the fore Burke's concerns that the original intentions of her movement were being overlooked. In the case of #TimesUp, the concern was that workplace harassment was not limited to Hollywood. No one individual leads #TimesUp, and the Hollywood actresses who signed the letter wanted to use their fame to expose broader problems across America for working women. In the article, producer Shonda Rimes (b. 1970) stated that "'It's very hard for us to speak righteously about the rest of anything if we haven't cleaned our own house. . . . If this group of women can't fight for a model for other women who don't have as much power and privilege, then who can?'"[18] It is meaningful that Buckley quoted a prominent Black producer in her article, drawing attention to the tendency for Black women to be overlooked in these movements and addressing the problem by centering Rimes's voice.

There are many similarities between the #MeToo and #TimesUp movements. For one thing, the proximity in the timing of the #TimesUp letter in early January 2018 to the resurgence of the #MeToo movement in 2017 suggests a close relationship of the two movements. For another, the website for #TimesUp prominently features women of color.[19] In the "About" section for #TimesUp, bold and largely sized text emerges to show that reads: "Safe, fair, and dignified work for women of all kinds."[20] The inclusion that Burke envisioned for #MeToo clearly played a role in how the website developers wanted to portray the women they wanted to protect. Namely, the founders "aim to create a society free of gender-based discrimination in the workplace and beyond" and "to be safe on the job and have equal opportunity for economic success and security."[21] At the Golden Globes on January 7, 2018, clothing functioned as a symbol for the #TimesUp movement, because attendees who supported it were encouraged to wear all black. The two groups share many goals. *TIME* reporter Alix Langone spoke to Burke and to one of the #TimesUp representatives, the Executive Vice President of WarnerMedia and *Latina* magazine founder Christy Haubegger (b. 1968), to discuss some of the overlaps in their visions for the movement.[22] Haubegger elucidated that "even though Time's Up is focused on what happens to people in professional realms . . . the organization's work is really in tribute to Burke and the remarkable work she did for a decade before #MeToo exploded globally."[23] At the heart of the matter, power imbalances adversely affect women in all kinds of circumstances, and women including Burke and Haubegger—and growing numbers of many, many others—want to rectify that.

#BLACKLIVESMATTER

In addition to the overlaps that I have discussed between the #MeToo and #TimesUp movements, the #BlackLivesMatter movement is another undercurrent for many of the examples in this chapter in addition to other examples throughout the book. It originated with a Facebook post by Alicia Garza (b. 1981) in 2013 that said "Black people. I love you. I love us. Our lives matter."[24] Garza's Facebook post spurred a number of responses, including one from her friend, Patrisse Khan-Cullors (b. 1983), who wrote "#BlackLivesMatter."[25] Khan-Cullors describes the experience in detail in her memoir *When They Call You a Terrorist: A Black Lives Matter Memoir* that she cowrote with Asha Bandele:

> And then my friend Alicia writes a Facebook post. Alicia, who I'd known for seven years at this point, who I'd met at a political gathering where at the end of the day our goal was to dance until we couldn't dance anymore. She and I danced with one another all night long and began a friendship that holds us together to this very day. . . . She writes . . . "btw stop saying that we are surprised. that's a damn shame in itself. I continue to be surprised at how little Black lives matter. And I will continue that. stop giving up on black life. black people, I will *never* give up on us. *never.*" And then I respond. I wrote back with a hashtag: #BlackLivesMatter.[26]

Opal Tometi (b. 1984) then joined Garza and Khan-Cullors to continue to turn the moment into a movement. All of the momentum of the #BlackLivesMatter movement on Facebook described above occurred after [redacted] (b. 1983) was acquitted for the shooting death of unarmed Trayvon Martin (1995–2012) on February 26, 2012. In the transcript of the shooter's phone call to the nonemergency number for the police, he mentioned that

Martin looked suspicious and was wearing a hoodie.[27] Martin was not doing anything suspicious; he was walking around and being targeted because of his skin color. Martin's killer subsequently chased him down, fought with him, and murdered him. The first sentence in the "About" section on the Black Lives Matter homepage states that "#BlackLivesMatter was founded in 2013 in response to the acquittal of Trayvon Martin's murderer."[28] Like #TimesUp, #BlackLivesMatter does not have any named leaders in a central position; the movement is meant to be as inclusive as possible. That said, it is representationally important that its three cofounders are all Black women, making it an especially meaningful movement to contextualize in this chapter about musical works that have in large part addressed the marginalization of women and minorities. Embracing actions of inclusivity that include both women and minorities, below a picture of Garza, Khan-Cullors, and Tometi, they make a statement noting their "commitment to placing those at the margins closer to the center," especially given the history of

> Black liberation movements in this country [that] have created room, space, and leadership mostly for Black heterosexual, cisgender men—leaving women, queer, and transgender people, and others either out of the movement or in the background to move the work forward with little or no recognition.[29]

The inclusivity in this statement means that #BlackLivesMatter is not only a pillar for many of the examples in this book but also for the #MeToo and #TimesUp movements.

Although I have discussed these three movements of #MeToo, #TimesUp, and #BlackLivesMatter in the separately labeled sections above in order to explore the origins of each and the central figures in establishing their goals and actions, it is clear that these movements have overlaps, the very types of intersections that address the quote from Giddens that I included in the chapter's title. All of the examples in this chapter focus not only on the empowerment of Black women and but also on the reclamation of space for other marginalized voices. For that matter, there are echoes of the effects of these movements in other examples throughout the book, such as the explanatory signs under Touba Alipour's neon light installation in chapter 1 (see figures 1.4 and 1.5 and their language of exclusion: "Keep in mind your gender, race, color and religion may be used against you"), along with Laurie Anderson's comments that I included that are about the marginalization of women near the end of chapter 1 ("Since we don't have much authority . . . we don't have that much to lose"). In chapter 3 I discuss the contributions of women in hip-hop in a largely male-dominated industry, and in chapter 4 I include a brief discussion about the power shift of women with strong female leads in *Hamilton*. So why single out the specific examples below from Beyoncé, Giddens, and

Monáe relating to the movements in a separate chapter? The examples that I have selected are products of Black women who are deliberately incorporating and enacting the messages of #MeToo, #TimesUp, and #BlackLivesMatter through encoded symbols and gestures.[30] In all of the examples, it can be understood that the women are performing the messages of these movements.

BEYONCÉ AND "FORMATION" (2016)

In her appearance at the Super Bowl on February 7, 2016, Beyoncé Giselle Knowles-Carter (b. 1981) created one of the most-watched and memorable performances of her career to that point in her performance of "Formation," which would later appear as part of the full album *Lemonade* that she released in June 2016. In addition, Beyoncé released the video for "Formation" one day before she would perform it at the Super Bowl. At once, both the Super Bowl performance and the release of the video became an icon for minorities, for the #BlackLivesMatter movement, for the underrepresented women that comprise #MeToo, #TimesUp, and #BlackLivesMatter, and for a challenge to persistent brutality against Blacks, all too often at the hands of Whites who continue to discriminate against them. In a book of essays devoted entirely to the *Lemonade* album, the recording artist Maiysha Kai wrote that "the debut of her *Formation* video—and subsequent Black Panther-inspired Super Bowl performance—displayed an unexpected streak of activism in a woman better known for her performances than her politics."[31] Given Beyoncé's deliberate change to her usual approach to performing, a change from performing-as-entertainment to performing-as-protest, I will first address critical reception—both positive and negative—of the video and the performance of "Formation" a day after the video's release. Kai hinted at the potential for negative reception of the performance. She added after acknowledging the political significance of Beyoncé's two performances: "Even as she pulled back the curtain on her famously private life with a work more personal than anything she'd offered before, there was a suspicion that it was just another layer of the façade. Were her politics performative?"[32] Kai's implication is that if Beyoncé's politics were performative, it would mean that her gestures were insincere. Kai did not interpret the gestures as such, and I agree. Beyoncé's inclusion of symbolic gestures delivers a message of resistance in a most formidable manner. The timing of Beyoncé's release of the video to her Super Bowl performance was a provocative political statement, and after reviewing the reception of both, I will consider many symbols in both the music video and the live performance. In her clothing and use of props, movements, and delivery of language—some of the elements that I have been discussing as repeated tropes and symbols for fighting social injustices—she offered and strengthened the foundation of one of her most potent political commentaries.

The music video for "Formation" includes several references to the #BlackLivesMatter movement through the lens of the devastation of Hurricane Katrina that hit New Orleans on August 23, 2005. In addition to the Black Lives Matter references in "Formation," Beyoncé regularizes the fight for Black justice throughout *Lemonade*.[33] After Hurricane Katrina devastated New Orleans, the city was subsequently filled with displaced residents who felt the effects of being overlooked simply by virtue of being a minority. The aftereffects of the storm were particularly catastrophic, because several levees collapsed and created further damage; experts estimate that the storm caused more than $100 billion in damage.[34] As tens of thousands of refugees had no place to go after the storm destroyed their homes, in the midst of a natural disaster, the government response was painfully slow. References to the #BlackLivesMatter movement became a powerful tool to express the rage and desolation that so many New Orleans residents felt.

Before considering additional details in the video that can be associated with the #BlackLivesMatter movement, it is helpful to put the video in the context of other responses to Hurricane Katrina. An article in *Ebony* plainly states one response in its title: "The Black Lives Matter Movement Started with Hurricane Katrina."[35] According to the article, this association of the #BlackLivesMatter movement with a national disaster happened in large part because of the images that began to surface after the hurricane struck. The public first saw images of "low-income Black Americans, stranded and desperate to escape," with no other viable option than to go to the overcrowded Superdome and convention center.[36] Systemic, structural racism that already kept Blacks below the poverty line that existed in the heart of the city—and in the heart of America—led them there. The *Ebony* article expanded on this idea, stating that "they were there because in a city defined by decades of poverty, segregation, and deep disenfranchisement, poor and working-class Blacks (including the elderly, and children) would largely shoulder the burden of the storm."[37] In another association of the nation's undue acceptance of Black suffering, the Reverend Jesse Jackson stated in an interview with CNN's Anderson Cooper that "We have an amazing tolerance for Black pain and for too long after our slave ships landed in New Orleans. . . We have great tolerance for Black suffering and Black marginalization."[38] Musical responses, too, were just as critical in their association of Hurricane Katrina's effect of exposing continued demoralization of the Black community. One reference to race in the wake of the Katrina disaster was Beyoncé's soon-to-be husband Jay-Z's track "Minority Report" (2006), which opens with news accounts of "people . . . being forced to live like animals," "no one say[ing] the federal government is doing a good job," and, perhaps most cutting, a sample of Kanye West declaring that "George Bush doesn't care about Black people."[39] All of these reactions spread widely on the news and on social media. With the knowledge that such responses were widespread, Beyoncé's choice to shoot the video in New Orleans and to reenact images after the storm was a statement to raise attention to the continued mistreatment of Blacks, a way of performing an important component of the vision of #BlackLivesMatter.

Created eleven years after Hurricane Katrina, Beyoncé's video for "Formation" (directed by Melina Matsoukas, b. 1981) includes speech samples with distinctive timbres by well-known figures in New Orleans in addition to hairstyles, clothing, and body movements that celebrate Black female beauty. The video opens with her sitting on top of a flooded police car, precariously floating on top of the water (by the end of the video, the car sinks), with a voice asking "What happened at the New Wildins?"[40] The voice is a cappella, answered by a solo sitar that plucks a wavering note repeated twice before moving to a note roughly a minor third above that, repeated in the same rhythm. The vocal sample turned out to be controversial, because the voice that she was sampling belonged to Anthony Barré (1987–2010), a New Orleans bounce rapper who went by the name of Messy Mya, hugely popular on social media and beloved by many in New Orleans before being shot in a still-unsolved murder on November 14, 2010. He became well known in New Orleans for videos that he would create to conduct impromptu interviews with people who talked about what living in the city was like. Sadly, his characteristic sign-off for these videos was "Now, who gonna pop me?"[41] Some saw Beyoncé's gesture as an homage to Messy Mya, but others have critiqued the presence of the voice and the absence of the image of Messy Mya.[42]

This same type of sonic dissonance occurs about midway through the video, at which point Beyoncé samples another New Orleans legend, the bounce music artist Big Freedia (b. 1978), whose voice can be heard saying "I did not come to play wit you ho's . . . Ha ha! I came to slay, bitch!"[43] Women and gender studies scholar Jennifer DeClue has named the inclusion of voices like Messy Mya and Big Freedia as "sonic vivication" without visual representation.[44] Although DeClue's criticism has merit, one could also interpret Beyoncé's inclusion of marginalized voices as samples as the very way of amplifying these voices, especially since their voices would likely be well known to many New Orleans residents. DeClue also talks about the important function of clothing, hairstyles, and body movements that we see in the video after the sample "I did not come to play." These elements foreground the Big Freedia sample, as DeClue explains:

> Big Freedia's illustrious declaration introduces a plantation-style porch scene in which Beyoncé, flanked by a multigenerational group of handsome Black

men who don tuxedos as they stare into the space just beyond the camera, is dressed in a Black satin off-the-shoulder top; long, full black satin skirt; and a wide-brimmed hat with two long blond braids that extend well past her waist. Beyoncé bobs her head incisively to the tickling pluck of the sitar.[45]

To punctuate the appearance of the long braids at her sides, Beyoncé takes one and starts twirling it as she sings about her heritage. It is the only movement that we see in the porch scene—everyone else is completely still—and the braid-twirling stands out for that reason, as though Beyoncé cannot help but introduce some sort of movement in a celebratory and defiant way as a contrast to the stillness. This scene occurs between moments of Beyoncé and her dancers lined up in formation and dancing together. All of these elements—the inclusion of marginalized voices as samples and the encoded movements, dress, and hairstyles, are celebrations and centerings of Black womanhood.

Throughout the *Lemonade* album and throughout the video, she uses several visual signifiers of celebrating what it means to be both Black and female. This remains a connecting thread for #MeToo, #TimesUp, and #BlackLivesMatter. Beyoncé's choice to highlight aspects of her Black femininity reflects her lived experience: she is a Black woman. Put another way, the way that she portrays her performance carries personal meaning for her. She is aware of the significance of the presentation of her performance, so she includes recognizable elements that will make it even more meaningful for the Black female community. Her gestures in the video support her self-love of the features that make her who she is: as she sings "I like my negro nose with Jackson Five nostrils," she touches her own nose and turns her head upward. She celebrates Black girlhood, too: the line "I like my baby hair with baby hair and Afros" is accompanied with a turn to a group of three young Black girls dressed in beautiful white dresses, the one in the center with her hands on her hips and a shy smile on her face. The two girls at her sides look straight at the camera, unsmiling, powerful, strong, and confident in their self-worth.[46] And while the word "slay" is used at points in the video in the context of police brutality, it is also used to depict a no-nonsense mentality from the outset of the video. The African and African Diaspora scholar Omise-eke Tinsley highlights symbolic moments in the video, including the significance of clothing, props, and nonmovement in the act of staring at the camera to exclaim this defiance:

> As the final sitar note punctuates the end of the line, the video cuts—first to a shot of women's feet in slides that read UH HUH HONEY—then to a medium close-up of a chocolate-skinned woman with cascading teal hair. The camera eventually pans to a full-body shot of these women standing shoulder to

shoulder with a third, posed like the Black Three Graces in the aisle of a hair store where shelves of wigs frame their stance.⁴⁷

The likening of these women to the "Black Three Graces"—the three young Black girls could be included too—is a meaningful reference and subversion of an ancient Roman tradition of (typically) representations of White women who, as the scholar Jane Francis explains, were "worshipped as minor goddesses" and who even in their original appearances in art featured "considerable discrepancies in hairstyle, pose, clothing, attribute, and, evidently meaning."⁴⁸ The ways in which both Tinsley and Francis describe the Three Graces show that elements of appearance can affect the meaning of the art itself. Tinsley talks further about the significance of transforming Black women into goddesses in "Formation," a lengthy passage full of meaningful critical details about the significance of the images that the audience sees:

> For all that getting hair and doing hair means to Black trans* and cis sisterhood, pairing Freedia's voiceover with the endless styling possibilities of the hair store means something in New Orleans queer culture. But my favorite part about the wig-loving (cis? trans*?) Graces of "Formation" is the teal color hair of the actress captured in medium close-up. Her saturated aquamarine tresses look like the mermaid hair popularized by singer Azealia Banks (and coopted by Kylie Jenner): a fantastical look that imagines Black women are magic, that the art of being a Black woman is turning ourselves into goddesses and sirens and back again daily. Yes, yes, yes.⁴⁹

Throughout the video for "Formation," Beyoncé shows the possibility for Black women to transform themselves into goddesses as much as she shows their humanity. The video is filled with images, moments, and movements of joyful celebrations of inclusive Black womanhood and girlhood.

In all of her representations of Black joy, one might wonder if Beyoncé is representing a positive change in the past decade that addresses the mistreatment of Blacks, particularly since she set the video in New Orleans, a city in transition and a city in need of change. But her joyful signifiers are paired with more disturbing elements, just as Gambino would do two years later in his video for "This Is America" in a similar juxtaposition and flux of joy against terror. In one moment of the "Formation" video, a young Black boy dressed in all-black attire breakdances in front of a row of heavily armed police, also dressed in black, somber and apparently unmoved, at least until the boy stops dancing and stretches his arms out widely to his sides. At this point, the camera focuses to the police, and they all raise their hands silently. This body movement is not only representative of a power reversal—the boy has caused the police to raise their hands, not vice versa—but also a gesture representing the "Hands up, don't shoot" reference after the August 9, 2014, killing of Michael Brown (1996–2014) and the subsequent momentum of the Black Lives Matter movement. Elaine Richardson and Alice Ragland explain that the body movement of raised arms and hands has become regularized at protests as a visual marker of resistance, stating that "Protestors putting their hands up (a symbol for surrender intended to notify police officers not to shoot) . . . is a widely recognized symbol used to raise awareness that many Black people have been shot by police even when they had their hands up."[50] The "Hands up, don't shoot" is a body movement seen in many other examples, notably in hip-hop, as a repeated gesture of resistance that I will revisit in chapter 3. After the image in the "Formation" video of the police with their hands and arms raised, a visual of graffiti reads: "Stop shooting us."[51] The timing of the camera shots with all of these movements is all carefully matched to the words that Beyoncé is slowly speaking: "Slay, trick, or you get eliminated."[52] When she says "slay," that is the point that the young boy outstretches his arms; when she says "trick," the police raise their hands (the boy has "tricked" them into doing so through the power of his breakdancing); and when she says "or you get eliminated," the view moves to the graffiti. After this point, the view shifts back to Beyoncé on top of the sinking police car as it becomes fully submerged in water. Beyoncé goes underwater with the car.

Water is a regular feature in the video for *Lemonade*, suggesting both a liminal space in the transitions between songs and a space for transformation. Water not only represents the devastation that Katrina caused, but it also offers the possibility of change, a trope that Beyoncé would return to in her 2020 release of the film *Black Is King*, in which she makes a powerful statement about reclamation of Black identity and the role of water: "You're swimming back to yourself. You'll meet yourself at the shore. The coast belongs to our ancestors. We orbit. Make joy look easy."[53] The flooding of the coasts of Lake Pontchartrain and Lake Borgne in New Orleans disproportionately took the homes and lives of many Black people, and the deluge of water in New Orleans became a symbol for broken systems in America. At the same time, water offered an opportunity for the personal transformation that she describes, as Beyoncé says herself, for joy and for overcoming. The transformations that Beyoncé represents in the "Formation" video go beyond the state of New Orleans just over a decade after Katrina. The transformations are also about the brutality that has continued to happen to Black bodies. The juxtaposition of the police presence amidst the suffering of Black bodies is as powerful as celebrating the women of color that she includes in the video. The duality of joy and sorrow in juxtaposition to represent images of America in the "Formation" video is the visual reminder of an enduring struggle.

One day after her video release of "Formation," she performed at the halftime show in the Super Bowl.[54] Beyoncé's performance became a hot topic of discussion, both in news headlines and in scholarship that followed. In an article discussing the performance's significance for Black women's agency, racism, misogynoir, police brutality, and classism, the self-proclaimed Wombanist Cherise Charleswell named the performance a "shift" in its representation of "the most politically charged and socially aware work of her career," adding that "Beyoncé defiantly, unapologetically, and without invitation brought such topics of racism, sexism, misogynoir, police brutality, and the devaluing of Black lives onto one of the most-watched shows and biggest platforms in the United States."[55] In an instance of one commentator using the word "performative" in a positive sense, as contrasted to the negative interpretation that Maiysha Kai used that I referred to earlier in this chapter, the editor-in-chief of the website verysmartbrothas.com, Damon Young, stated in a reaction to her Super Bowl performance that "I think you're hard-pressed to find that demonstrative an example of performative Blackness on stage, on such a high profile stage," clarifying his interpretation of performative in the positive sense of the word by adding "Between the dancers coming out dressed as Black Panthers to the lyrics to the song, again . . . I can't recall another time you saw that unambiguousness with a performance on a large scale."[56] In another positive review of Beyoncé's performance, the #BlackLivesMatter activist and Pan-African scholar Melina Abdullah commented that "it's wonderful that artists like Beyoncé 'are willing to raise social consciousness and use their artistry to advance social justice.'"[57] The platform was particularly important; over 112 million people watched the Super Bowl halftime show.[58] Given the already inestimable influence of Beyoncé and her legions of fans known as the "Beyhive," it was significant that she would be the one to make such a statement at the place where she chose to carry out the statement.

Beyoncé commanded full attention in her performance. At the same time, she received much backlash for her performance. It is possible that the initial backlash might have had more of an effect than did praise, especially in the rapid sharing of comments and reactions on social media. In an article entitled "Pop Culture without Culture: Examining the Public Backlash to Beyoncé's Super Bowl 50 Performance," the Africana studies scholar Marquita Gammage examined how "the public took to social media, not in the usual fan craze, but to condemn and damn Beyoncé for her celebration of Black culture."[59] Whereas the positive reception to the performance highlighted Beyoncé's ability to celebrate Blackness, the negative reception to the performance focused on Beyoncé's lack of patriotism in a misguided focus on fighting for a cause. Gammage explained that "immediately after" the performance, "Beyoncé's featured performance was classified as an anti-American act of terrorism because her performance was perceived as social justice oriented."⁶⁰ This kind of negative reception is doubly problematic in its condemnation of both Black culture and Black women. Americans equated a performance promoting social justice—Black power, specifically Black female power—with un-American values and, worse, with terrorism. Another critique in the form of a Facebook post arose from the Republican New York Congressman Peter King, who posted that "Her pro-Black Panther and anti-cop video 'Formation' and her Super Bowl appearance is just one more example of how acceptable it has become to be anti-police."⁶¹ In the context of this chapter that focuses on the intersections of the #MeToo, #TimesUp, and #BlackLivesMatter movements, unlearning these kinds of critiques is foundational if there is any kind of social change that might be able to happen. In another piece of evidence suggesting that Beyoncé received fallout on social media because she was both Black and female, Beyoncé had performed just three years earlier in the 2013 Super Bowl to much wider acclaim than her 2016 appearance. In fact, as Gammage notes, that performance "labeled her as a feminist and women's rights supporter."⁶² This discrepancy once again draws attention to the continued efforts that must occur to ensure the inclusion of women of color in movements that are seeking to protect them.

With the reception of Beyoncé's Super Bowl halftime performance in mind for context, many details stand out, including repeated references to elements associated with the Black Panther Party and to the Civil Rights activist Malcom X (1925–1965). Dressed in all black, wearing berets that called to mind one of the accessories worn by the Black Panther Party of the 1960s—a trope that I will also address in the following chapter in several hip-hop performances—Beyoncé and her cadre of female backup dancers arrived defiantly on the scene. To punctuate the defiant appearance, Beyoncé also wore a bandolier made of bullets. Many observers commented on the significance of the clothing, appearance, and body movement as a tribute to the Black Panther Party. The musicologist Sarah Lindmark has observed that there is another clothing association to Michael Jackson's attire at the 1993 Super Bowl.⁶³ The association that seemed to be most identifiable to most of her audience, however, was the reference to the Black Panthers. Beyoncé and her dancers wore leotards that facilitated hip-hop dancing. While the leotard itself is not tied to something associated with the Black Panther Party, the color of the leotard was, along with the beret and the freely afro-styled hair. Figure 2.1 is a still from the performance showing the clothing of Beyoncé and the dancers.

In addition to the all-black clothing, berets, and militant gear, Beyoncé and her dancers each raised a clenched fist to the sky, another gesture evoking the Black Panther Party. Midway through the performance, she and her dancers moved to stand in the shape of the letter "X," a reference to Malcom

Figure 2.1 Beyoncé in "Formation" at the 2016 Super Bowl. "DSC09776" by Arnie Papp is licensed with CC BY 2.0.

X, who was assassinated on February 21, 1965, and whose assassination led to the establishment of Oakland's Black Panther Party by Huey Newton (1942–1989) and Bobby Seale (b. 1936).[64] All of the indicators evoking the appearance and actions of a party established decades before became a positive way of asserting and celebrating identity through performance, affecting the meaning and subsequent interpretation.

The timing during which the performance occurred provided another historical connection to the Black Panther Party, as did the significance of the geographical location of Oakland for the Super Bowl. The Super Bowl performance took place in February, which is also Black history month. The year of the performance, 2016, was also the fiftieth anniversary of the founding of the Black Panther Party. Geographically, the performance was located at Levi's Stadium in Santa Clara, California, part of the larger San Francisco Bay area. The Black Panther Party began under a different name in Alabama, the Lowndes County Freedom Organization, and it had such momentum that the movement began to spread.[65] After that, another epicenter for the celebration of Black power, the Black Panther Party for Self Defense, took place in Oakland, California. One of its founders, Stokely Carmichael (1941–1998), who wanted to streamline the two organizations, stated the significance of the panther emblem for the movement as it gained geographical momentum:

> In Lowndes County, we developed something called the Lowndes County Freedom Organization. It is a political party. The Alabama law says that if you have a Party you must have an emblem. We chose for the emblem a Black panther, a beautiful Black animal which symbolizes the strength and dignity of Black people, an animal that never strikes back until he's back so far into the wall, he's got nothing to do but spring out. Yeah. And when he springs he does not stop.[66]

Similar to the significance of the Super Bowl's location in the San Francisco Bay area, the inclusion of the Black Panther's apparel and gestures recalls the growing popularity of the movement in the same area. Beyoncé performed visual, geographical, and chronological signifiers of the Black Panther movement and a broader celebration of Black history, and this was one of the most powerful markers of resistance that she offered.

Marching was another symbolic marker of resistance in both the video for "Formation" and the Super Bowl performance. Through what would become a signature feature of certain moments in the video for "Formation," the Super Bowl performance, and her documentary *Homecoming* three years later, marching became emblematic of taking control and assuming order. Beyoncé and her accompanying dancer's marching was an act of resistance to the status quo and also an important marker of Black identity. Unlike the live Super Bowl performance and the deliberate use of marching bands from Historically Black Colleges and Universities for the *Homecoming* documentary, the video alludes to marching without using it as a centerpiece of choreography.[67] For example, about halfway through the video, the scene cuts to a festive Second Line parade moving along a New Orleans street. The image is a staple feature of New Orleans culture, particularly for post-Katrina New Orleans culture. In a recent publication about the topic, the African American religious historian Richard Brent Turner quoted words uttered at an African American healing ceremony before a Second Line was about to take place in commemoration of the tenth anniversary of Hurricane Katrina, words that mark the lasting devastation still felt in minority communities a decade after the storm:

> We feel the pain . . . We ain't even gained. . . . We come here today to pay homage to those who cross over, to ask for healing upon the families. We mustn't forget the babies and elders who crossed over here and everywhere in the city, and we want to give thanks to them, because their transition is hopefully bringing us light. . . . We ask right now . . . that no police force come upon us. . . . We ring a bell for the ancestors. We ask that all of them be made well where they are and help us to keep well where we are. We thank you and we ask for peace.[68]

In the solemnity of this statement preceding a Second Line parade, we see a similar juxtaposition of threats to Black livelihood and images of Black joy that Beyoncé highlighted in her video: ongoing police presence and surveillance amidst celebration of Black lives and culture. In addition, in the context of the geographical setting of New Orleans for the video, marching is a movement that occurs within a multicultural flux of traditions. The ethnomusicologist John Storm Roberts talked about the mixture of Haitian traditions, Mardi Gras Indians traditions (images of Mardi Gras Indians also appear in the video for "Formation"), and the marching bands in New Orleans Second Lines:

> Parades . . . associated with dancing and . . . carnivals [of] the rara bands of Haiti . . . [and] the New Orleans marching bands . . . seem to be part of a loose tradition associating dance, music, religion, social function, and royalty . . . [that] is to be traced to [central] African origins in royal and religious ceremonial.[69]

In combining the images of this culture together with the political statements that she is making about #BlackLivesMatter in the "Formation" video, marching is transcendent. Other moments in the video capturing the fundamental aspect of marching as a part of daily life in New Orleans happen in moments: a group of four young men in marching band outfits, bandleaders leaping in their march movements from left to right as each carries a marching baton, along with the parades associated with marching as participants wear Mardi Gras masks; and the all-white outfits that are traditional in the Second Lines accompanying jazz funeral parades. Especially for Black culture, marching becomes a transformational art. In a stunning collection of photographs of Black marching bands taken by Jules Allen and an accompanying article written by Gail Reid, Reid talks about how this kind of transformation might apply, stating that "Black marching bands are a marching history book of culture, keeping alive our connections to the past, ennobling the struggles and triumphs of everyday life, inspiring us to adapt, succeed, and celebrate cultural potency."[70]

Whereas the video for "Formation" primarily features Black men marching, and the images of marching are brief, in the Super Bowl performance, all-Black, all-female marching served to be a symbol of Beyoncé's political statements, and it stands out in the context of this chapter focusing on activist groups whose common goal is advancing the status of minorities and women. Beyoncé again took the stage—technically, the football field—after Bruno Mars (b. 1985 as Peter Gene Hernandez) began a rousing performance of "Uptown Funk." Mars's performance was upbeat, up-tempo, peppy, and all-male. The men wore all black and danced elaborate choreography. When Mars uttered "Stop! Wait a minute," a lyric in the song, Mars and his group stopped dancing, and the camera panned to Beyoncé on the field with her backup of female dancers. Cue to the marching band references: a drumroll, women in formation marching along on the football field. Gradually they revealed Beyoncé, who said "Okay ladies, now let's get in formation."[71] Add to this another use of clothing as a symbol, this time of Beyoncé's business acumen, in the form of a sly commercial reference to her to-be-revealed athleisure line of Ivy Park, which was emblazoned on the face of one of the marching bass drums. As Beyoncé and the dancers performed, they began to form the shape of an arrow directed toward Beyoncé at the center. Incredibly, they made the arrow appear to be animated as they moved their bodies forward and backward. The arrow is powerful, implying movement and direction, and it might have also functioned in this moment as a subversion of the traditional male gender sign, since Beyoncé and her dancers had taken over the spotlight from the all-male group. The arrow pointed toward her, a Black female. Mars's troupe consisted of all-Black men; Beyoncé's was all-Black women. Beyoncé's ability to make this kind of statement in a halftime show at a football game where she and the dancers were taking over the football field, not the stage, was momentous. As she approached the literal stage on the football field, she began a call-and-response with Mars. She began again with "Okay ladies, now let's get in formation" and Mars responded with "Fellas! Let's get this stadium shaking" before an onstage dance-off occurred, in the spirit of a dance battle that would be central to a hip-hop or breakdancing standoff. Although the number ended in a recap of "Uptown Funk" with everyone on stage, the vibe was distinctly one of Black female empowerment. Given the all of overt political references in the performance—the Black female bodies moving to create the shape of the letter "X," the Black Panther attire, the inclusion of marching—together with the intentionally timed release of the music video, Beyoncé made a resolute statement that commanded and received attention around the world.

RHIANNON GIDDENS

The pioneering artist and musician Rhiannon Giddens has such a diverse and multicultural effect that she could easily be the subject of an entire book. Before I briefly talk about the symbolic elements of defiance and resistance in her song "At the Purchaser's Option" (2017), her Smithsonian Folkways album *Songs of Our Native Daughters* (2019), and one of the tracks from that album that has a behind-the-scenes video as specific examples of works that dovetail with #MeToo, #TimesUp, and #BlackLivesMatter, I will briefly discuss the impact of her broader work as a cultural historian. She recently posted on Facebook that "My work as a whole is about excavating and shining a light on pieces of history that not only need to be seen and heard, but that can also add to the conversation about what's going on now."[72] For Giddens, the conversation is not only about race but also about her role as a woman promoting this message. She has made tireless efforts to share her music and to educate her audiences about the origins of her music. Specifically, many Americans have clung to a narrative about the country genre in which she performs the most: that its origins are White and rural. This narrative is reinforced in many history books and in documentaries alike, especially with the influence that Ralph Peer (1892–1960) had in collecting and distributing recordings beginning in the 1920s, perhaps most famously with the renowned Carter family. When asked in a *Rolling Stone* interview about the profusion of folk festivals and the increasing popularity of country music during this time, Giddens directly associated both with White supremacy. As one example, she stated that "Henry Ford would hold fiddle competitions and forbid Black people from entering. . . . Folk festivals were thinly-veiled attempts to recast the music as White mountain music, as part of a project to create a White ethnicity."[73] Peer marketed "race records" to Black audiences and "hillbilly music" to White audiences, even though the music of both groups shared "the same songs . . . with the same instruments."[74] As part of this recasting, many White musicians and record producers appropriated the banjo as an association of an instrument that matched their self-believed and manufactured country roots. As she explains, Giddens's efforts to educate the public about the details of this narrative are ongoing and sometimes exhausting for her. She stated in the interview that "I get tired of carrying the ancestral weight of what happened. . . . I keep having to explain every night at every concert: this is our music."[75] If she is tired, though, she does not let that stop her. She regularly posts on social media to help spread the message and to create a heightened social awareness, reinforcing the critical role that digital resources play for artists who might offer an interpretation of the sentence "This is America."

"At the Purchaser's Option" (2017)

The video for "At the Purchaser's Option" features the gesture of stillness as a challenge to the status quo in an innovative combination of a still photo and animation. The video opens with a view of a road between two cornfields, with Giddens seated barefoot in a chair in the center, her gaze fixed upon us and her hands calmly on her knees. Like many of the videos that I have included in the book, it begins with a message. But this message is different, because it is a historical archive: a record of a newspaper advertising a slave for sale, specifically a "negro wench."[76] Animation begins to appear alongside her, suggesting that Giddens's seated posture is a still frame of a photo. The animation is an abstract visualization of the description of the woman for sale in the ad: "About 22 years of age . . . sold for no fault but for want of employ. She has a child about 9 months old, which will be at the purchaser's option."[77] The animated figures of a woman dancing with her child on her knee move around Giddens as she remains fixed in the chair. The image of the ad disappears off of the video at the same time that the animated figures do, with Giddens still in the chair. Her ancestral ghosts dance around her, but as she has explicitly noted, she carries the weight of that ancestry. Her seated posture helps to convey that message. As she begins singing the lyrics, which are not coming from her seated position in the video (her mouth remains closed), each line of the lyrics appears in a scroll at the top of the frame in a way that allows the viewer to maintain direct eye contact with Giddens in the center of the video. The message of the chorus reinforces that a static, unmoving posture such as sitting can symbolize a challenge to authority: "You can take my body, you can take my bones," the chorus hauntingly begins, but the soul triumphs in the end, because Giddens adds that "you can take my blood but not my soul," a message that she repeats.[78] In the start of the second verse, the animated woman appears again briefly. The focus remains on Giddens, looking at us. Each verse shows the animated woman moving in an increasingly joyful way; the third verse begins with her moving in an arc above Giddens; her back is arched and her arms are flung above her head, and a brief interlude shows alternating images of all of the animations that we have seen so far, ending with an enlarged version of the image in the third verse. After the final chorus and an instrumental interlude, the image of the ad reappears along with the lyrics of the first line of the first verse: "I have a babe but shall I keep him?" The song ends with this question haunting her and haunting us as joy persists within the memory and continued presence of injustices against Black women and children.

Songs of Our Native Daughters (2019)

This album's title speaks volumes: in addition to the reference to James Baldwin that I noted at the beginning of the chapter, the album celebrates women and children, specifically women of color who are native to America and who comprise its roots. The "daughters" reference is also an important ancestral link; it recalls the child–parent perspective in the closing line of "At the Purchaser's Option" and is a recurring theme throughout many of the song's titles and lyrics on the album. Giddens collaborated with three other women for the project, and all four of them are featured prominently on the album's cover: Giddens, Amythyst Kiah (b. 1986), Allison Russell (b. ?), and Leyla McCalla (b. 1985). All four women are banjo players. They share a cultural heritage and legacy that emboldens their message. In an *NPR* review of the album, Jewly Hight notes the significance of the four of them joining forces, "exemplify[ing] the power of solidarity" in such a way that "will lead to shared insight, buoying empathy or freer, brasher expression."[79] She adds that the visual element of them holding their banjos also makes an impression, because it offers them an opportunity "to explain their connection to string-band lineages falsely presumed to be the historic domain of White men."[80] This collaboration rewrites that misunderstood history and is critical for advancing the role of women of color.

One of the band's members recently made it her mission to reinforce this message of inclusivity, speaking from the point of view of her own mixed-race heritage and as someone who crossed the border from Canada to America in search of the American dream. Four days before the 2020 American presidential election, the *Native Daughters* member Allison Russell released a spoken-word essay about race, identity, and voting that spoke directly to her experience as a Black woman.[81] The video begins with an image of the American flag amidst a vast sky, with Russell's words: "I don't believe in the American dream, but I believe in the dream of America."[82] After a long pause, she lists women in chronological order whom she envisions having the same dream, with still images of the women that she names: "Sojourner Truth's dream. Harriet Tubman's dream. Ida B. Wells's dream. Audre Lorde's dream. Marcia P. Johnson's dream. Breonna Taylor's dream. Ruth Bader Ginsberg's dream."[83] She then introduces herself with a prerecorded text while she looks directly at the camera, blinking but not moving her lips. As she explains that "I'm not a college graduate; I'm not famous; I'm not rich; But I am the hero of my own story," an image of a Black Wonder Woman appears, with an afro and the characteristic crossed arms in an "X" in front of her body, reinventing the iconic White superhero. "We who stand at the intersections of the margins have the clearest view of the page. Our vision is needed. Representation does matter." In a list of things that give her hope, she includes "the anti-racism mission led by Black Lives Matter, all the movements to dismantle bigotry, our radically inclusive intersectional communities." She concludes her speech, which was released not only digitally on YouTube but also began as a speech for the Women's March in Nashville on October 17, 2020, by singing part of "We Shall Overcome" and stating "We march. We vote. We rise." In releasing this video, Russell amplified her already powerful voice on the *Songs of Our Native Daughters* album.

The liner notes for *Songs of Our Native Daughters* are an important means of engaging with the audience, an additional educational resource besides the audience engagement that Giddens regularly encourages in her performances and on her social media platforms. All four women are contributors for the notes, and they include personal stories about what their America looks like given that they are Black women, in a similar way that Russell depicted in the video of her spoken-word essay. Giddens offers a bibliography at the end of her liner notes, something that is rarely done.[84] Her list of resources ranges from histories of minstrelsy and slavery in the United States, Black music during the Civil War, to timeless writings such as Baldwin's 1955 work *Notes of a Native Son*. The list of sources implies that the listener can be actionable beyond just listening to the album. By including references, Giddens offers a way for listeners to be active and to engage. This inclusion of resources and references on a digital platform is similar to the way in which Laurie Anderson, Taynya Selvaratnam, and Laura Michalchysyn included resources that interested participants for Art Action Day might read, as I discussed in chapter 1. In this kind of act, Giddens is impelling her listeners to act in a similar manner. And like Russell, she is creating a next step directed to her audience beyond just listening to the album: What will you do? Who is in charge?

She also directly addresses the question: Whose story will you tell? In the first part of the liner notes, she writes that the album "shines new light on African American stories of struggle, resistance, and hope" in order to show the value of reinterpreting history.[85] At the time of the album's production in 2019, many Americans were uncomfortable talking about race, slavery, and sexism. Many Americans still are; these are difficult topics to address. A renewed discussion has begun in the context of many of the inequalities laid bare in 2020 and the protests taking place around the world, specifically protests against police brutality against Blacks. #The BlackLivesMatter movement has taken on a new urgency in this context. The urgency of that movement alongside #MeToo and #TimesUp must continue to be in the foreground, and Giddens talks about the importance of choosing to put the discussion in the foreground: "This album confronts the ways we are culturally conditioned to avoid talking about America's history of slavery, racism, and misogyny, knowing that what's past is prologue—but only if we let it be."[86]

In addition, she specifically refers to the #MeToo movement in her liner notes and how the growth of the movement in part led to the creation of the album as a means of creating positive change in American society. Giddens was in a theater in New York City watching a 2016 remake of the original 1915 movie *The Birth of a Nation*, which depicted slavery in a positive manner and celebrated the Ku Klux Klan. Most disturbingly, according to one account of the movie in *The New Yorker*, it "asserts that the white-sheet-clad death squad served justice summarily and that, by denying Blacks the right to vote and keeping them generally apart and subordinate, it restored order and civilization to the South."[87] The actor Nate Parker (b. 1979), who directed the 2016 film, changed the point of view to be that of Nat Turner (1800–1831), a slave who led a rebellion. At first glance, this would seem to be the kind of historical rewriting for educational purposes—that is, a more historically accurate retelling—that Giddens seeks to do in her own work. The 2016 film, however, was enshrouded in controversy because of a previous rape allegation against Parker in 2012. The release of the movie caused divisiveness among many Blacks, according to one account by Rebecca Carroll: "those who will see the movie, and those who will not."[88] As Giddens watched the movie, she found one scene in particular appalling, and it stayed with her as a reminder of the ways in which Black women's voices are silenced, including a passage that appears as part of this chapter's title. She described what happened in the moment and how it related to the creation of her album in the liner notes:

> The second moment [of the album's creation] was during a screening of *The Birth of a Nation*, the much-heralded but little-seen movie by Nate Parker—taken down, along with him, due to some unsavory behavior in a prequel to the #MeToo movement. In the scene, one of the enslaved women on the plantation is forced to make herself available for a rape by the plantation owner's friend; afterwards, she leaves his room, in shame, while the others look on. The gaze of the camera, however, does not rest on her, the victim's face. It rests on her husband, the man who was "wronged" as an impetus for him to rebel against his White oppressors—and as I sat in the little theater in New York City, I found myself furious. Furious at the moment in a long history of moments of the pain and suffering of Black women being used to justify a man's actions; at her own emotion and reaction being literally written out of the frame. The idea of taking historical words and notions and observations about slavery and making art with them then came to me. . . . There is surely racism in this country—it's baked into our oldest institutions—just as there is sexism, millenia old. At the intersection of the two stands the African American woman.[89]

Giddens's description of the video not only highlights the role of the #MeToo movement affecting her view of how one might go about portraying such a scene in a film, but it also centers upon the important topic of gaze. Again the questions arise of who is being watched, and of who is watching whom. In the film, this gaze became a detail in need of change. For Giddens, who is both Black and female, the very intersection of amplifying the voices and perspectives of Black female women is a starting point for change.

There are also many captivating points in another video describing the behind-the-scenes process for one of the tracks on the album, "Mama's Cryin' Long."[90] The track itself is a call-and-response of a horrific account of a enslaved woman who was raped and who subsequently killed her attacker, eventually chased down by a group of men who hanged her in front of her children. Giddens repeats each line and Kiah, McCalla, and Russell in turn repeat a new phrase in response, creating the effect of a relentless and persistent cycle. The response consists of limited intervals, often spanning a minor third and rarely going past a fourth, and the three women sing in unison response. The accompaniment is a spare, syncopated, repeated pattern. At several points, the grief in Giddens's voice is clear. In the video describing the process of putting the track together, Giddens is shown alone doing the call-and-response with the syncopated pattern that she claps. Her eyes are closed and at points her facial expressions suggest that she is in pain. She interrupts herself after singing the line "Mama's flying free / and she won't come down" four times, scratches her head, eyes still closed, as if trying to imagine how to put into words how it feels to carry the emotional weight of the song that she sings.[91] The camera then pans to Kiah, McCalla, and Russell, who listen attentively as Giddens describes the source of the song: a slave narrative. The child—again, the child's perspective is centered—who watched the mother die came up with the song to describe what happened, resulting in, as Giddens said, "a warped idea of a kid's song."[92] She added, "This song has been looking for a home for a long time . . . and this felt like the place to bring it."[93] As she says these words, the camera shifts from focusing on her to focusing on the four women preparing for the image that would become the album's cover: standing side by side, getting their banjos ready. They are on a dusty road with trees behind them and little in the way of buildings, reminiscent of the central positioning of Giddens, alone in nature, looking at us, in the video for "At the Purchaser's Option." Their solidarity and sisterhood are defiant and resistant, and the timing of seeing this image of them together with her words "This felt like the place to bring it" once again points to the importance of the African American woman—the one today just as much as the one yesterday—standing in the crossroads. Giddens also personifies the song, noting that it "wanted to be found," a feeling that was reinforced for her when it took only one take for her to record it; it made her feel as though "the spirits were" there.[94]

Although she does not explicitly refer to the #MeToo experience that she felt while viewing *Birth of a Nation*, she mentioned that "Mama's Cryin' Long" was originally to be included in the music for *Birth of a Nation*, but she withdrew it. It is clear in the video that Giddens is putting as much effort as she can into performing the song in such a way that might capture the perspective of the child, so the aural effects of the very pattern of the words in the call-and-response are critical. For example, the lyrics "and she can't come down" and "and she won't come down" are continually altered. As she talks about her reasoning for that text pattern, Giddens looks off into space, unblinking, holding back tears, describing how she imagines the child: "I just imagine him going . . . why isn't she saying anything, when, like, she's in the tree, and he just doesn't understand."[95] The video then pans to the musical layers added to the song when they created it, showing it in different stages of production, from Giddens alone to when the group joins her. Just as the pan to the image of the four African American women standing together created solidarity in community, so, too, does the performance of this solidarity enrich the meaning and experience of the song. And it is this solidarity that pervades Giddens's works as a whole, particularly in her ability to center Black female voices.

JANELLE MONÁE, 2018 GRAMMY SPEECH AND "AMERICANS"

Like Giddens, Janelle Monáe (b. 1985) regularly invokes politics into her performances, and she uses her fame as a platform to deliver her message. One notable instance of her active engagement with politics and specifically with promoting women's rights occurred at the 2018 Grammys, during which she delivered a speech that was about equal rights for all. She referenced the #TimesUp movement specifically: "We come in peace, but we mean business. And to those who would dare try and silence us, we offer you two words: Time's up."[96] After her speech, Kesha (b. 1987 as Kesha Rose Sebert) delivered a powerful performance of the song "Praying," a personal story of her own sexual abuse, as she was joined onstage by women in all-white clothing in a show of solidarity. This performance emphasized Monáe's powerful words. Although she did not explicitly mention the #MeToo and #BlackLivesMatter movements in her address, she did refer to #TimesUp in her closing sentence, and the crossovers of the movements that I discussed in the beginning of the chapter are implicit for her speech in that Monáe is a Black woman. The majority of the press coverage of the speech referenced #MeToo and #TimesUp without mentioning #BlackLivesMatter, reinforcing the too-often tendency to overlook the vital role of women of color in the #BlackLivesMatter movement. A quick online search for "Janelle Monáe's 2018 Grammy speech" yields several returns that all mention #TimesUp, and in some cases #MeToo, but none reference #BlackLivesMatter.

Monáe first performed the song "Americans" from her 2018 album entitled *Dirty Computer* on The Late Show with Stephen Colbert on July 21, 2018.[97] The premise for the album is that Monáe herself feels like a "dirty computer," and in the opening eponymous track of the album she sings that "I'm broke inside / Crashing slowly, the bugs are in me."[98] She produced the track with Brian Wilson (b. 1942), and the track is full of distortions and warped sounds to draw attention to the metaphor. Every track on the album makes some kind of statement about the persistence of racism, misogyny, and inequality in America. "Americans" is no exception, and there are symbols for resistance, empowerment, and the promotion of gender and race equality that Monáe included in her Colbert appearance that suggest that she was speaking the loudest to the mistreatment of Black American women.

In the video of the performance, as with all of the videos that I have discussed, body movement, clothing, props, and lighting serve to symbolize nonmajority groups standing up to groups that are perceived to be in control. The camera focuses first on a group of singers—Monáe is not yet in view—who sing the introduction, "Hold on," visibly supporting each other as they have arms wrapped around each other, hands held. Not all of the group is singing: two of the people stand still in the center of the group, surrounded by their supporters. The two standing still are Black women, a visual representation of Giddens's aforementioned powerful description about African American women being at the crossroads. One wears a shirt that says "snatch" in capital letters, using clothing as a signal to question authority. It is not clear if the reference is to the verb "snatch," as in wresting something from someone else, perhaps a symbol of wresting authority, or to the noun "snatch," as in the off-color euphemism for a vagina.[99] In the second interpretation, the woman standing still looking directly at the camera could be implying the hurtful ways in which women are treated, objectified, and vilified by showing a potentially offensive word to the audience on her clothing. That gesture itself is a form of reclamation and of wresting authority, so it is possible that the word "snatch" could signify here as both the verb and the noun. The other woman stands with her arms folded in front of her, also a gesture of resistance, with one of her hands held tightly by the woman in the "snatch" shirt. A digital screen of a red-lit and enlarged American flag becomes visible behind the group.

The camera pans to Monáe, seated news-anchor style (perhaps at Colbert's desk?), and as she sings into the microphone "War is old, so is sex," she points one finger at the audience and lays her other hand flat on the desk.[100] She is telling the audience how it should be; she will not continue to endure how it is. As she moves to the stage that is a checkered floor, she says "Jim Crow Jesus, rise again." A seemingly mismatched upbeat, synthesized, and jaunty accompaniment begins as Monáe and her backup dancers begin the song. The accompaniment is ironically jaunty, because she sings about ways in which it has become regularized and normal to subjugate and idealize women, so much so that no one seems to notice or take care. We keep snapping our fingers to the beat. We keep dancing amidst trouble, as Gambino does in "This Is America." Lyrics such as "I like my woman in the kitchen," and "seventy-nine cents to your dollar" reinforce the perpetuation of these stereotypes.[101] Monáe also refers to race, specifically the implicit, if unintended, racism of a claim of colorblindness: "Sometimes I wonder if you were blind / Would it help you to make a better decision?"[102] From the start of the performance, Monáe commands attention.

At points in the video, two other body movements are meaningful: marching and kneeling. Marching serves as a symbol for justice, as we saw with the Beyoncé "Formation" examples: the group marches to the stage in order to prepare for a musical bridge that includes a quoted speech. The timbre, tone, and delivery of the voiceover sound like Martin Luther King, Jr. (1929–1968), although it is not actually his voice. As he says, "Until women can get equal pay for equal work, this is not my America," Monáe raises a fist in the air, joined one by one by the other members of her group. To emphasize the gesture of resistance, they take their arms and cross them over their chests, fists still closed, to accompany the words "not my," and then they lower their arms back down on the word "America." One performer stands out after this, keeping an open hand on her heart while she kneels, eyes closed, head bowed, an implicit reference to Colin Kaepernick (b. 1987), the football quarterback and civil rights activist who began kneeling in protest of the national anthem in 2016. As I discussed in the Introduction, the reference to Kaepernick is a trope repeated across many examples in this text. In an interview with National Football League media, Kaepernick explained his choice to kneel:

> I am not going to stand up to show pride in a flag for a country that oppresses Black people and people of color. To me, this is bigger than football and it would be selfish on my part to look the other way. There are bodies in the street and people getting paid leave and getting away with murder.[103]

The connection of kneeling as protest in Monáe's performance to Kaepernick's is clear, especially given the lyrical content that occurs as the performers are kneeling. As the intoned speech continues, each phrase concludes with the words "This is not my America," accompanied by another performer who kneels, a silent resistance that speaks volumes. Monáe is the last standing as she begins the final chorus. The impassioned speech comes in one more time and Monáe herself performs the kneeling gesture, mouthing the words and shaking her head while she remains kneeling: "Until Latinos and Latinas don't have to run from walls / This is not my America."[104] The performance ends with all of them dancing and embracing, draping a large American flag around them. With actions throughout the song that include marching and kneeling, the body-movements-as-protest in the song render a powerful message: Until this can be everyone's America, it is not their America. Monáe thus performs her interpretation of "This Is America"—notably including a quote that states "This is not my America"—through such gestures that are associated with opposition to authority.

Curiously, "Americans" is one of the songs that the critic Chris Richards, to whom I refer in the Introduction, chose as a poor example of an innovative approach to a protest song. He claims that the song is a repeat of music of the past, an example of "recycling the sounds of Ronald Reagan's America" in that it sounds like Prince.[105] If his only measure of the worth of the song is that

Monáe evokes Prince (1958–2016, born Prince Rogers Nelson)—something that she frequently deliberately does in homage in both her movements and her manner of singing—it defeats the entire purpose of the irony with which she delivers the deceptively peppy song. It also misses the point that Monáe is intentionally and successfully evoking the stunning artistry of Prince, a feat in and of itself. The content of the lyrics combined with the way that she performs the meaning of the lyrics is as powerful a protest as ever. To add to that, she is delivering the message as a Black female in the United States. Contrary to Richards's glib dismissal of her stunning work, we should continue to listen to and watch carefully what she is saying and how she is saying it.

The examples from Beyoncé, Giddens, and Monáe are among many that are calling increased attention to the central role of the Black and African American female in American culture. Their performances and actions include shared gestures and symbols that celebrate Black women and Black girls, especially as considered within the context of the foundation of the #MeToo, #TimesUp, and #BlackLivesMatter movements. In chapter 3 in which I address hip-hop as resistance in the Trump era, I will also at times address the tendency to disregard Black women in the genre of hip-hop and how that is beginning to change. In closing, and in a tone of optimism and resilience, the following lyrics from the track "Moon Meets the Sun" from *Songs of Our Native Daughters* symbolize both the social movements in addition to the gestures that Black women such as Beyoncé, Giddens, and Monáe have begun to regularize in their performances, all of which have been central to this chapter: "Brown girl in the ring / raise your voice and sing."[106]

NOTES

1. Rhiannon Giddens, Amythyst Kiah, Allison Russell, and Leyla McCalla, "Songs of Our Native Daughters," liner notes, 2019 Smithsonian Folkways Recordings, https://folkways-media.si.edu/liner_notes/smithsonian_folkways/SFW40232.pdf.

2. Elaine Richardson and Alice Ragland, "#StayWoke: The Language and Literacies of the #BlackLivesMatter Movement," *Community Literacy Journal* 12, no. 2 (Spring 2018): 46.

3. Among her list of other groups of people who have experienced "intersecting oppressions," she includes "Puerto Ricans, U.S. White men, Asian American gays and lesbians, U.S. White women, and other historically identifiable groups." Patricia Hill Collins, *Black Feminist Thought: Knowledge, Consciousness, and the Politics of Empowerment* (New York: Routledge, 2000), 245.

4. Linda S. Greene, Lolita Buckner Inniss, and Bridget J. Crawford, "Talking about Black Lives Matter and #MeToo," *Wisconsin Journal of Law, Gender & Society* 34, no. 2 (2019): 177.

5. The pendulum effect of the news makes it hard to keep these songs' meanings and interpretations fixed. It seems like something is happening in America every day that sheds new light and interpretation on the musical statements. One such example is the postponement until at least 2026 of the $20 Harriet Tubman bill. This was an initiative begun in the Obama presidency and the symbolism of the delay during the Trump presidency has been too much for many Americans to bear. As one *New York Times* reader put it, "To say these times are disorienting is to put it mildly. Still, I am trying not to give up. I have a seven-year old spitfire of a daughter who needs to grow up believing anything is possible and that Tubman on the $20 is as politically correct (in the literal sense of the word) as Washington on the $1 or Hamilton on the $10 or Grant on the $50" (Online in "Comments" section under "NYT Picks," "MBD," in Virginia at https://www.nytimes.com/2019/05/22/us/harriet-tubman-bill.html).

6. Daniel Victor, "Janelle Monáe Brings a 'Time's Up' Message to the Grammy Awards," *The New York Times*, January 28, 2018, https://www.nytimes.com/2018/01/28/arts/music/janelle-monae-kesha-grammy-awards-metoo.html?login=email&auth=login-email.

7. Alyssa Milano, Twitter post, October 15, 2017, 4:21 p.m., https://twitter.com/Alyssa_Milano/status/919659438700670976.

8. Alix Langone, "#MeToo and Time's Up Founders Explain the Difference between the 2 Movements—And How They're Alike," *Time*, March 22, 2018, https://time.com/5189945/whats-the-difference-between-the-metoo-and-times-up-movements/.

9. "me too," *2020 me too.*, https://metoomvmt.org.

10. Ibid.

11. Ibid.

12. *The Founder of #MeToo Doesn't Want Us to Forget Victims of Color*, Films On Demand, 2017, https://fod.infobase.com/PortalPlaylists.aspx?wID=237067&xtid=145897.

13. Ibid.

14. Ibid.

15. Elizabeth Adetiba, "Q&A Tarana Burke," *Nation* 305, no. 15 (December 2017): 5.

16. "Time's Up," *2020 Time's Up Now*, https://timesupnow.org.

17. Cara Buckley, "Powerful Hollywood Women Unveil Anti-Harassment Action Plan," *The New York Times*, January 1, 2018, https://www.nytimes.com/2018/01/01/movies/times-up-hollywood-women-sexual-harassment.html.

18. Ibid.

19. "Time's Up."

20. Ibid.

21. Ibid.

22. Langone, "#MeToo and Time's Up Founders Explain the Difference."

23. Ibid.

24. Carly Jennings, "The Love Note That Launched a Movement," *ASA Footnotes: A Publication of the American Sociological Association* 48, no. 4 (July/August 2020): https://www.asanet.org/news-events/footnotes/jul-aug-2020/features/love-note-launched-movement.

25. Monica Anderson, "The Hashtag #BlackLivesMatter Emerges: Social Activism on Twitter," *Pew Research Center*, August 15, 2016, https://www.pewresearch.org/internet/2016/08/15/the-hashtag-blacklivesmatter-emerges-social-activism-on-twitter/#fn-16486-9.

26. Khan-Cullors and Bandele, *When They Call You a Terrorist*, 179–80.

27. Joel Rose, "911 Tapes Raise Questions in Fla. Teen's Shooting," *NPR*, March 19, 2012, https://www.npr.org/2012/03/19/148902744/911-tapes-raise-questions-in-fla-teens-shooting-death.

28. "Black Lives Matter," 2020, https://Blacklivesmatter.com/about/.

29. "Black Lives Matter: Herstory," 2020, https://Blacklivesmatter.com/herstory/.

30. The North Carolina rapper and hip-hop artist Rapsody also performs the message of these movements, as I discuss in chapter 3.

31. Maiysha Kai, "Interlude A: What Do We Want from Beyoncé," in *The Lemonade Reader: Beyoncé, Black Feminism, and Spirituality*, edited by Kinitra D. Brooks and Kameelah L. Martin (Milton: Routledge, 2019), 5.

32. Ibid., 6.

33. The video for "Freedom," for example, opens with Black mothers holding pictures of their sons who were unlawfully killed at the hands of police, representing the momentum of the Black Lives Matter movement, as Omise'eke Tinsley discusses in *Beyoncé in Formation: Remixing Black Feminism* (Austin: University of Texas Press, 2018), 119. Beyoncé, "Freedom," *YouTube Video*, 4:49, April 22, 2019, https://www.youtube.com/watch?v=7FWF9375hUA.

34. Michael Appleton, "Hurricane Katrina," *History*, August 9, 2019, https://www.history.com/topics/natural-disasters-and-environment/hurricane-katrina.

35. Slate, "The Black Lives Matter Movement Started with Hurricane Katrina," *Ebony*, August 24, 2015, https://www.ebony.com/news/the-Black-lives-matter-movement-started-with-hurricane-katrina-981/.

36. Ibid.

37. Ibid.

38. CNN transcript, "Anderson Cooper 360 Degrees," *CNN*, September 2, 2005, http://edition.cnn.com/TRANSCRIPTS/0509/02/acd.01.html.

39. Jay Z, "Minority Report," track 13 on *Kingdom Come*, November 21, 2006, Roc-A-Fella Records and Def Jam Recordings, Apple Music. Beyoncé and JayZ (b. 1969 as Sean Carter) married on April 4, 2008.

40. Beyoncé, "Formation," *YouTube Video*, 4:53, February 6, 2016, https://www.youtube.com/watch?time_continue=267&v=LrCHz1gwzTo&feature=emb_logo.

41. Travis M. Andrews, "Beyoncé Controversially Sampled New Orleans Culture in 'Lemonade'. Now She's Being Sued for It," *The Washington Post*, February 8, 2017, https://www.washingtonpost.com/news/morning-mix/wp/2017/02/08/beyonce-controversially-sampled-new-orleans-culture-in-lemonade-now-shes-being-sued-for-it/.

42. See, for example, Mari E. Ramler, "Beyoncé's Performance of Identification As a Diamond: Reclaiming Bodies and Voices in 'Formation'," *constellations: a cultural rhetorics publishing space* 1 (May 2018): 1–20.

43. Beyoncé, "Formation."

44. Jennifer DeClue, "To Visualize the Queen Diva!: Toward Black Feminist TransInclusivity in Beyoncé's 'Formation'," *Transgender Studies Quarterly* 4, no. 2 (2017): 220.
45. Ibid.
46. Ibid.
47. Tinsley, *Beyoncé in Formation*, 149.
48. Jane Francis, "The Three Graces: Composition and Meaning in a Roman Context," *Greece & Rome* 49, no. 2 (October 2002): 180.
49. Tinsley, *Beyoncé in Formation*, 152.
50. Richardson and Ragland, "#StayWoke:" 40–41.
51. Beyoncé, "Formation."
52. Ibid.
53. Beyoncé, *Black Is King*, directed/performed by Beyoncé (Los Angeles and Burbank, Parkwood Entertainment and Walt Disney Pictures, 2020), movie.
54. NFL, "Beyoncé & Bruno Mars Crash the Pepsi Super Bowl 50 Halftime Show," *YouTube Video*, 4:37, February 11, 2016, https://www.youtube.com/watch?v=SDPITj1wlkg.
55. Cherise Charleswell, "Getting into Formation: Beyoncé, The Affirmation of Blackness, and Black Women's Agency over Their Bodies," *ProudFlesh: New Afrikan Journal of Culture, Politics and Consciousness* no. 13 (2016, online): ISSN: 1543-0855. According to wordpress.com, "Wombanism is a new way of being for women who want to celebrate their femininity yet embrace their strength as well as the men in their lives" (https://wombanism.wordpress.com/about/).
56. CBS News, "Beyoncé's Super Bowl Show Brings Praise and Criticism, *CBS News*, February 9, 2016, https://www.cbsnews.com/news/beyonces-super-bowl-show-brings-praise-and-criticism/.
57. Ibid.
58. Richard Deitsch, "How the Super Bowl 50 Ratings Stack Up," *Sports Illustrated*, February 8, 2016, https://www.si.com/nfl/2016/02/09/super-bowl-50-tv-ratings-media-circus.
59. Marquita Gammage, "Pop Culture without Culture: Examining the Public Backlash to Beyoncé's Super Bowl 50 Performance," *Journal of Black Studies* 48, no. 8 (2017): 715–31.
60. Ibid., 716. This kind of misperception—associating social justice for Black people with terrorism— is all too common in the Black Lives Matter movement, as Khan-Cullors and Bandele describe in *When They Call You a Terrorist*.
61. CBS New, "Beyoncé's Super Bowl Show."
62. Ibid.
63. Sarah Lindmark, "'Watching Their Souls Speak': Interpreting the New Music Videos of Childish Gambino, Kendrick Lamar, and Beyoncé Knowles-Carter," MA thesis (University of California Irvine, 2019), 51–2.
64. History.com editors, "Black Panthers," *history.com*, June 6, 2019, https://www.history.com/topics/civil-rights-movement/Black-panthers.
65. "Origin of the Black Panther Party Logo," source material from the H.K. Yuen Archive, http://www.docspopuli.org/articles/Yuen/BPP_logo.html.

66. Ibid.

67. She also prominently features marching bands in the track "Black Parade" from the *Black Is King* documentary, in which she sings that "My history is her-story." Beyoncé, "Black Parade," track 17 on *The Lion King: The Gift [Deluxe Edition]*, Compilation (P) 2020 Parkwood Entertainment LLC, under Exclusive License to Columbia Records, A Division of Sony Music Entertainment., Apple Music.

68. Richard Brent Turner, *Jazz Religion, the Second Line, and Black New Orleans after Hurricane Katrina*, rev. ed. (Bloomington, Indiana University Press, 2017), xiii.

69. John Storm Roberts, *Latin Jazz: The First of the Fusions, 1880s to Today* (New York: Schirmer Books, 1999), 7–8.

70. Gail Reid, "Black Marching Bands," *Black Renaissance/Renaissance Noire* 14, no. 2 (Fall 2014): 166–73.

71. Ibid.

72. Rhiannon Giddens, "My Work as a Whole Is About Excavating and Shining a Light on Pieces of History That Not Only Need To Be Seen and Heard, But That Can Also Add to The Conversation About What's Going On Now," *Facebook*, February 27, 2020, https://www.facebook.com/pg/RhiannonGiddensMusic/posts/?ref=page_internal.

73. Elamin Abdelmahmoud, "Rewriting Country Music's Racist History," *Rolling Stone*, June 5, 2020, https://www.rollingstone.com/music/music-country/country-music-racist-history-1010052/?fbclid=IwAR2ZnjDB-RNMP5pl1KEwaLoTLN-JpaYbCL-T3ZSahh26mBTnLU9zgIe2FIw.

74. Ibid.

75. Ibid.

76. Rhiannon Giddens, "At the Purchaser's Option," Rhiannon Giddens, *YouTube Video*, 4:16, January 13, 2017, https://www.youtube.com/watch?v=6vy9xTS0QxM.

77. Ibid.

78. Ibid.

79. Jewly Hight, "'Songs of Our Native Daughters' Lays Out a Crucial, Updated Framework for Americana," *NPR Music*, February 14, 2019, https://www.npr.org/2019/02/14/693624881/first-listen-our-native-daughters-songs-of-our-native-daughters.

80. Ibid.

81. Allison Russell, "Allison Russell – Dream of America," *YouTube Video*, 9:38, October 30, 2020, https://www.youtube.com/watch?v=cgMj1hb1_c0&feature=emb_logo.

82. Ibid.

83. Ibid.

84. Giddens, Kiah, Russell, and McCalla, "Songs of Our Native Daughters."

85. Ibid., 5.

86. Ibid.

87. Richard Brody, "The Worst Thing about 'Birth of a Nation' Is How Good It Is," *The New Yorker*, February 1, 2013, https://www.newyorker.com/culture/richard-brody/the-worst-thing-about-birth-of-a-nation-is-how-good-it-is.

88. Rebecca Carroll, "The Birth of a Nation: How Nate Parker Failed to Remake History," *The Guardian*, October 10, 2016, https://www.theguardian.com/film/filmblog/2016/oct/10/the-birth-of-a-nation-problems-nate-parker.

89. Rhiannon Giddens, liner notes, 5–6. This is the quotation that led to the first part of the title of this chapter.

90. "Mama's Cryin' Long (feat. Rhiannon Giddens, Amythyst Kiah, and Allison Russell)," track 7 on *Songs of Our Native Daughters*, 2019, Smithsonian Folkways Recordings, Apple Music.

91. Smithsonian Folkways, "The Making of 'Mama's Cryin' Long' from 'Songs of Our Native Daughters'," *Smithsonian Folkways, YouTube Video*, 7:47, December 13, 2018, https://www.youtube.com/watch?time_continue=25&v=M7PvWw97Cq0&feature=emb_logo.

92. Ibid.

93. Ibid.

94. Ibid.

95. Ibid.

96. CNN, "Read Janelle Monáe's Empowering Grammy Speech," *CNN*, January 28, 2018, https://www.cnn.com/2018/01/28/entertainment/janelle-monae-grammy-speech/index.html.

97. The Late Show with Stephen Colbert, "Janelle Monáe Performs 'Americans'," *YouTube Video*, 4:23, July 21, 2018, https://www.youtube.com/watch?v=9ivqFkLYxp8.

98. Janelle Monáe, "Dirty Computer," track 1 on *Dirty Computer*, 2018, Bad Boy Records LLC for the United States and Wea International Inc. for the World outside of the United States, Apple Music.

99. In the music video for another track from the album, "Pynk," Monáe and her accompanying dancers wear pants that are designed to look like vaginas, so the use of clothing to make a political statement—drawing attention to the ways in which women are seen—is a fundamental concept for the album. The song was also recently featured in the ending credits of the HBO show "I May Destroy You," as the show's central character Arabella (stunningly played by Michaela Coel, b. 1987) had just outed a man who raped her and began a #MeToo social media sensation that went viral in the episode. "I May Destroy You," Spotify playlist, 2020, https://open.spotify.com/playlist/37i9dQZF1DWUcT0QzTFbgH.

100. Janelle Monáe, "Pynk," track 7 on *Dirty Computer*, 2018, Bad Boy Records LLC for the United States and Wea International Inc. for the World outside of the United States, Apple Music.

101. The "seventy-nine cents to your dollar" refers specifically to the wage gap between men and women, although this number itself varies based on a woman's race, once again disproportionately affecting BIPOC women. For one of many recent articles discussing this discrepancy, see Stephen Miller, "Black Workers Still Earn Less than Their White Counterparts," *Society for Human Resource Management*, June 11, 2020, https://www.shrm.org/resourcesandtools/hr-topics/compensation/pages/racial-wage-gaps-persistence-poses-challenge.aspx.

102. Ibid.

103. NFL, "Colin Kaepernick Explains Why He Sat During National Anthem," *NFL*, August 27, 2016, https://www.nfl.com/news/colin-kaepernick-explains-why-he-sat-during-national-anthem-0ap3000000691077.

104. "Janelle Monáe Performs 'Americans'," The Late Show with Stephen Colbert.

105. Richards, "It's a Brave New World," https://www.washingtonpost.com/lifestyle/style/its-a-brave-new-world-why-is-our-protest-music-stuck-in-the-past/2019/09/03/7d9c1056-ca97-11e9-a4f3-c081a126de70_story.html.

106. "Moon Meets the Sun (feat. Rhiannon Giddens, Amythyst Kiah, and Allison Russell)," track 2 on *Songs of Our Native Daughters*, 2019, Smithsonian Folkways Recordings, Apple Music.

Chapter 3

"We the People?" Hip-Hop as Resistance in the Trump Era

In the previous chapter I addressed the influential role of #BlackLivesMatter among other social movements, particularly focusing on powerful Black women. #BlackLivesMatter has had an extraordinary trajectory in recent years. Many artists have specifically linked the genre of hip-hop and its social topicalities to the #BlackLivesMatter movement. As the hip-hop artist Bun B (b. 1973 as Bernard James Freeman) plainly summarized in a recent *The Breakfast Club* podcast interview, "Before #BlackLivesMatter, there was hip-hop."[1] In an essay recently published in *The Hip Hop and Obama Reader* (2015), the political economist and sociologist Sujatha Fernandes speaks similarly of this very power of hip-hop artists' savviness in cutting through the noise of politics. She asks:

> Why has rap—an American music that in its early global spread was often demonized by local media, governments, and the conservative right as violent and criminal—come to be so highly influential and respected as a medium of political communication? One reason could the oratory style it employs: rappers report in a direct manner that cuts through political subterfuge. Rapping can simulate a political speech or address, conventions that are generally inaccessible to the marginal youth who form the base of the movement.[2]

Since the publication of *The Hip Hop and Obama Reader*, along with the ensuing political transition from the Obama administration to the Trump administration, hip-hop has become an even more potent rhetorical genre. As the musicologist Mark Katz has noted in his recent publication *Build: The Power of Hip Hop Diplomacy in a Divided World*, anti-Trump sentiment in hip-hop is not geographically exclusive to America. He states that "Solidarity can be a form of shared resistance, directed toward oppressive systems, inequality, and bigotry. Since late 2016, solidarity also emerged around a more specific object of resistance: Donald Trump."[3] In addition to sharing a feeling of solidarity in their anti-Trump sentiment, many artists have used the rhetorical power of hip-hop as an opportunity to critique the current Trump administration, revealing a curious shift. As a businessman before being elected as president, Trump garnered near-ubiquitous praise in hip-hop; his name became synonymous with the prerequisite swagger of the genre. This association has all but disappeared in the wake of the 2016 election, with notable exceptions including hip-hop artists Kanye West (b. 1977), Ice Cube (b. 1969 as O'Shea Jackson), 50 Cent (b. 1975 as Curtis James Jackson), and Lil Wayne (b. 1982 as Dwayne Michael Carter). This chapter is subdivided into the years of Trump's presidency, beginning in the year he was elected (2016) and concluding in the final year of his presidency (2020). Arranged in chronological order, the examples that I highlight feature a variety of techniques to draw attention to what many perceive to be a dissolution of American democracy through at least one or more of the components that I explore throughout the book: especially props, accessories, lighting, clothing, body movement, vocal inflections—in many cases, distortions—and audience engagement, both in examples taken from live performance and in examples released only by video. In the case of tracks that I discuss that do not yet have an accompanying video to observe body motion, I will consider the role of vocal inflection and audience engagement along with the dynamics of the group or solo performer that is performing. The directness of rapping paired with such tropes levels criticism against a government that these artists believe is exclusionary and dangerous. The artists use the popularity of their respective digital platforms to promote further their calls for social justice. While hip-hop is and always has been a genre that challenges the status quo, the increased potential for the ability to see live performances, social media reactions, and connections to social movements has tremendously increased its potential to serve as a tool for social justice.

2016

February 15: Kendrick Lamar's Grammy Performance

At the Grammys on February 15, 2016, rapper Kendrick Lamar (b. 1987) was a symbol of Black and African American empowerment when he performed two numbers from his album *To Pimp a Butterfly* (2015) and concluded with a debut from his album *untitled unmastered* (2016). Lamar's art draws upon deep-seated themes of prejudice and injustice in American history. The scholars Christopher Driscoll, Monica Miller, and Anthony Pinn have recently devoted an entire book centered upon the notion that themes of Black identity are ongoing throughout Lamar's oeuvre, beginning with the 2011 album *Section 80* an ending with the Pulitzer-prize winning 2017 album *DAMN*.[4] During the early months of 2016 that coincided with Lamar's Grammy performance, Trump already had a commanding lead in the presidential primaries. In the context of this chapter that considers hip-hop in the era of Trump, Lamar's masterful performance at the 2016 Grammys speaks to the fear that many minorities felt as they watched Trump ascend to power.[5] At the same time that he performed what it means to be Black in America, he also performed his African American identity. Lamar took a trip to South Africa to perform a series of concerts in February 2014 and has often spoken about how much the trip influenced his musical and aesthetic style. In an interview with the comedian Dave Chapelle, Lamar talked about the personal meaning of this trip:

> I went to South Africa—Durban, Cape Town, Johannesburg—and those were definitely the "I've arrived" shows. . . . Outside of the money, the success, the accolades . . . This is a place that we, in urban communities, never dream of. We never dream of Africa. Like, Damn, this is the motherland. You feel it as soon as you touch down. That moment changed my whole perspective on how to convey my art.[6]

Body movement (including stasis and lack of movement), facial expressions, clothing, visual effects, vocal inflections, and audience engagement intertwine throughout Lamar's 2016 Grammy performance as a means of articulating his Black and African American identities and the complexities of negotiating those identities in today's America.

Lamar first leads the artists out in a single-file line onto the stage in darkness, and accompanying performers and dancers appear in prison cells. All of the artists wear prison uniforms, and Lamar and the men in his line are bound in chains, handcuffed. They walk slowly with a slight limp, limited in their movement by the shackles that bind them. Along with the reference to mass incarceration in America that overwhelmingly and disproportionately affects people of color, an additional reference here is to the American chain gang. The African American historian Dennis Childs has argued that the chain gang is one way that slavery has persisted in the United States even after the supposed abolishment of slavery in 1865 with the ratification of the Thirteenth Amendment; Lamar is visually representing this type of argument.[7] The accompaniment is spare as Lamar raps in a call-and-instrumental-response fashion with saxophonist Kamasi Washington (b. 1981), who is in a prison cell onstage. The motionless Black simulated inmates stand behind Lamar, as Lamar drapes the chains between his handcuffs around the mic, when a loud and rapid two-beat percussive passage that sounds like a gunshot interrupts the silence, matched with bright blinking lights, and Lamar raps "I'm the biggest hypocrite of 2015," the opening words from the track "The Blacker the Berry." Washington's response is dissonant wails on sustained notes. The immediate impression in the opening moments of the performance is bleak.

The role of body movement onstage at this point also contemporizes Lamar's message that racism is real and thriving in America and that art can be a tool of resistance. When the lights blink and the gunshot-percussion sounds, the men in shackles shake their fists in rhythm toward the floor, changing position on the stage, sometimes raising their arms, clearly starting to gather momentum. At several points when the lights blink, Lamar closes his eyes tightly as though he is feeling pain. When he raps "your plan is to terminate my culture," the men in shackles behind him turn to face to the right, then to the left, then to the front, hands raised in resistance, moving more and taking up more space on the stage. Quoting The Notorious B.I.G.'s rap "Who Shot Ya?" Lamar imitates the same vocal inflections of the original as he shouts "As we proceed to give you what you need." Lamar and his crew begin to remove their shackles. Bodies freed, their movements become more fluid. Lamar begins swaying his hips side to side, stepping along with his feet more joyfully as contrasted to the opening slow, stilted gait when he was in chains. "Trap our bodies but can't lock our mind," he continues, hands in the air and gesturing to his head to emphasize the word "mind," he yells "everybody just stop!" On the word "stop," he holds his hands high in the hair, open palms, a reference to the "Hands up, don't shoot" gesture that began after the August 9, 2014, shooting of Michael Brown in Ferguson, Mississippi.[8] At this point, movement and sound cease briefly before an explosion of activity onstage occurs. The lights change to blacklights, highlighting bright white stripes and colors on the dancers; the effect is electrifying. The musical texture thickens to reinforce the effect. These elements all occur in just the first minute and a half of the six-minute masterpiece.

The scene then shifts to darkness along with tribal dress for the dancers, colorful painting on the body that is even more enhanced in the blacklight, and lively percussive polyrhythms. In the darkness, Lamar struggles to find his way to a new area on the stage; his walking stride is more limited, although he is no longer in chains. He walks as though he is having trouble seeing where he is going and trying to get his footing, as though he is making his way into a new world, the "motherland" to which he referred in the above-mentioned interview with Chapelle. "We gon' be alright," we hear in repeated chants as Kendrick moves across the stage. This phrase is meaningful in and of itself because it is frequently repeated at #BlackLivesMatter protests. Elaine Richardson and Alice Ragland talk about the phrase as a hashtag, its unique syntax in the context of African American Language

(AAL), and Lamar's profound influence.[9] Surrounded by dancers and the jazz musicians who accompany him—this time grouped together, no longer in cages—Kendrick raps "Alright" alone while the dancers respond in energetic and engaged movements to his verses. The transition serves as a tool of freedom, resistance, and defiance, in stark contrast to the opening of the performance that began with the performers in locked chains. He centers upon "Alright" not only as a message of hope but also as a reclamation of power. Here again, his persuasive skills as a performer and the symbols that he pairs with his words offer answers to hypothetical questions such as the ones posed by Laurie Anderson in chapter 1: "What is suffering? What is justice? What is language? What's a story? Whose story are you going to believe? Who's in charge?"[10] Lamar brilliantly performed symbolic answers to questions such as these and negotiated with them during the six minutes that he took the Grammy stage—by fire, no less. As he moved across the stage in the transition to "Alright," a huge onstage fire improbably consumed the space behind the performers. This would not be the only time that Lamar would perform before an audience of millions—estimates are that 24.95 million people watched the 2016 Grammys—because he again performed with a fiery stage as a backdrop at the 2017 Video Music Awards on August 27, 2017.[11] The fire in Lamar's performances is a trope for the urgency of his message; it is difficult—perhaps impossible—to turn your eyes away from something that is on fire, similar to the way in which neon served to draw the viewer's attention in Touba Alipour's image of "America" that I discussed in chapter 1 (see figures 1.3, 1.4, and 1.5, and this book's cover).

Four minutes in, the lights dim, the camera focuses just on Lamar, we are back to the melancholy saxophone accompaniment, and as Lamar crosses his chest and says "God," Lamar is walking back to where he started, shaking his head as though trying to make sense of what just erupted onstage. Under a spotlight, this is when Lamar debuts his new track, "Untitled 3," including lyrics such as "On February 26th I lost my life too," and "2012 was taken for the world to see," referring to the shooting of Trayvon Martin (1995–2012), another Black man in a racially divided United States who was killed by an angry and suspicious White man [redacted] (b. 1983). As Lamar raps, the camera rapidly shifts focus so that Lamar appears to be in multiple places at once, as though there is a glitch in the recording. It happens so rapidly that it is difficult to process what we are seeing; it becomes too much to take it in. But Lamar continues to command attention, often gesticulating by raising both hands, palms facing each other, emphasizing words including "2012," "set us back another 400 years," and "this is modern day slavery." As he increases the tempo of his rap, the perceived camera glitches happen even more quickly than before and the angle starts to zoom in closer to Lamar's face, along with a flickering light that appears to be getting closer and closer to his face, as though he is being tracked in some way. When he concludes, a white, blank map of Africa appears behind him, marked with the word "Compton." The superimposition of Compton on Africa represents not only Lamar's dislocation of home amid gang violence in Compton but also in the roots of apartheid in Africa and the negotiation in America of his Black identity with his African American roots.[12] In all of the vivid representations that he creates onstage, we are called to listen even more intently to what he is saying and how he is saying it.

Finally, it is significant that Lamar chose "The Blacker the Berry" and "Alright" to perform his message of a representation of a Black American and an African American struggle, that these were the two examples that he chose among many others on what would be a tremendously popular album. The scholar Sayeed Joseph has mapped "The Blacker the Berry" and "Alright" in the center of a Venn diagram that he developed to show his interpretations of songs that represented the following categories: "'To pimp' (structural racism), 'The cocoon' (self-examination), and 'The Butterfly' (reaffirmation)."[13] In Joseph's interpretation, these two songs embody all three characteristics. As for the album as a whole, in the original concept for the album's title, Lamar said that he wanted it to be "To Pimp a Caterpillar," both a reference to Tupac in the sounding of the first part of his name "u" and in the following acronym formed by the first letters of the following part of his name, or "-pac."[14] He changed the album title from caterpillar to butterfly, because he thought the image of a butterfly was even more beautiful than a caterpillar. In his words, the word "pimp" represented aggression and stood in contrast to the brightness of the butterfly. In an interview with MTV's Rob Markman, Lamar said that he wanted to use his celebrity for good rather than to be pimped by the industry. His performance of these songs was another way of demonstrating his artistic goals in addition to the message of the album.

April 18: YG's Video Release of "FDT"

Ahead of his June 2016 album release *Still Brazy*, the rapper YG ("Young Gangster") (b. 1990 as Keenon Dequan Ray Jackson), and Nipsey Hussle (1985–2019, born Ermias Joseph Asghedom), released the official video for "FDT" ["Fuck Donald Trump"]. The opening credits of the video are just as powerful as the music that follows. The video opens with the following words in stark white font against a black screen:

> As young people with an interest in the future of America. . . . We have to exercise our intelligence and CHOOSE who leads us into it wisely . . . 2016 will be a turning point in this country's history. . . . The question is . . . in which direction will we go?[15]

We hear distant sounds of traffic as the next screen opens with continued text marking the progress made during the Obama administration, from "inclusive foreign policy" and "prison reform" to healthcare becoming a "public service."[16] A third screen encourages the viewers to register to vote, concluding with the hashtag "#fdt."[17] This introduction lasts for almost a full minute. There is near-complete silence to accompany the opening. There is the sound of cars speeding by and lightly squealing brakes, a sonic forecast of some of the action that we will eventually see once the rap begins. The activism encouraged by the opening words underscores the idea that what we see is just as important as what we will hear.

The introduction concludes with what sounds like news footage of a young woman saying:

> I think we got kicked out because we're a group of Black people, and what's going on in America . . . they're afraid we're gonna say something or do something but we really just want to watch the rally. And to get kicked out because we're a group of Black people shows you how racist our own school is.[18]

Although the specific event isn't cited in the video, the young woman is likely talking about a rally that took place on February 29, 2016, in Valdosta, Georgia. The police asked a group of almost thirty Black students to leave a Trump rally. According to Valdosta Police Chief Brian Childress, "these folks were told to leave the PE complex by the Trump detail . . . [Trump] had the right to tell folks he didn't want to be there, that they had to leave."[19] Childress shot down the notion that the controversy could be interpreted as a "Black issue," stating that "they were using profanity" and by doing so, were "violating Georgia law."[20] It is beyond disturbing that the Trump crew would cite profanity as the reason to eject the protestors given the regularity of Trump's own profanity at his rallies. A recent analysis shows Trump's profanity to be "part of a trend of trash talk that began with the Republican candidate back on the campaign trail in 2016."[21] Further, this account contradicts comments from the students, one of whom claimed that "We came in quiet, we weren't starting any trouble. . . We just came in together as a group to see what the presidential candidate had to offer not only our campus, but the community as well as our country."[22] Brooke Gladney, another student, added that "the only reason we were given [about being asked to leave] was that Mr. Trump did not want us there."[23] The Valdosta students planned to sit in silent protest at the rally, and their protest came on the heels of another protest that occurred the same day at Radford University in Radford, Virginia. At that protest, security officers escorted a group of Black students who were shouting "No more hate! No more hate! Let's be equal, let's be great!"[24] Tensions were especially high, because these protests occurred shortly after Ku Klux Klan leader David Duke

(b. 1950) openly endorsed Trump, and Trump subsequently failed to disavow Duke. Added to the message of the words that open the video, the news footage of the young woman condemning her school as racist is another call to action, specifically to vote for leaders who would find such actions to be reprehensible.

The video transitions to capture the scene of another protest, a specific protest against someone who could be in charge in an election year, that grows in the number of people participating as the music begins. A syncopated groove of a minor sixth interval that sounds dissonant is filled in with a perfect fourth, major second, and minor second (E-flat–A-flat–B-flat–B natural). As with the opening of Beyoncé's "Formation" that I discussed in chapter 2, the plainness of this groove in its limited range and in the absence of other instruments brings even more attention to the words laid bare. Men, women, and children hold their middle fingers high to accompany the refrain "Fuck Donald Trump." They walk along a street, holding signs that say the same and gathering momentum as the number of people in the crowd grows. Graffiti is central to the protest; we see the protestors creating the graffiti, a videographic detail that was also present in Beyoncé's "Formation" video. We also see the completed graffiti—for example, a stop sign with the word "Can't" spray-painted above "Stop" and the word "Us" spray-painted below. During the first verse, YG raps, and the image is in grainy black-and-white, save for red details. In the second verse, Hussle raps, and the previously red-color detail shifts to blue. There could be at least two interpretations of the color change. It could be a reference to the red, white, and blue of the American flag, used as a visual symbol of resistance in the video at the beginning of this verse (someone holds it upside down in front of a police car). Then again, the color shift could also be a reference to the colors associated with two Los Angeles gangs, the Crips (blue) and the Bloods (red). The latter interpretation is supported by the color emphasis on stereotypical accessories such as jackets, ball caps, shoes, and clothing. In addition, YG joined the Bloods in 2006 and remains a member, whereas Hussle joined the Rollin' 60s Crips and later got out. The divisiveness of this gang rivalry is set aside for the sake of the video's message to unite against Trump. The camera then focuses in to a news report of Trump proclaiming, "I will build a great, great wall on our southern border and I will have Mexico pay for that wall," at which point a close-up of what appears to be a Mexican man holding both middle fingers in the air continues the message of disdain toward Trump. He then holds a Mexican flag as YG raps, "It wouldn't be the USA without Mexicans / Black love, Brown pride." As the crowd grows, the police presence becomes stronger, and we see helicopters flying above. Meanwhile, protestors engage in car-spinning contests on the street. Throughout the video, our perspective continually shifts from feeling as though we are seeing the perspective of the crowd to seeing the perspective of the surveillance surrounding them, both on the ground and in the air. The haunting question "Who's in charge?" persists.

It turns out that YG's focus on surveillance in the video would have an ironic consequence for him, because it led to a visit from the Secret Service. The notion of representing surveillance in the hip-hop world is common. The scholar Erik Nielsen, who often serves as an expert in court trials that examine rap music as evidence, has stated that "rap music has always been under surveillance."[25] Originating from a specific task force in the New York Police Department, as Nielsen explains, a "black binder" created by officers consisted of

> a six-inch-thick compendium of dossiers on well-known rappers and producers—complete with photos, license plate numbers, and social security numbers—that they distributed to other police departments across the country.[26]

In the late 1970s and early 1980s when hip-hop began to flourish, hip-hop artists had trouble finding space to practice key elements of their craft, including practicing break dancing and the art of graffiti, because they were constantly being monitored by the police.[27] A wealth of scholarship exists detailing the the effects of police surveillance on hip-hop artists, and this surveillance has become regularized.[28] Along with YG, there are other artists—21 Savage and Eminem—whom I feature in this chapter and who were also detained by authority figures for questioning.[29] In the case of "FDT" the Secret Service contacted Def Jam, the label for the album. According to an interview with TMZ, "YG's got a new audience hanging on to his every word, and snooping to find out his lyrics before they're released to the public, and that would be the Secret Service."[30] In a clip of the brief exchange between YG and the TMZ reporter, during which YG was walking through an airport, the interviewer asked: "You have 20,000 people singing your song at Coachella . . . Did the Trump campaign ever try to get at you in a negative way about it?"[31] YG's response: "Secret Service hollered at the label. They asked to see the lyrics on my album to see if I'm talking about him on my album, cause if I talk about it on my album, they gonna try to take it off the shelf."[32] He continued to note the importance of spreading the message of the rap as a motivation to try to get young people to vote, not to suppress voices but to encourage people to use them and express themselves, reinforcing the rhetorical power of the opening credits that the viewers see at the beginning of the video.

2017

February 12: A Tribe Called Quest's Grammy Performance

In chapter 1, I discussed the impact of Trump's proposed immigration bans in 2017 and responses in the artistic world, including, for example, Touba

Alipour's work "America" that directly addressed the ban. Alipour was one of many artists to use her art as a form of protest to this ban. In the hip-hop world, one of the most stunning and evocative performances of resistance occurred at the 2017 Grammys on February 12, 2017. A Tribe Called Quest performed "We the People," including these lyrics in the chorus: "All you Black folks you must go, all you Mexicans you must go."[33] Others excluded are "poor folks," Muslims, and "gays." The highlighted groups are all purportedly "bad folks." The hate behind these words was eerily prescient—the original album release was on November 9, 2016, the day after the United States presidential election—in the proposed travel bans on immigrants that Trump would introduce just months later. The Grammy performance occurred a little over two weeks after the initial travel bans for seven countries on January 27, 2017.

Dressed in aviators and black militaristic attire that resembled the dress of the 1960s revolutionary organization of the Black Panther Party, rapper and vocalist Q-Tip (b. 1970 as Jordan William Davis) began the performance by engaging with the audience, pointing his finger at the audience in an inclusive, all-embracing manner while speaking the following words, both to the live audience itself and the 26 million others who were watching: "We would like to say to all of those people around the world, all of those who are pushing people who are in power to represent them tonight: we represent you." He emphasizes certain words with his index finger pointed closer at the audience and with his voice inflected: "pushing," "people," "them," and "you." When he includes the audience on "you," his arm is fully outstretched for the first time, representing a gesture of inclusion in his body movements and implied audience participation.

The rapper Consequence (b. 1977 as Dexter Raymond Mills, Jr.), who in a yellow jacket that has a panther on the back and two smaller panthers on the front is also dressed in Black Panther attire, then joins Q-Tip in a tribute to the recently passed Phife Dawg (1970–2016, born as Malik Izaak Taylor), for whom there is an empty microphone. The segment is both moving and lighthearted. Audience engagement is in full effect with call-and-response as they revisit Tribe classics such as "Award Tour" and "Can I Kick It?"[34] The focus turns to Anderson .Paak (b. 1986) on drums, singing "I don't want to move backwards, somebody just give me direction" (another track from *We Got It from Here . . . Thank you 4 Your Service*).[35] Throughout this segment, the iconic black, green, and red artwork—the colors of the Pan-African or Afro-American flag—that appears on all of the album covers serves as a colorful backdrop for the lively tribute.

About two and a half minutes in, several visual and audio clues shift the mood to blatant political protest in a scathing critique of Trump's immigration ban. Visually, the backdrop changes from the vibrant album cover to the new cover for *Thank You 4 Your Service*. But there are other important changes in the background to symbolize the chaos: the digital images are continually shifting, showing different messages such as "Build bridges not walls" along with intentional glitches in the video that creates visual distortion. Musically, the texture shifts to the low, distorted, fuzzy ostinato of the bass guitar with the ostinato groove at the opening of "We the People": a syncopated G-sharp minor triad that is interrupted with eight rapid drum beats (it could also be a low pitch on the bass guitar, but the player is out of view at this point in the video). Busta Rhymes (b. 1972 as Trevor George Smith, Jr.), clad in all black, joins Consequence. "Hey yo, what up Consequence?" he asks. He continues: "I'm not feeling the political climate right now." Waving his hand to accentuate certain words for emphasis, he says "I just want to thank President Agent Orange—"What up, Cheeto?" Consequence interjects—for perpetuating all of the evil that you've been perpetuating throughout the United States." As he speaks, he waves his right hand rapidly to the side and in front of him as if to push away the evil of which he speaks. Then, he continues: "I want to thank President Agent Orange for his unsuccessful attempt at the Muslim ban. Where we come together." He concludes, repeating "We the people!" four times. When Busta finishes his speech, the groove continues as in the song, moving between the syncopated G-sharp minor triad and a C-sharp minor triad, implying a tonic-subdominant stasis without resolution.

Right before the conclusion of the speech, we continue to see several visual markers in the choreography, particularly the role of movement versus the absence of movement, another key element to reinforce the message of music as a tool for social justice. As Busta speaks the word "unsuccessful," the Tribe members break through a wall that appears to be made of stacked foam blocks, a wall that the audience was not aware of until that moment. A woman in a hijab walks out, hand-in-hand with Q-Tip. Her face resolute, she stands defiantly still with her hands on her hips and her feet spread apart, behind the performers. Q-Tip wags his index finger back and forth in a scolding manner as he says, "We don't believe you, 'cause we the people." The message: She is not going anywhere. She is one face of a Muslim who has broken through a border to become part of the performance. She is also one of the first women to appear on the stage. Her role as both a woman and a Muslim represents two minority groups. The inimitable DJ Ali Shaheed Muhammad (b. 1970) and Q-Tip, also Muslim, have been present throughout. At one point, Busta turns his back to the audience to face her and the others who have broken through the wall. The group is all standing still, unsmiling and resilient. The visual effect is incredible. The performance stage itself seems to have no borders. As Busta roars his characteristic "Rahhhhh!" sound, a timbral growl, the Tribe performers stomp their feet. All of the visual and sonic markers reinforce the message of resistance.

Once again, the contrast of bodies in motion versus bodies that are still illustrates the power of this trope. The only questionable exception to the perceived lack of borders present in front of the Tribe performers are a group of dancers that are also in Black Panther gear; they seem to suggest an authoritative presence even as they are just as energetic and defiant in joining the dance and movement of protest. As Q-Tip sways his hips back and forth, hands up in the air, feet tapping "you gots to go," the guards (if they are guards?) have turned to face the back of the stage, feet spread wide, unmoving, and we see yet another border changing. Their pose suggests the stance of figures who might oppose resistors, such as a wall of police officers at a protest, the same visual marker, for example, that Beyoncé used in her music video for "Formation" that I discuss in chapter 2. Throughout the aisles of the audience, dozens of people are walking to join everyone on stage. All of the minorities spoken of in the song—those "No Bodies" that Anderson spoke of that I referenced in chapter 1—become the very embodiment of the music. As the chorus chants "must go," more people walk on stage. They do not go. They join. They stop moving once they walk onstage. The constantly fluctuating juxtaposition of the explosion of movement and dance amid the diversity from the performers to the stillness of everyone who is joining them on stage amplifies the message of inclusion. During Phife Dawg's verse presented as the camera pans to a standing microphone with no one in front of it to commemorate the passing of Phife, the Tribe members first listen closely and then raises their fists, heads lowered, in both a tribute to Phife and as a Black Power salute. The guards have faced the audience as the number of people joining Tribe continues to grow. The effect of the audience engagement is undeniable, from those who are clearly in awe and energized by the moment (notably Beyoncé, who as I discussed in chapter 2 also included these types of gestures in her live "Formation" performance) to those who are fully feeling the vibe and also seemingly near tears (DJ Khaled). "Resist!" chants Busta, four times, at the end of the performance.

Apart from the remarkable performance at the Grammys, the release date of the album itself is worth noting, as I mentioned above. The album release occurred the day after Trump's election. Given the title of the album and the timing of its release in its proximity to Trump's election, one interpretation of the title could be that it was a direct address to Trump. It could also be a tongue-in-cheek remark to the hip-hop world at large, since the album was the Tribe's sixth and final one and since it included so many major figures in its guest performances, including André 3000, Kendrick Lamar, Jack White, Elton John, Kanye West, Anderson .Paak, Talib Kweli, Consequence, and Busta Rhymes. There is also the possibility that there are multiple coexisting interpretations for the album title. Regardless, the symbolic role of the album and of the Grammy performance shows the effects of these musicians asking

"Who's in charge?" reversing the script so it is clear that the answer is "We the people."

2017–2018: ARTICULATED ANTI-TRUMP SENTIMENT IN WORKS BY EMINEM AND A VISIT FROM THE SECRET SERVICE

In what is possibly one of the most blatant examples of a hip-hop star using Trump as an exemplar of influence and swagger and then ending up condemning his mannerisms, Eminem (b. 1972 as Marshall Mathers) included a video of Trump appearing at Eminem's mock 2004 convention in order to endorse Slim Shady's presidential bid at the "Shady National Convention." The implication was clear: if someone as influential as Trump endorsed Slim Shady, Eminem's alter ego, then Slim Shady must be a legitimate powerhouse. In the brief video showing Trump's appearance at the Shady National Convention, Trump characteristically gestures toward the audience by pointing fingers at different members, opening his palms to the sides, and repeating the phrase "Nice group."[36] He goes on to say that "I'm Donald Trump. I'm always right. I know a winner when I see one . . . and Slim Shady is a winner . . . He's got Donald Trump's vote. Ladies and gentlemen, our candidate: Slim Shady!"[37] As the crowd begins chanting "Shady! Shady!" Donald Trump mouths along in support. When the tables turned and Trump was actually running for president, Eminem outrightly and repeatedly excoriated him. Eminem's hatred of Trump is a regular feature of his music, and as such this chapter contains several examples from Eminem. Following are just a few of many examples of Eminem's praise-turned hatred of Trump and his politics.

The Secret Service has taken note of Eminem's hatred. In January 2018, the Secret Service interviewed Eminem over lyrics that they perceived to be as threatening in the song "Framed" from the 2017 album *Revival*.[38] In the track leading to allegations, Eminem refers to Trump as the cartoon character Donald Duck and imagines violence toward his daughter Ivanka: "Donald Duck's on as the Tonka Truck in my yard / But dog, how the fuck is Ivanka Trump in the trunk of my car?"[39] Allegedly added to the Secret Service's concern, Eminem had released a freestyle rap on October 6, 2017, during the airing of the BET Hip-Hop Awards. He opened with the lines: "That's an awfully hot coffee pot / Should I drop it on Donald Trump? Probably not."[40] As he continues, he raps about the inherent dangers of having Trump as president, especially in the wake of Obama's presidency: "But we better give Obama props / 'Cause what we got in office now is a kamikaze that'll probably cause a nuclear holocaust."[41] As he raps, a cappella, his gestures become even more important in conveying the urgency and anger behind his rhetoric. At points his rapping timbre changes to growls and his index finger moves rapidly, diagonally across his body, then moving toward the ground. A half-cypher of listeners group behind Eminem and clearly sympathize with his words and gestures, indicated by nods and rapt attention. Eminem raps "From his endorsement of Bannon," as his arm is outstretched to the right, palm down, "support for the Klansman," as he keeps his arm out and steps rapidly to the side to emphasize his point.[42] As discussed in chapter 1, the critique of Bannon and the connection to the Ku Klux Klan is similar to the criticism that the artist Joel Tretin also considered in his original title for "Donald Trump's First Snowman," which was "Stephen Bannon's First Snowman" (see figure 1.1). As was the case for YG, who also received a visit from the Secret Service for anti-Trump rhetoric and for lyrics that were perceived to be violent, Eminem would come to find his artistic expression to be under surveillance, a regular occurrence for hip-hop artists.

In another scathing example from Eminem featuring Alicia Keys (b. 1981 as Alicia Augello Cook) on piano, "Like Home" (released on the album *Revival* on December 15, 2017) opens with a reference to Trump's implicit support of the Ku Klux Klan, and it also makes reference to the video of the 2004 Shady National Convention, showing his complete reversal in his opinion of Trump. "Someone get this Aryan a sheet," Eminem angrily raps; he uses the tone of his voice as a sonic marker of resistance as he issues the command while referencing an item of clothing associated with the KKK.[43] He also repeats the hard "e" sound heard in "sheet" several times throughout the first stanza, in effect creating a sound of distress: "prepare to get impeached," "square off in the street," "barely even sleeps," "All he does is watch Fox News like a parrot and repeats / While he looks like a canary with a beak," culminating in the final phrase "Why you think he banned transgenders from the military with a tweet?"[44] In "Like Home," Eminem also refers to the tragic events in Charlottesville in 2017. Eminem speaks directly about the killing of the paralegal Heather Heyer, calling her name: "Band together for Charlottesville / And for Heather, fallen heroes, fill this wall with murals." Eminem specifically refers to meeting Trump at the Shady convention and raps that he should have spat on Trump's hand rather than shaken it.

The musical and lyrical content of the chorus has a fascinating role as it pertains to body movements that function as symbols of resistance. Though we might not see the movements, we can envision them. In the chorus, he repeatedly shouts "Hands up" as Keys sings, another reference to "Hands up, don't shoot" that we have seen in so many examples so far. But the "hands up" gesture also takes on a positive tone, because Eminem insists that those against Trump will rise up, "even if it means sitting when they raise the flag / To sing 'The Star Spangled Banner'," another Kaepernick reference.[45] He simultaneously invokes the act of standing up as rising up and also the act of kneeling as simultaneous gestures of resistance. Keys sings "There's no place like home" in the chorus, giving another take on the duality of the meaning of "This is America" / This can't be America. The phrase "there's no place like home" became popular in the nineteenth century with the success of the beloved parlor song "Home Sweet Home" (music by Henry Bishop (1787–1856) and lyrics by John Howard Payne (1791–1852), 1821). "There's no place like home" is also a phrase made famous by the character Dorothy in the film *The Wizard of Oz* (1939, 1956). When Dorothy utters the words and clicks her ruby slippers together, she is finally able to return to the comfort of her home. When Keys sings the phrase, the expression sounds sincere—there is hope built into her voice and in the consonant, full sonorities of the chorus. But the words also have a function alongside the content of Eminem's rap that adds a duality to them, implying sarcasm. These kinds of rhetorical dissonances amid the musical consonances fit in with all of the juxtapositions of joy versus sorrow that are the basis of this book. In the "2020" subsection of this chapter, I will explore how Eminem broadens his anti-Trump sentiment to make a broader statement about his desire for stricter gun control laws in America.

2018

May 5: Childish Gambino's Video for "This Is America"

At several points throughout this book I have mentioned specific moments in Gambino's video for "This Is America," directed by the Japanese-American filmmaker Hiro Murai—who is also Gambino's codirector for the television show *Atlanta*—and choreographed by Rwandan-born Sherrie Silver (b. 1994), who included many dances in the video that had already gone viral. The dances include the "nae nae," BlocBoy JB's "shoot" dance, Ghanaian *alkayida* and *Azonto*, the South African *gwara gwara*, the Nigerian *Shoki*, and other new dances that Silver created herself.[46] There is a ceaseless juxtaposition of celebration in the form of these dances and violent chaos throughout Gambino's video, violence often made more shocking with Gambino's impassive expressions after the violence occurs.

In an article portraying Gambino's "complicity" with violence in the video, *Vulture* reporter Frank Guan considers the constant, relentless, merciless threat that has always existed in America against people of color. Every time that gunshots happen in the video, Gambino is holding the gun, with an unreadable and expressionless stare back at his viewers. This expressionless stare morphs into another scene with jubilant dancing, as though nothing had happened. At the same time, these joyful moments are hard to resist, problematizing what it means to value the viewing and listening experience.

They are embedded in a never-ending cycle of violence, an effect of which Black Americans are all too aware, and an effect that was exacerbated after Trump's election. Guan explained how the threat of violence in Black communities became particularly amplified after Obama's departure in office and with Trump's subsequent arrival.[47] Guan explains:

> Created by guns, overflowing with guns, America had always been a sort of rhetorical weapon, its greatness a cudgel applied to recalcitrant people of color at home or abroad. What the Trump campaign and election signaled was an abolition of all alternative Americas, the permanent reduction of the nation to a weapon directed at people whose skin is not pale.[48]

In each case of violence, Gambino embodies the weaponization of America; he holds the gun and aims it toward people of color. Since the juxtaposition of gun violence and dance happens over and over again in the video, we are never sure when to trust if it is safe to settle into the groove. And at no point do we actually feel safe, since we can assume that the violence will happen again, especially in the context of joy.

As I have alluded, another problematic layer for interpretation is the ongoing concept of who is watching whom that is ongoing throughout the video, relating to the questioning of power and control that is at the heart of this book. At many points during the dancing, Gambino's face contorts into a smile, as if forced, and he moves his face closer to the camera and lowers his chin as he maintains eye contact. When Gambino moves his face closer or keeps it turned toward the camera even if his body is turned another way, it feels as though he is also watching us watch him. On top of that, the dances are as irresistible as the groove, so it is an altogether complicated listening and viewing experience. The visual effect is that it seems as though his body is being controlled by something else and that he is aware of being watched, reinforcing both the minstrel Jim Crow references and also W. E. B. Du Bois's conception of the "double consciousness" of the Black man seeing himself through the eyes of how a White person would see him.[49] In this sense, and in the same way that Gambino moves his body in the Jim Crow caricatures, Gambino is using the element of dance and body movement as a negative connotation here. The acts of violence are against minorities, but this is no mere comment about violence within traditionally disadvantaged groups. It is also a commentary about the violence they regularly experience from non-minorities, made more complex because Gambino himself is Black, and he holds the gun. In the moment that he shoots the gospel choir, as discussed in the Introduction, the association is implicit to the shooting that occurred at the Emanuel African Episcopal Church in Charleston, SC in 2015. That shooter was White. At once, Glover manages to call to mind both a specific event and a perpetual cycle of violence against Blacks. The violence itself becomes a kind of performance. And the fact that it is performed by a Black man who is acting as a White man within the context of references to minstrelsy, Jim Crow, Zip Coon, and the suffusion of dance in the video adds another layer. As the dancer Theresa Ruth Howard noted, his contorted expressions after the first shooting "reminded [her] of the idea of Black people constantly having to be in a performative state. The smile drops and comes back. It's the mask of double consciousness. In the midst of chaos, the Black body fights for its humanity."[50] The concept of the Black body having to be constantly in motion is the basis for another study by Jennifer Lin LeMesurier, in which she explores how Gambino "performs the contradictory expectations for Black male embodiment as both hyper-violent and hyper-talented by juxtaposing African and African American dance forms with gun violence."[51]

Gambino's adept way at portraying this duality is captivating. In addition to the way in which Gambino captures the violence regularly experienced by disadvantaged groups, he simultaneously critiques America's obsession with social media as a means of trivializing prevalent injustice. At one point, for example, children are absorbed in their phones as windows smash behind them. Later in this chapter I will discuss the role of the song as it became a TikTok trend, looped over and over again to capture moments during protests that turned violent in America in the summer of 2020. Ironically, the digitization of this video as it was mapped to capture violence across America was part of a revival of the song. In this case, the gaze shifts to the app user who watches the violence unfold as the song plays and who views the struggle against those perceived to be in control pitted against those who are not in control and who are marginalized, making the song and Gambino's message as starkly relevant now as it was in 2018.

2019

January 29 and February 3: 21 Savage's Performance of "a lot" on *The Tonight Show* with Jimmy Fallon and His Subsequent Detention by U.S. Immigrations and Customs Enforcement (ICE)

When I originally searched for the video of the Atlanta rapper 21 Savage's 2019 performance of "a lot" in the summer of 2019, I was able to access the video. I am no longer able to find the video of that specific performance. The song would go on to win the award for best rap song at the 2020 Grammys on January 26. It is possible that the timing of this performance on January 29, 2019, along with the content of the lyrics, including the ways in which he delivered his message, was part of what drove ICE to detain him just days later for allegedly overstaying his Visa as a citizen of the United Kingdom. This arrest came as a surprise to his fans, because so many of his lyrics center upon his experience growing up in Atlanta, including a track with Gambino about growing up in Zone 6 in Atlanta, where by one account it is "the trappest of all possible zones."[52] After his arrest, his lawyer, Dina Lapolt, stated that he should be released, because he was a "role model to young people."[53] Eventually he was released on bond on February 13. In the absence of being able to see the aspects of language, body movements, and audience engagement during 21 Savage's performance on *The Tonight Show*, I will instead use accounts of the performance along with a discussion of the lyrical content along with visual elements in the music video in order to consider the possibility that the very skill of 21 Savage's performance, along with the powerful symbols that he included in the performance, in part led to his subsequent detention by ICE.

21 Savage, whose real name is Sha Yaa Bin Abraham-Joseph (b. 1992), performed the track "a lot," the opening track for his recent album *i am > i was*, which was released on December 21, 2018, and the performance signified a challenge to authorities.[54] According to one account of the performance, "the Atlanta MC mostly sat on a stool as he delivered the bars of 'A Lot,' bathed in red and white light. Behind him, a storm flashed on the screen, but 21 Savage's performance was calm and assured, elevated by a trio of backup singers."[55] The red effect might be a reference to 21's affiliation with the Bloods gang, whose associative color for accessories is red, as I explained for the role of the color contrast of red and blue in YG's video "FDT" earlier in this chapter. Once again, the lack of body movement proves to be a powerful gesture of resistance. At first glance, the backdrop of a screen with visually distracting and busy images conjuring a storm might seem to be better paired with a storm of movement onstage. But the absence of movement again draws closer attention to the words that 21 Savage says and the way that he says the words. He employs a similar approach toward stillness in the official music video featuring J. Cole (b. 1985 as Jermaine Lamarr Cole).[56] Amid a group of visibly wealthy Black Americans who are congregated at a mansion (another signifier of Black wealth that also appeared in Beyoncé's "Formation" video that I discussed in chapter 2), 21 Savage stands still in the front lawn as more and more people go to join him, standing still and looking at the camera. Throughout the chorus, their movements are more animated and joyful, but as the camera focuses on each individual, we see a picture of their former lives—some were behind bars, some were in abusive relationships, some were attending funerals of family members. The contrast in circumstances is clear, and 21 Savage's stillness brings closer attention to these discrepancies. His stillness at the *Tonight Show* employs the same kind of trope, a squaring off to authorities, another means of asking "Who's in charge?"

The lyrical content of "a lot" is similarly dissenting, and his questions are not merely out-loud musings to himself, but also to his audience. The track opens with a sample of East of Underground's soulful 1971 track "I Love You," and 21 Savage begins to catch the beat by responding on syncopated beats with repeated utterances of "yeah."[57] This call-and-response is recurrent throughout the track. 21 Savage responds to all of the questions he asks in the lyrics, a kind of call-and-response that he does with himself (something that we also see with the character King George in *Hamilton*, which I explore in further detail in chapter 4). He repeats the question three times: "How much money you got? / (a lot)" before delivering the questions without as much repetition, creating a perceived shift in tempo by varying the rate of change of the words that we hear.[58] Other questions include "How many problems you got?" "How many people that doubted?" and "left you out to rot."[59] The backstory of this song is not a simple rags-to-riches celebration. In his words, it is a picture of a bigger systemic problem in America that leaves people of color at a disadvantage ("how many n*****s done died? / a lot").[60] Although the questions become increasingly urgent, making the repetition of "a lot" feel increasingly exhausting, the speed of 21 Savage's delivery remains consistent. He repeats a rapid triplet pattern before ending on the first beat of the second repetition and maintains this cadence throughout the track. The effect of the repeated rhythms paired with the content of the lyrics is thus also "a lot" to take in, and that is precisely the point. The timbre of 21 Savage's voice remains uncompromisingly consistent throughout the performance; he often raps with only very subtle frequency changes in the pitch of his voice. One reviewer has described the timbre of his speech as a "trademark villainous monotone drawl."[61] In the case of the *Tonight Show* performance, 21 Savage draws our attention closer to questions such as these by juxtaposing them with his stillness amid the chaos of the images behind him. He does this in order to flip the perspective from apparently asking and answering questions that he says to himself to questions posed to the audience, in order to demand that we ask ourselves questions in turn about what we can do to change the relentless answer to all of his questions.

The Rise of Rapsody

There is an ongoing inequity in the hip-hop world for the representation of Black female artists, similar to the paradox of the lack of representation for Black girls and women in the social movements that I discussed in chapter 2. In an attempt to counterbalance this inequality, I am including an entire album by the North Carolina artist and 2020 Black Entertainment Television (BET) Lyricist of the Year Rapsody (b. 1983 as Marlana Evans), but this is just a beginning for the scholarship that can possibly address this disparity.

Part of the difficulty in this discrepancy is that there are not as many examples from female hip-hop artists as there are for male hip-hop artists with explicitly or implicitly anti-Trump language. In 2020, this changed for Rapsody when Public Enemy released a music video for a new version of the 1989 classic "Fight the Power," explicitly stating their agenda by means of a blistering critique of current events. The video and lyrical content for "Fight the Power: Remix 2020" features performances by Nas, Black Thought, YG, Jahi, QuestLove—and Rapsody, the only female performer. During her verse and appearance in the music video, she wears a camouflage jacket with "Kaepernick" spelled in all-capital red letters on the back and speaks out against police brutality against minorities, specifically referencing the recent killings of George Floyd (1973–2020), Rayshard Brooks (1993–2020), and Breonna Taylor (1994–2020).[62] She is also the first featured rapper in the 2020 Stevie Wonder (b. 1950 as Stevland Morris) release "Can't Put It in the Hands of Fate," immediately calling out the negligence of American government by spitting lyrics such as "Gotta defend ourselves when the laws ain't equal."[63] Turning back to the lack of implicit or explicit calls to challenge authority for female hip-hop artists, another part of the problem is the gender politics of hip-hop and the popularity of lyrics that often deliberately exclude women or express violence or misogyny.[64] Many of the women in the hip-hop world tend not to direct their voice directly to Trump as, say, Eminem often does. Rather, they use their voice and platform to address a broader societal ill (coincidentally, something that Eminem does in his video for "Darkness" that I discuss near the end of this chapter, in which he critiques the lack of a government response to mass shootings in America). Recently the musicologist Tammy Kernodle developed a powerful methodology for a way to include women—specifically Black women—in these types of discussions. Kernodle argued that Black women, including specific examples by Lauryn Hill, Rhiannon Giddens, and Janelle Monáe, have created "spaces of resistance" in their work.[65]

The majority of examples that I have discussed in this chapter have so far been predominantly male, and many have featured rightful expressions of anger in a number of engaging ways. Not all of the hip-hop examples in the Trump era that make a political statement, however, are rooted in this kind of anger. Rapsody's album *Eve* is worth mentioning in its entirety in this light, because she positively channels an inclusive message for women of color. A concept album that celebrates historical achievements of Black women, *Eve* is stunning in its scope and diverse in its range of characters. Rapsody named each track after a famous Black woman. As she described in an interview with NPR's Rodney Carmichael, "I wanted to make an album and name every song after a Black woman, because I'm an extension of every Black woman."[66] As Carmichael summarized, the list of tracks is "a virtual hall-of-fame of living and luminous Black women, most iconic enough to be recognized by mononym: Oprah, Aaliyah, Whoopi, Serena, Tyra, Maya, Iman, Myrlie, Michelle, Sojourner, Afeni, Hatshepsut."[67] In the picture used for the interview, Rapsody is dressed in all black, with a "thug life" cap and a Black Panther jersey similar to the one that Busta Rhymes wore during the "We the People" 2017 Grammy performance and Beyoncé's attire in the 2016 Super Bowl performance that I discuss in chapter 2. Rapsody's long braids flow down, also a symbol for Beyoncé in the "Formation" video, and gold hoops decorate her ears. The picture is at once a celebration of her identity with Blackness and with womanhood.[68] Rapsody prefers to be identied as a womanist rather than as a feminist. In an interview with Talib Kweli, she suggested that feminism excludes men "in the same way that pro-Black is not anti-white" and explained to Kweli why she preferred to use Alice Walker's term "womanist."[69] Her inclusion of prominent Black women on this album promotes the audience engagement that I have explored for male hip-hop artists so far in this chapter.

One of the tracks entitled "Ibtihaj" refers to the Olympian athlete Ibtihaj Muhammad (b. 1985), a Black Muslim American who was the first athlete at the Olympic games to wear a hijab and thus explicitly identify as Muslim. In her appearance at the 2016 games, there was already established unrest directed toward Muslim Americans, particularly after the so-called "war on terror" had been fully established after the September 11, 2001 terrorist attacks in America carried out by the radical Islamic terrorist group al-Qaeda. Thus, on one level, Muhammad's story fits into the larger narrative of the negative stereotypes that she encountered just by virtue of her living in America. In an interview about her Muslim identity and her choice to wear the hijab, Muhammad commented that she wanted to "challenge the narrative that Muslim women are meek and docile and oppressed, [by] being unapologetically Muslim, Black, a woman, and . . . you either like it or you don't. I don't really care either way."[70] She expressed that fencing was one of the first sports in which she participated that allowed her to look like her teammates, given the long sleeves, long pants, and masks that fencers wear. Her very story is one of challenging American stereotypes against Muslims.

On another level, Rapsody's choice to feature her in the music video and in the track amid others celebrating the achievements of Black women everywhere is also another subversive statement against Trump's stringent anti-immigration policies proposed in 2017, particularly against people from Muslim countries. In her interview with Carmichael, Rapsody said that "that song [was] the only song on the album that I didn't go in with a specific content."[71] Rapsody's producer 9th Wonder (b. 1975 as Patrick Denard Douthit) came up with the title of the track, and she knew that she wanted to incorporate a Wu-Tang sample. 9th Wonder chose the track "Liquid Swords" (1995), and Rapsody began the track the same way that GZA did: "When the MCs came."⁷² 9th Wonder had another idea, Rapsody explained:

> Then 9th said, "Yo, since I flipped Liquid Swords," why don't we name it after Ibtihaj Muhammad, because she's a fencer with a sword. It's just that literal. She's a Muslim-American fencer and she's the first one to perform in a hijab. The correlation is that we're two very strong, confident, fearless women who, in our own sports, never compromise.⁷³

Directed by Jay Scorsese (b. ?), the video celebrates inclusion. It opens with a close-up of a telephone pole covered in pictures of Ibtihaj.⁷⁴ We see several copies of just one picture of her, edges overlapping, as she is in action, fencing. As the camera angle moves out, a young Muslim girl in a hijab is staring at the pictures. Her expression is serene, unsmiling, and captive, similar to the expression of the hijab-clad woman in the 2017 Tribe Called Quest Grammy performance that I discussed earlier in this chapter. Throughout the video, vibrant images are juxtaposed with Muslim women standing still, their facial expressions suggesting that they are the ones in control rather than the ones being controlled. We are in the midst of a busy city, and each subsequent close-up features another woman in a hijab. Some are brightly decorated—the second one that we see is a vivid fluorescent yellow with black polka dots—some are plainer and not as colorful. But there is a sense of growing momentum as we see more images of these women. Save for the opening frame of the girl looking at the picture of Ibtihaj, they are all moving toward something. The vividly colored hijab belongs to a woman on an ATV headed somewhere; other frames show women getting up out of their restaurant chairs to go somewhere. Then we get the coordinates for the exact location: Harlem, 40.8116 degrees North, 73.9465 West. As the two women leave the restaurant, they pass by a group of Black men; then the camera turns back toward the first girl, who is hit in the back of the head with a plastic bottle that two young Black boys have just thrown at her, and she begins to run after them. They all run past Rapsody, sitting on the front steps of a brownstone with two other Muslims in hijabs behind her, arms crossed defiantly, having none of the drama they are watching in front of them. Their dress suggests resistance as well: in addition to the hijabs, they have camouflage joggers on, and their legs are crossed, one foot swinging lazily over the other leg. Rapsody scolds the young boys: "Boy! Boy you sharp boy! Look that fade on you, boy!"⁷⁵ She compares the experience to "back in the day" when this hairstyle was part of an identity and part of "tryin' to catch a wave," playing on the double entendre of the wearing a wave hairstyle and catching a moment in time, and she moves her arms in a waving motion as she sings.⁷⁶ By scolding the young boys for taunting the young Muslim girl and by incorporating elements such as dress, mannerisms, and hairstyles that combine Black and Muslim heritage, she implies that one does not have to be separate from the other. In the chorus, the Muslim women sitting with her are clearly into the vibe as all of their heads move with the beat, side-to-side, looking at the camera with determination and strength in solidarity. Then we see the ATV driver doing wheelies again. The chill Wu Tang sample continues. This is music of resistance as much as it is of celebration. The video cuts frequently to clips of Ibtihaj's stunning skills and victories. To reinforce this concept of inclusivity, GZA raps in his verse that "an emcee should electrify, beautify, empower, inspire, transform a world view."[77]

Once again, stillness and the absence of body movement is a call to action, to the "empowerment" of which GZA speaks. When the Muslim women in the video do move, it is very subtle, such as with the minimal head gestures. But it is joyful. This is one of the ways in which body movement (or lack thereof) is an important symbol in Rapsody's video. This is as true for the example that I have discussed here as it is for the other examples that have featured a similar juxtaposition of movement and nonmovement. But the key difference here is how Rapsody is channeling positive energy in the resistant dress, movement, color, and lyrics featured in the video. Her words are a statement of resistance, but her approach is more melodic, less distorted, less percussive, with a slower tempo than some of the other examples that I have considered in this chapter. Juxtaposed with the moments of stillness and of silence, the message of resistance has a latent anger and feeling of being fed up with the status quo. By incorporating such vibrant colors, melodic grooves, and alternating moments of singing with rapping, put alongside with more disturbing moments, such as when the young girl is hit with the empty plastic bottle for no other reason than that she is Muslim, Rapsody is expressing how she is fed up with stereotyping and exclusion.

In 2020, with the release of her black-and-white video for "12 Problems" (a reference to Jay-Z's "99 Problems" from 2003), Rapsody's exasperation is much blunter and more deliberate than in the previous examples. It is unclear what the number "12" signifies in the title; she does not state so specifically in the lyrics, but she associates the problems with ongoing issues in Black and Brown communities throughout the lyrics. The number could symbolically represent the number of people on a jury, especially because she includes examples of disproportionate sentences leveled against minorities ("Black men in jail for an ounce or two . . . White man makin' beaucoup, in Timbuktu").[78] Most likely, though, the number refers to slang for the police, specifically as an expression of "Fuck the police." The phrase has been used in a number of hip-hop tracks, although its origins are unclear. Elaine Richardson and Alice Ragland have explained the symbolic significance of this phrase on apparel. Incorporating an argument from Distinguished Professor Emerita

Geneva Smitherman, they state that "#Fuck12 T-shirts highlight a slang phrase that means fuck the police and the anti-Black establishment.... This lyric evinces residue of the traditional African worldview shared by non-westernized Africans, wherein 'there is fundamental unity between the spiritual and the material aspects of existence.'"[79] While Rapsody does not use the full phrase "Fuck 12" in her lyrics, the number is easily associated with the police—specifically, the misdeeds of police—in the visual content of the video. In addition, the lyrics call immediate attention to injustices in the Black and Brown communities within the context of police brutality, a global pandemic, and protests around the world. The black-and-white video directed by Patrick Lincoln (b. ?) opens with the distant sound of police sirens as the camera pans in toward a little Black girl dressed in a frilly black dress, what we will eventually learn is a tutu.[80] The girl lifts her head, eyes closed, before slowly opening them to look directly at the camera. As the camera pans out, solo piano music begins to accompany a sample from the singer Ambré's track "Revolution," and we see the little girl in ballet attire preparing for a dance in the middle of an open parking lot with few cars in it. A picture of two hands clasping each other appears behind her; the hands are pictured such that one arm is above the other while that hand grasps the hand below it, as if the lower arm was signaling trouble. The photo is from Atlanta artist Yvette Glasco (b. ?) and is entitled "Don't Let Go." It was featured in Sprite's #CREATEYOURFUTURE campaign, designed to encourage young people to vote in the 2020 presidential election by means of creating a platform for Black artists to share their art and encourage others to vote, very similar to the organization of Art Action Day that I discussed in chapter 1 but with a stated focus on Black artists. According to the website, "Young Black creators share their reasons to vote through their art."[81] In Glasco's photograph that Rapsody used in the "12 Problems" video, the photograph is turned on its side; this simple gesture creates a different effect than the original, used now in the video as a call for help. The girl walks slowly toward the photograph and extends her arms above her head, palms facing each other, before slowly lowering her hands to be on each side of her face as she gazes at the photograph. Rapsody talked about the central role of the photograph "Don't Let Go" with *Billboard* reporter Heran Mamo, noting that "You have these two hands grasping each other. And some people will see that, and everybody will think something different. I know when I saw it, it made me think about community and how much we have to stick together. And it's kind of like each one, teach one, each one hold each other up, each one call the next person."[82]

After the young girl stands in front of "Don't Let Go" with her back turned to us, the video transitions to Rapsody's appearance and her performance of "12 Problems." She appears alone amid a flurry of shooting range paper silhouettes hanging in the air before the video transitions to a backdrop of all-female dancers and two other enlarged photographs by Glasco, "The Same Dance" and "Faceless." As Rapsody raps, the embellished face mask that she wears signals not only the suggested face protection in the global pandemic of 2020 but also the repeated and enforced attempts by authority figures to silence minority voices—she is being dragged by the police as she raps in this attire. The dancers that accompany Rapsody wear all black; the twelve-girl choir wears all white, save for the picture of a target in the center of the choir robes, the same target that appeared in the shooting range paper silhouettes in the background of Rapsody's first entrance in the video. The video alternates with dynamic movement and stasis; Rapsody's next appearance involves her standing still, lips not moving even though we hear her rapping (a similar effect used by Rhiannon Giddens and Allison Russell that I discuss in chapter 2), at the center of a circle of police officers who all have their guns aimed directly at her head; the scene repeats later in the video with a Black man at the center when she raps "Black men in jail for an ounce or two." The transitions in the video seem deliberately grainy and distorted and flicker to the white sheet of paper with a brief image of a bullet mark; after one such transition, Rapsody is still in the center of the circle of police but again has the mask on. As she raps in the chorus, "I got 99 problems, but 12's still the biggest / I got 99 problems, batons, bullets, triggers." Not until the end of the video do we see her in the center of the same circle, this time with her lips speaking the words and her gaze turned directly toward the camera as she raps "They tryin' to take us out" before uttering "We don't die, we multiply," the famous phrase first spoken by the comedian Robin Harris (1953–1990). Rapsody concludes by silently holding one of her fists in the air. Rapsody's overarching message is not only to resist but also to encourage people to vote and to use their voices as an agent of change. When asked about the power of the video as a means of encouraging young voters to vote, Rapsody noted the specific appeal of hip-hop videos and performances in a manner that recalls Fernandes's words at the opening of this chapter about hip-hop's rhetorical power:

> Hip-hop has always been a voice of the people. . . . So it has to be me, it has to be Snoop, it has to be Anderson .Paak, it has to be Reason, 9th Wonder, whoever to connect with our audience, because we speak our language, we know how to talk to our people in a way that they get it, that they feel heard, they feel seen, and they feel like, "Yo, I understand you, and you understand my issues. And this ain't no just fluff and puff and bluff."[83]

Throughout the videos for "Ibtihaj" and "12 Problems," the images and lyrical content reinforce the lack of protection for minorities in the face of authorities, specifically by centering the voices of Black females, featuring recognizable tropes that signify resistance as an agent of change.

2020

Eminem's Video "Darkness," January 16

In Eminem's most recent album release to date of this publication, *Music to Be Murdered By* (2020), the video for the track "Darkness," directed by James Larese. (b. ?), is ostensibly about the Las Vegas shooter at the Mandalay Bay Casino in 2017 who killed fifty-eight people and wounded 489 others, but it is also a statement about changing the current gun laws in America and a metaphor about Eminem's own anxieties around fame, performance, crowds, noise, and violence, both in his concerts and in the news cycles that seem to feed off of gun violence.[84] The music video contains a warning for its viewers that it is a reenactment of a mass shooting.[85] The camera's perspective shifts so that in one room, we see Eminem, seated in a folding chair with a lot of space around it, isolated, similar to the solitude of Calvin the Second sitting alone on a chair in the beginning of the video for "This Is America." Eminem faces us with his head lowered in a darkened room. A low reverberating tone that sounds like static interference begins; the sound is similar to the moment that the trap beat—and the first shooting—begins in "This Is America." He sings "I don't wanna be alone in the darkness" and lifts his head as the camera briefly switches perspective to another room. Eminem turns to walk away and the perspective shifts to the shooter's view from the Mandalay Bay Casino.[86] When Eminem inhabits the killer's persona, his back is turned to us. When the perspective shifts back to Eminem in the dark room, he is turned toward us, at times with his head in his hands in despair, at other times pacing in circles around his chair as he raps, gestures, and, in some cases, pantomimes the killer's movements such as opening the curtains in the hotel room, drinking, and aiming to shoot. Throughout the video, these two scenes alternate. Near the end of the video, Eminem as Eminem turns his back on us for the first time and begins walking away. The once-darkened room begins to light up, as though we see his perspective performing at a concert.

Literally and figuratively, the role of silence versus noise in "Darkness" is also effective. In the video, after brief news footage appears that was taken from the hotel after the killer's suicide, the track fades into silence, similar to the moment of silence as violence that first occurs in "This Is America." To this point, the entire track has quoted a portion of Simon & Garfunkel's "The Sound of Silence" as a static, distorted ostinato; the portion of the track that is quoted is "Hello darkness my old friend / I've come to talk to you again."[87] The effect is ironic, because a mass shooting is anything but silent. But it is not merely the presence of the quotation that sends the ironic message. The irony is also in how the quotation is used. Eminem attempts to put himself in the mind of the killer preparing for the shooting, which took place at a concert, yet another level of interpretation for the album's title, *Music to be Murdered by*, along with its reference to Alfred Hitchcock's appearance on the 1958 album of the same name. When we hear the gunshots burst out in the song, the ostinato moves from what accompanies the lyric "Hello darkness my old friend" to the accompaniment in the Simon and Garfunkel original that would match these lyrics: "People talking without speaking, people hearing without listening" at the same time that Eminem raps "But I'm a licensed owner."[88] In this ostinato shift, Eminem's implication here is that the violence happens, it gets reported, everyone is upset, nothing changes, and then it happens again. In his words, he's "just trying to show you the reason we're so fucked."[89] The almost-complete silence (there is a distant siren that continues) near the end of the song and video augments the effect of the track fading right back in with news stories that become aurally impossible to distinguish from each other. The news reports come in, rapid-fire—disturbingly in the overdramatized expressions that characterize the voices of so many news reporters—and hard to distinguish from each other as a new siren begins with each new announcement: "A school shooting," "another school shooting," "breaking news: another deadly school shooting," "twenty-six killed and twenty others wounded," "opening fire outside the church," and "a deadly shooting at a food festival in northern California."[90] The overlay and deluge of news stories calls to mind Laurie Anderson's observation that Americans are "drowning in our own stories," as Anderson described the relentless cycle of American news stories (see chapter 1). In Eminem's video, screens with news headlines appear atop each other, to the side of each other, so that it is as though we are watching several TV screens at once. As the camera's view widens, we learn that we are standing with Eminem, who is also watching the screens multiply. The TVs are slowly forming a shape that resembles the United States of America. Some screens show protest signs for gun rights; some show proposals for anti-gun legislation. Eminem then walks away, and the TVs shaped as America slowly turn into an American flag waving in the wind. A question is then directed to us that appears on the screen: "When will this end?" An answer: "When enough people care." The music stops, the screen fades to black, and the video continues with the text "When enough people care." The silence continues to reinforce the song's message: "Register to vote at vote.gov. Make your voice heard and help change gun laws in America." The silence behind the message as the viewers read it is deafening.

To some, Eminem's gestures have translated not as agents of change and resistance but as a sympathetic voice to White Americans who voted for Trump. In the title of an article "We Are Living in Eminem's White America," the reporter Justin Charity refers both to the song "White America" from Eminem's 2002 album *The Eminem Show* and to Trump's White America.[91] Although Eminem is vehemently anti-Trump, argues

Charity, his "hypermasculine provocations" from his earlier albums stand in contrast with his newfound cynicism in the Republican party and his critique of Trump.[92] To this end, Charity concludes:

> The problem with adopting this sort of cynicism, especially as early in life as Eminem did, is that once you're ready to repudiate it, it's already gone and betrayed you. Suddenly, your country's overrun with Nazis, and your costar has become their new role model. It's too late. The bully won. Apathy prevailed. White America abided.[93]

This is a provocative argument worthy of addressing. Charity's view of Eminem, however, is limited only to the interpretation of his bodily gestures and his lyrical delivery simply as angry for the sake of being angry. The content of what Eminem is saying goes much past his anger. In fact, his more recent gestures and lyricisms augment the depth of his concern and fear about what is currently plaguing America. Eminem has also largely been received positively in the Black hip-hop community, although not without exception, another important marker for his credibility and identity. As the musicologist and hip-hop scholar Loren Kajikawa has argued for Eminem's rise to fame in the early 2000s, Eminem emerged "as a lightning rod for public opinion on issues such as homophobia, misogyny, and violence in popular culture" and at the same time "had to negotiate [racial boundaries] in ways that made sense to his audiences."[94] Miles White also talks about the problematic nature of Eminem's early popularity with White audiences. In a discussion of the album *Encore* (2004), White concludes that "Eminem is guilty of the same kind of brutal equation that fueled the 'hood fantasies of the Beasties and Vanilla Ice, all of whom invoke the subtext of racial transgression and the imagery of the brute in order to stroke anxiety among White adults and glee among adolescent White males."[95] Any early struggles that Eminem might have had with identity and the possibility that he was appropriating from the Black community take on a different meaning when Eminem's current work is considered in the backdrop of the injustices that he protests. It is meaningful, for example, that when he performed his freestyle rap, he had a group of minorities standing behind him in full solidarity not only for the issues he protested but also for his manner of delivery. Further, since one of the conditional requirements for racism to exist is anger, any person wishing to justify racist thoughts or actions by turning to an artist could simply use anger as the justification for the means. Eminem's anger of the early twentieth century is directed much differently than his anger in his recent works. There is much more of a sense of urgency to his words. Eminem's Whiteness does not absolve him of some of the more detrimental effects of his anger, but the way that he has recently expressed his anger is an ideological shift, one that is rooted in the gestures and the language of his resistance.

Afterward: February–May 2020: Recent Responses in the Hip-Hop Community to Police and Civilian Brutality against Blacks

As I complete this chapter about gun violence, racism, xenophobia, and sexism in America and how it has been represented in selected examples from the hip-hop world, racism has been especially alive and thriving in the 2020 pandemic. In fact, African American studies professor Kihana Miraya Ross argues that racism is no longer the term that we should be using to describe the prejudices in America. She believes that the word is no longer sufficient to capture the fear that minorities feel, because each type of prejudice against each person of color should be considered on its own terms. Thus she argues that we should call the problem what it really is: "anti-Blackness."[96] She acknowledges the importance of the word racism and is not arguing to do away with the word, but according to her it is a "catch-all" word that lacks specificity.[97] In referencing one of the recent victims of "anti-Blackness" that I have included in the last part of this chapter, she notes that

> Many Americans, awakened by watching footage of [the police officer] killing George Floyd by kneeling on his neck, are grappling with why we live in a world in which Black death loops in a tragic screenplay, scored with the wails of childless mothers and the entitled indifference of our murderers. And an understanding of anti-Blackness is the only place to start.[98]

The afterward to this chapter exists not only to remember the names of innocent lives lost—those named here who have been killed, along with the unnamed souls they join—but also for the impact of the response in the hip-hop community. Hip-hop artists reacting to incidents of police brutality is not new. The public access to videos and reactions on digital media platforms is, and there is an increased digital presence and focus for Americans as many of them are quarantined at home in a global pandemic. As *Washington Post* reporter Elahe Izadi describes,

> Hip-hop commenting on police brutality is not new terrain. N.W.A. did it and earned the ire of the FBI. Ice Cube released an entire album in the aftermath of the Rodney King beating and verdict and Los Angeles riots. KRS-One, Public Enemy. The list goes on. But in recent years, videos showing fatal police encounters with Black civilians have become more frequent. Technology has allowed bystanders to capture and distribute footage of these shootings with a

speed and ease that were impossible before. The videos have become headline news, fueled a national conversation and given rise to the Black Lives Matter movement.[99]

Rest in peace and in power, Ahmaud, Breonna, George, and the countless others—those names and lives senselessly cut short that we know, that we will come to know, and that we do not know—who have suffered from racist acts of violence.

February 23: Murder of Ahmaud Arbery (1994–2020)

In an article providing a timeline for the killing of Ahmaud Arbery, *New York Times* reporters grimly summarized the event: "Ahmaud Arbery loved to run. A former high school football standout, he had been jogging near his home on the outskirts of Brunswick, Georgia, when he was shot and killed after being pursued by two White men with guns."[100] Arbery's shooters were not charged with murder until more than two months after their crime, and their arrest occurred after the release of a graphic video of the shooting was released. As the article accounting the timeline stated, "The case has generated a wave of outrage and raised concerns about persistent racial inequities in the justice system."[101]

These inequities are what led artists with millions of followers on their digital platforms to issue statements against racism and to inspire their followers to fight for social justice. BET Staff compiled several reactions in the hip-hop community after Arbery's death.[102] Atlanta rapper Jeezy (b. 1977 as Jay Wayne Jenkins) offered one moving response:

> My heart goes out to the family of Ahmaud Arbery. Prayers goes out to all of us that look like him too. This could be you, me, your brother, uncle. Maybe your son or your father. Truth of the matter is, if he is a suspect based off of the way that he looks, then I guess I'm a suspect too. No one deserves to be hunted like a wild animal. Outnumbered, then murdered in cold blood. Racism is still very real. And it has killed more of us than any pandemic. It's time for us to find a cure. This has to stop. One word. Justice![103]

Snoop Dogg (b. 1971 as Calvin Cordozar Broadus Jr.) posted a picture of Arbery with the following words: "I was murdered by an armed father and son who hunted me down and shot me as I jogged in a Georgia neighborhood. Neither of my killers has been charged. My name is Ahmaud Arbery."[104] Countless other artists and celebrities emphasized the importance of naming the victims in order to acknowledge the persistence of racism in America that led to the senseless death of these victims. In addition, there exists an insidious form of racism that results when no one acts as an agent of change. The artists used their digital presence both as an agent of change and a call to their followers to enact change.

March 13: Murder of Breonna Taylor (1994–2020)

During the midst of the global coronavirus pandemic in a time when America's medical personnel were and continue to be extremely strained, Breonna Taylor was an essential worker and served as an emergency medical technician for two hospitals in Louisville, Kentucky. In the middle of the night on March 13, Taylor and her boyfriend, Kenneth Walker, were awakened by noises that sounded like a break-in. Dressed in plain clothes, police officers broke down her door with a battering ram and did not identify themselves when they entered the home, nor did they wear body cameras.[105] Acting in defense, Walker retrieved a weapon and fired a single shot that hit one of the officers in the leg, at which point the officers released over twenty rounds of gunfire in the apartment. Walker was originally charged, but prosecutors eventually dropped the charges.[106] According to a lawsuit that Taylor's family issued, the officers are accused of "wrongful death, excessive force, and gross negligence."[107] An added layer of grief to this story is that Taylor's death occurred in the midst of a social media firestorm over what had just happened to Ahmaud Arbery. When the video of Arbery's killing was released on May 5, it initially seemed to attract the public's eye—as well as the eye of many reporters—more than her own death. This reflects the dire narrative of the way that Black women are often treated, not only in history but also to this day, as I explored in more detail in chapter 2. As reporter Alexandria Neason stated, "Taylor's name . . . went largely unspoken. The journalism industry . . . was now serving a changed world; it made its choice about which stories, which lives, deserved focus."[108] Neason continued that "In doing so, it did what it often does: erase Black women from the narrative of America's stubborn history of police violence and vigilante murder against people with skin like Taylor's."[109]

Just as the hip-hop community benefits from a stronger female presence in a genre stereotypically defined by men, the reactions in the community after what happened to Taylor are just as important to evaluate, especially in the context of historical negligence. I had more difficulty finding endless lists of immediate reactions in the hip-hop community to Taylor's death than I did for Arbery's or Floyd's. In the immediate aftermath of her death, TI (b. 1980 as Clifford Joseph Harris Jr.) was one of the only hip-hop artists to have a consistent presence as he commented on the collective grief of his Black brothers and sisters. He posted on Instagram that "There is no way in hell the officers responsible for murdering #breonnataylor can be allowed to walk free. Our brothers are already being killed daily, but murdering our sisters can not be tolerated!"[110]

May 25: Murder of George Floyd (1973–2020)

After a storeowner called 911 due to a counterfeit $20 bill—"Think about it / That's 2,000 pennies," raps Rapsody in the 2020 remix of "Fight the Power"—that George Floyd had just used, police quickly came to the scene to arrest Floyd.[111] Although the arresting officers claim that Floyd resisted arrest, there is no evidence to suggest that he did. After Floyd was already in handcuffs, one of the police officers proceeded to pin him down on the ground, putting his knee against Floyd's neck. Floyd repeatedly told the officer "I can't breathe," a haunting echo of Eric Garner's last words in 2014 when he died due to excessive force by chokehold at the hands of a New York City police officer. Despite pleas from nearby witnesses for the police officer to take his knee off of Floyd's neck, even though Floyd was visibly struggling and his nose began bleeding, the officer persisted. Floyd stopped breathing and lost his life just seventeen minutes after being arrested.

In a recent account of the response in the hip-hop community to Floyd's death, *XXL* reporter Aleia Woods stated that "members of the hip hop community are making calls to action on social media to seek justice for the former artist. Rappers are demanding justice for Floyd, his family, and other Black people whose lives have been taken at the hand of police officers."[112] Some of the highlights featured in this article follow. Cardi B's reaction on Instagram was swift: "Enough is enough! What will it take? A civil war? A new president? Violent riots? It's tired! I'm tired! The country is tired! You don't put fear in people when you do this you just show how coward you are! And how America is really not the land of the free!"[113] Her words echo the sentiment that I referred to in the Introduction, in which the sentence "This is America" can be interpreted as "This must not be America." TI's response was also immediate: "So fuckin sick of posting this shit Maaaaan . . . But then if we don't, it goes unnoticed. I'm ready when y'all is. It won't stop until we stop it!"[114] 2 Chainz (b. 1977 as Tauheed Epps): "I can't post the video, I can still see the killer with his hands in his pocket and knee on the neck of a handcuffed black man."[115] Shortly after she posted her initial reaction, Cardi B (b. 1992 as Belcalis Marlenis Almánazar) began a "Justice for George Floyd" petition on Change.org. In an article featured on *The Breakfast Club's* website, "As per a press release, which was sent out on Friday (May 29), the viral petition has obtained over five million signatures, with a growing rate of one signature every two seconds."[116] Change.org spokesperson Alaina Curry said that the enormity of Cardi B's influence was not to be overestimated, stating that "Reaching five million signatures has been an incredible milestone for not just the site but for the millions of Americans who have joined together to stand up against racism and police brutality. The fight is not over, but we celebrate an unforgettable and historic moment on Change.org today."[117]

LL Cool J (b. 1968 as James Todd Smith) released a more extensive response in a freestyle rap made in the form of a video from his home, facing his computer screen.[118] Like so many of the artists featured in memorable performances that I have discussed in this chapter, he wore (almost) all black: a black cap, black T-shirt with yellow lettering for "Black Lives Matter," and a black jacket. The digital medium for his message allowed him to be as blunt and close to us as possible. As many Americans are still quarantined, sitting at home in front of their computers—if they are fortunate enough to be employed—video calls have become the new norm for communication, whether through meetings, family gatherings, or happy hours. LL Cool J thus doubly encodes his performance by using the platform that so many Americans are using while they are quarantined and already feeling stuck. There is nowhere else to turn. If you watch the freestyle, there is nowhere else to look but directly into his eyes (or perhaps the background of his home). There is no accompaniment. All of this draws close attention to the words that he raps. "For 400 years you had your knees on our necks," he begins, his face visibly angry as his eyes narrow. "I can't be bought with a $1,200 check," he says at one point, referring to the recent stimulus package passed in Congress that distributed $1,200 to every American (a check for which many Americans waited to receive longer than others).[119] LL gestures toward his neck in reference to Floyd's death but also as a more general reference to racism run rampant in America. His palm is facing down, and, if his hand was on a turntable, it would be very close to resembling the movement of a DJ: a rapid back-and-forth motion. But his hand is at his neck, and he is angry, and his words reinforce it: "After [redacted] killed Floyd we got necks." His choice of the word "necks" is sonically forecasting the word "next" as an implicit threat to disadvantaged groups. Later, he brings his fingers to his mouth and then opens his hand while making a kissing sound. The gesture is both a kiss-off to authorities and an homage to his ancestors to accompany the lyrics "Harassed by cops / Word to my ancestors' souls."[120] As he moves his head from side to side to follow the pulse of his rap, he yells "America's a graveyard full of Black men's bones," but lest the women are forgotten, he honors Breonna at this point as well, continuing that "I ain't got to tell ya that Breonna Taylor got slayed in her own home."[121] He then follows in a brilliant listing of double entendre by imagining what victims of racism might have been able to do with their lives if they had not been killed: "Sean could have rocked bells," referring to the 2006 shooting of Sean Bell (1983–2006); "Eric could have garnered attention beyond the T-shirts and obituary mentions," referencing the 2017 shooting of Eric Garner (1970–2014); and "Tamir coulda went to Rice," referencing the 2014 shooting of the twelve-year-old Tamir Rice 2002–2014). When he completes his rap by saying that "Black lives matter / forever," his voice is notably softer and he lowers his chin slightly. All of these gestures ask his audience—intended to be virtual, since he performed the freestyle that way—both to reckon with horrible truths in our America today and to take action against them.

Across the country, protests began happening in response not only to Floyd's death but also to Taylor's, because the offending officers had not been arrested. The public release of Walker's 911 call on May 28 renewed attention to Taylor's death on social media. Many of these protests turned violent, incited in some occasions by the protestors, in others by the police, and still in others, by Whites who supported racist organizations and tried to make it look like Blacks were causing violence. On social media, TikTok videos began trending with none other than a portion of Gambino's "This Is America" chorus repeated in a loop, at the same time visually showing damage caused by the protests, from broken glass to burning buildings to protestors who had been hit with rubber bullets and tear gas. In one example, protestors holding signs saying "I can't breathe" and holding their fists up in solidarity are next to a burning building while Gambino's chorus sounds: "This is America / Don't catch you slippin' now."[122]

In the quote from Sujatha Fernandes that opened this chapter, she noted that "rappers report."[123] But they also play with words and gestures in such a way that allows for the meaning of their message to be amplified. As the examples in this chapter have demonstrated, these messages have been particularly amplified in the age of Trump. The artists deliver their messages of resistance through all types of media—digital, live, millions watching, intimate performances—using such markers as dance, dress, movement, lighting, rhetoric, delivery style, and engagement. They turn their gaze toward us, so that we are not only watching them perform, but they are watching how we will respond, and in some cases, they are providing suggestions for how we might respond. The directness of the genre of hip-hop is a central component for the messages of these artists. Hip-hop signifiers and rapping also play a central role in the musical *Hamilton*, the subject of the following and final chapter. *Hamilton* ends with similar questions about how we will live, how we will die, and who will tell our stories. As with all of the works in this book, the artists who pose such questions do so in a way that subverts authority and directly challenges the status quo.

NOTES

1. Bun B, interview with DJ Envy, Angela Yee, and Charlamagne tha God, The Breakfast Club, podcast audio, September 22, 2020, https://podcasts.apple.com/ca/podcast/wedding-charge-rate/id1232428553?i=1000492131770.

2. Sujatha Fernades, "'Obama Nation': Hip Hop and Global Protest," in *The Hip Hop and Obama Reader*, edited by Travis L. Gosa and Erik Nielson (Oxford: Oxford University Press, 2015), 91–2.

3. Mark Katz, *Build: The Power of Hip Hop Diplomacy in a Divided World* (Oxford: Oxford University Press, 2020), 132.

4. Christopher M. Driscoll, Monica R. Miller, and Anthony B. Pinn, *Kendrick Lamar and the Making of Black Meaning*, Routledge Studies in Hip Hop and Religion Series (Milton Park, UK: Taylor & Francis Group, 2019).

5. As one example, the following article discusses this growing fear in the context of Latino communities: Ben Newman, Sono Shah, and Loren Collingwood, "During the Election, Trump's Racist Rhetoric Activated the Fears of People in Areas with Growing Latino Populations," *USApp – American Politics and Policy Blog*, January 24, 2018, http://blogs.lse.ac.uk/usappblog. As another, see Lawrence D. Bobo, "Racism in Trump's America: Reflections on Culture, Sociology, and the 2016 US Presidential Election," *The British Journal of Sociology* (November 8, 2017), https://onlinelibrary.wiley.com/doi/full/10.1111/1468-4446.12324.

6. Dave Chappelle, "Kendrick Lamar by Dave Chappelle," *Interview Magazine*, July 12, 2017, https://www.interviewmagazine.com/music/kendrick-lamar-cover#_.

7. Dennis Childs, *Slaves of the State: Black Incarceration from the Chain Gang to the Penitentiary* (Minneapolis: University of Minnesota Press, 2015).

8. Many questions surround the case of the shooting of Michael Brown, but the killing raised widespread concern about the police treatment of black and brown bodies. According to some accounts that were disproven by the FBI, Brown yelled "Don't shoot" before a police officer then fired twelve shots at Brown. Six of the bullets hit Brown. Mitch Smith, "New Ferguson Video Adds Wrinkle to Michael Brown Case," *New York Times*, March 11, 2017, https://www.nytimes.com/2017/03/11/us/michael-brown-ferguson-police-shooting-video.html. Although Brown might not have uttered the words, they became a cornerstone of the Black Lives Matter movement.

9. Elaine Richardson and Alice Ragland, "#StayWoke:" 44.

10. The Laura Flanders Show, "Laurie Anderson & Mohammed el Gharani."

11. Oriana Schwindt, "Grammy 2017 Ratings Rise from the Last Two Years," *Variety*, February 13, 2017, https://variety.com/2017/tv/news/tv-ratings-grammy-ratings-2017-1201986602/.

12. Lyrics from "Mortal Man," the outro on *To Pimp a Butterfly*, support this point: "But while my loved ones was fighting the continuous war back in the city, I was entering a new one / A war that was based on apartheid and discrimination / Made me wanna go back to the city and tell the homies what I learned / The word was respect / Just because you wore a different gang color than mine's / Doesn't mean I can't respect you as a black man." Kendrick Lamar, "Mortal Man," track 16 on *To Pimp a Butterfly*, Top Dawg Entertainment, 2015, Apple Music.

13. Sayeed Joseph, "'We Gon' Be Alright': Mental Health and the Blues in Kendrick Lamar's *To Pimp a Butterfly*," *Ethnomusicology Review* (2017), https://ethnomusicologyreview.ucla.edu/journal/volume/21/piece/990.

14. MTV, "Kendrick Lamar Breaks down Tracks from 'To Pimp a Butterfly'," *YouTube Video*, 1:44, March 31, 2015, https://www.youtube.com/watch?v=AUE l_ep9iDs.

15. WORLDSTARHIPHOP, "YG & Nipsey Hussle 'FDT (Fuck Donald Trump)' (WSHH Exclusive – Official Music Video), YouTube Video, 4:57, April 18, 2016, https://www.youtube.com/watch?v=WkZ5e94QnWk.

16. Ibid. Although Obama preached inclusive and egalitarian language, he was often not able to match his words with policy. As the legal scholar and civil rights activist Michelle Alexander has noted, "President Obama publicly preached values of inclusion and compassion toward immigrants, yet he escalated the detention and deportation of non-citizens," continuing a system in America wherein, regardless of the political party in control, "highly racialized and punitive systems thrived under liberal presidents who were given the benefit of the doubt by those who might otherwise have been critics." Michelle Alexander, *The New Jim Crow: Mass Incarceration in the Age of Colorblindness*, 10th anniversary ed. (New York: The New Press, 2020), xliii.

17. "YG & Nipsey Hussle 'FDT'."

18. Ibid.

19. Jennifer Jacobs, "Black Students Ejected from Trump Rally in GA," *USA Today*, March 1, 2016, https://www.usatoday.com/story/news/politics/elections/2016/02/29/donald-trump-georgia-rally-valdosta/81129964/.

20. Ibid.

21. Steve Herman, "Trump's Public Expletives Another Break with Presidential Decorum," *VOA News*, October 12, 2019, https://www.voanews.com/usa/us-politics/trumps-public-expletives-another-break-presidential-decorum.

22. Colin Daileda, "Why Were 30 Black Students Kicked out of a Trump Rally in Georgia?," *Mashable*, March 1, 2016, https://mashable.com/2016/03/01/black-students-ejected-donald-trump-rally/.

23. Jacobs, "Black Students Ejected from Trump Rally in GA."

24. Ibid.

25. Erik Nielson, "'Can't C Me': Surveillance and Rap Music," *Journal of Black Studies* 40, no. 6 (July 2010): 1254.

26. Ibid., 1254–55.

27. Ibid., 1256–57.

28. See for example Joe Austin, *Taking the Train: How Graffiti Art Became an Urban Crisis in New York City* (New York: Columbia University Press, 2001), Craig Castleman, *Getting Up: Subway Graffiti in New York* (Cambridge: The Massachusetts Institute of Technology, 1982), Jeff Chang, *Can't Stop Won't Stop: A History of the Hip-Hop Generation* (New York: St. Martin's, 2005), and Tricia Rose, *Black Noise: Rap Music and Black Culture* (Middleton, CT: Wesleyan University Press, 1994).

29. Another example from YG in 2020 entitled "FTP" (which stands for "Fuck the Police") is bound to attract the attention of authorities because its title specifically calls them out.

30. TMZ, "YG Secret Service on My Ass over 'F*** Trump!'," *TMZ*, April 25, 2016, https://www.tmz.com/2016/04/25/yg-donald-trump-secret-service/.

31. Ibid.
32. Ibid.
33. Fatima Robinson, "A Tribe Called Quest Performs at the Grammys 2017," *Vimeo Video*, 5:28, November 26, 2018, https://vimeo.com/302978618. The original music video is also incredible. I analyze the live performance that took place at the Grammys because of its proximity in date to Trump's immigration bans and its viewer exposure. In 2017, 26.05 million people watched the Grammys, as contrasted to the nearly six million people who have watched the official video as of this writing (May 2020). A Tribe Called Quest, "A Tribe Called Quest – We The People (Official Music Video)," *YouTube Video*, 3:14, November 17, 2016, https://www.youtube.com/watch?v=vO2Su3erRIA. I credit the song's title for part of this chapter's title.
34. A Tribe Called Quest, "Award Tour," track 3 on *Midnight Marauders*, November 9, 1993, 1993 Zomba Recording LLC, Apple Music; A Tribe Called Quest, "Can I Kick It?," track 4 on *The Anthology*, October 26, 1999, 1999 Zomba Recording LLC, Apple Music.
35. A Tribe Called Quest, "Movin Backwards," track 5 on *We Got It from Here . . . Thank You 4 Your Service*, November 11, 2016, 2016 Epic Records, a Division of Sony Music Entertainment, Apple Music.
36. MTV News, "Donald Trump Says He Would Vote for Eminem at the Shady National Convention," *YouTube Video*, 2:04, October 11, 2017, https://www.youtube.com/watch?v=SuSkOQsv9fg.
37. Ibid.
38. The heavily redacted Secret Service document is available online at https://www.documentcloud.org/documents/6515270-LEOPOLD-Secret-Service-FOIA-Eminem.html.
39. Eminem, "Framed," track 12 on *Revival*, Aftermath/Shady/Interscope Records, 2018, Apple Music.
40. BETNetworks, "Eminem Rips Donald Trump in BET Hip Hop Awards Freestyle Cypher," *YouTube Video*, 4:34, October 10, 2017, https://www.youtube.com/watch?v=LunHybOKIjU.
41. Ibid.
42. Ibid.
43. Eminem, "Like Home," track 9 on *Revival*, Aftermath/Shady/Interscope Records, 2017, Apple Music.
44. Ibid.
45. Ibid.
46. Lynsey Chutel, "The Choreographer Who Brought Africa to Childish Gambino's 'This Is America' Had a Clear Message," *Quartz Africa*, May 17, 2018, https://qz.com/africa/1280777/childish-gambinos-african-pop-dance-moves-were-created-by-this-rwandan-choreographer/. For a great tutorial from Silver on the dances, see Sherrie Silver, "This Is America (Official Dance Tutorial Pt 1) by Choreographer Sherrie Silver," *YouTube Video*, 6:50, May 14, 2018, https://www.youtube.com/watch?v=9wBiZtW77AE, and Sherrie Silver, "This Is America (Official Dance Tutorial Pt 2) by Choreographer Sherrie Silver," *YouTube Video*, 7:48, May 30, 2018, https://www.youtube.com/watch?v=suRvNYrwaAY.

47. Frank Guan, "What It Means When Childish Gambino Says 'This Is America'," *Vulture*, May 7, 2018, https://www.vulture.com/2018/05/what-it-means-when-childish-gambino-says-this-is-america.html.

48. Ibid.

49. WEB Du Bois, *The Souls of Black Folk; Essays and Sketches* (Chicago, AG McClurg, 1903, New York: Johnson Reprint Corp., 1968).

50. Theresa Ruth Howard, "A Dancer's Take on 'This Is America': Is the Dance a Distraction or Something Deeper?," *Dance Magazine*, May 10, 2018, https://www.dancemagazine.com/this-is-america-dance-2567663747.html.

51. Jennifer Lin LeMesurier, "Winking at Excess: Racist Kinesiologies in Childish Gambino's 'This Is America'," *Rhetoric Society Quarterly* 50, no. 2 (2020): 139–51.

52. 21 Savage, "monster," track 13 on *i am > i was*, 2018 Slaughter Gang, LLC under Exclusive License to Epic Records, a Division of Sony Music Entertainment, 2018, and Thomas Morton, "Known Zones: The Noisey Guide to ATL's Trap Map," *Noisey*, February 9, 2015, https://www.vice.com/en_us/article/7b7yag/known-zones-0000575-v22n2.

53. Matthew S. Schwartz, "Rapper 21 Savage Arrested by ICE for Allegedly Overstaying Visa," *NPR Music News*, https://www.npr.org/2019/02/04/691210275/atlanta-rapper-21-savage-arrested-by-ice-for-allegedly-overstaying-visa.

54. 21 Savage, "a lot," track 1 on *i am > i was*, 2018 Slaughter Gang, LLC under Exclusive License to Epic Records, a Division of Sony Music Entertainment, 2018, Apple Music.

55. Ben Kaye, "21 Savage Gives Intimate Performance of 'A Lot' on Fallon: Watch," *Entertainment News*, January 29, 2019, https://consequenceofsound.net/2019/01/21-savage-performs-fallon/.

56. 21 Savage, "21 Savage – a lot ft. J. Cole," *YouTube Video*, 6:31, February 1, 2019, https://www.youtube.com/watch?time_continue=260&v=DmWWqogr_r8&feature=emb_logo.

57. 21 Savage, "a lot," and East of Underground, "I Love You," track 8 on *Hell Below: East of Underground, The Black Seeds, & The Sound Trek*, August 28, 2007, 2011 Now Again Records, Apple Music.

58. Ibid.

59. Ibid.

60. Ibid.

61. Thomas Hobbs, "DJ Khaled – 'Father of Asahd' Review," *NME*, May 17, 2019, https://www.nme.com/reviews/dj-khaled-father-of-asahd-review-2489183.

62. ChannelZERO, "Public Enemy – Fight the Power (2020 Remix) feat. Nas, Rapsody, Black Thought, Jahi, YG & Questlove," *YouTube Video*, 4:59, August 28, 2020, https://www.youtube.com/watch?v=nNUl8bAKdi4. At the end of this chapter I discuss the murders of George Floyd and Breonna Taylor in more detail, in addition to how members of the hip-hop community responded in the immediate days following the violence.

63. Stevie Wonder, "Can't Put It in the Hands of Fate," single, 2020 UMG Recordings Inc, Apple Music.

64. Recent scholars have sought to redress this imbalance. See for example Carrie Walker, "Disassembling the 'Matrix of Domination': Janelle Monáe's Transformative Vision," in *In Media Res: Race, Identity, and Pop Culture in the Twenty-First Century* (Lewisburg: Bucknell University Press, 2015), 215–38. See also Sarah Raine and Catherine Strong, eds., *Toward Gender Equality in the Music Industry: Education, Practice, and Strategies for Change* (New York: Bloomsbury Academic, 2019).

65. Tammy Kernodle, "No More Tears and Prayers: Black Women, Black Music, and the Mythology of Post-Racial America," paper presented at the annual meeting of the American Musicological Society, Boston, MA, November 2019. The examples that Kernodle discussed included Hill's "Black Rage," in which Kernodle argued that Hill subverted "My Favorite Things" from *The Sound of Music* "from White female pleasure to the dissonance of Black childhood"; Giddens's "Cry No More," demanding a response from the heartbreaking string of violence against people of color in America and the urgency of speaking out against it, and Monáe's "Hell You Taln' Bout," which addresses "silence as the enemy and sound as the weapon." She includes gestures that she labels as "sonic," such as "timbral changes" and "vocalizations"; "rhetorical," moving beyond a "normative use of words" to include "multiple meanings"; and "embodied," or "kinetic aspects of anger in the performing body."

66. Rodney Carmichael, "With 'Eve,' Rapsody Wields the Legacies of Legendary Black Women, from Nina to Serena," *NPR Music* (August 9, 2019), https://www.npr.org/2019/08/09/749645215/with-eve-rapsody-wields-the-legacies-of-legendary-black-women-from-nina-to-serena.

67. Ibid.

68. Beyoncé's *Lemonade* (2016) is another example of the celebration of black womanhood and is worth mentioning in this context, even though that album is not wholly in the hip-hop genre. For an excellent collection of essays about this work, see Kinitra D. Brooks and Kameelah L. Martin, eds., *The Lemonade Reader: Beyoncé, Black Feminism and Spirituality* (New York: Routledge, 2019).

69. UPROXX Video, "Talib Kweli & Rapsody Talk Rap Influences, Being Pro Black, Kendrick, Jay Z, Eve | People's Party," *YouTube Video*, 1:14:15, March 2, 2020, https://www.youtube.com/watch?v=HDL9fx9fBX0.

70. Vox, "Ibtihaj Muhammad Was the First US Olympian to Wear a Hijab," *YouTube Video*, 3:58, February 10, 2017, https://www.youtube.com/watch?v=mr5j-Lkk7rw.

71. Carmichael, "Rapsody Wields the Legacies of Legendary Black Women."

72. Ibid. The sampling is from GZA, "Liquid Swords," track 1 on *Liquid Swords*, January 1, 1995, 2015 Geffen Records, Apple Music.

73. Ibid.

74. Rapsody, "Rapsody–Ibtihaj ft. D'Angelo, GZA," *YouTube Video*, 5:14, August 2, 2019, https://www.youtube.com/watch?time_continue=44&v=jhMk_wLm07E&feature=emb_logo.

75. Ibid.

76. Ibid.

77. Ibid.

78. It is also possible that the number twelve could be some kind of play on the "Dozens" game within African American communities, but this game usually involves humor, sarcasm, and insults from one party directed at another, with an opportunity for the insulted party to respond, and Rapsody is not inviting the same kind of response in her delivery.

79. Richardson and Ragland, "#StayWoke," 37. The material and spiritual connection from Smitherman comes from Geneva Smitherman, *Talkin and Testifyin: The Language of Black America* (Detroit: Wayne State University, 1977), 75.

80. Rapsody, "12 Problems" (Extended Version), YouTube Video, 6:18, October 30, 2020, https://www.youtube.com/watch?v=_mkhkaw84k8.

81. https://www.sprite.com/createyourfuture/.

82. Heran Mamo, "Rapsody Captures Why This Election Gives Black Americans a 'Fighting Chance' in '12 Problems' Video: Watch," *Billboard*, October 30, 2020, https://www.billboard.com/articles/columns/hip-hop/9475390/rapsody-12-problems-video-interview.

83. Ibid.

84. A full list of the victims is available online: Alan Gomez and Kaila White, "Here Are All the Victims of the Las Vegas Shooting," *USA Today*, October 6, 2017, https://www.usatoday.com/story/news/nation/2017/10/06/here-all-victims-las-vegas-shooting/733236001/.

85. EminemMusic, "Eminem–Darkness (Official Video)," *YouTube Video*, 6:09, January 16, 2020, https://www.youtube.com/watch?v=RHQC4fAhcbU.

86. Ibid.

87. Simon & Garfunkel, "The Sound of Silence," track 1 on *Sounds of Silence*, January 17, 1966, All rights reserved by Columbia Records, a division of Sony Music Entertainment, Apple Music.

88. EminemMusic, "Darkness."

89. Ibid.

90. Ibid.

91. Justin Charity, "We Are Living in Eminem's White America," *The Ringer*, December 18, 2017, https://www.theringer.com/2017/12/18/16788430/eminem-revival-donald-trump-white-america.

92. Ibid.

93. Ibid.

94. Kajikawa, Loren, "Eminem's 'My Name Is': Signifying Whiteness, Rearticulating Race," *Journal of the Society for American Music* 3, no 3 (August 2009): 342.

95. Miles White, *From Jim Crow to Jay-Z: Race, Rap, and the Performance of Masculinity* (Urbana: University of Illinois Press, 2011), 114.

96. Kihana Miraya Ross, "Call It What It Is: Anti-Blackness," *The New York Times*, June 4, 2020, https://www.nytimes.com/2020/06/04/opinion/george-floyd-anti-blackness.html?action=click&module=Opinion&pgtype=Homepage.

97. Ibid.

98. Ibid.

99. Elahe Izadi, "'Rewriting the Black American Story': Hip-hop's Protest Anthems Respond to Police Shootings," *The Washington Post*, September 23, 2016,

https://www.washingtonpost.com/news/arts-and-entertainment/wp/2016/09/23/rewriting-the-black-american-story-hip-hops-protest-anthems-respond-to-police-shootings/.

100. The New York Times, "Ahmaud Arbery Shooting: A Timeline of the Case," *The New York Times*, May 21, 2020, https://www.nytimes.com/article/ahmaud-arbery-timeline.html.

101. Ibid.

102. BET, "Hip Hop Community Demands Justice after Video of Ahmaud Arbery's Shooting Death Surfaces," *BET*, May 7, 2020, https://www.bet.com/music/2020/05/07/hip-hop-reacts-to-footage-of-ahmaud-arbeys-shooting-death.html.

103. Jeezy (@jeezy), "My heart goes out to the family of Ahmaud Arbey. Prayers goes out to all of us that look like him too. This could have be you, me, your brother, uncle. Maybe your son or your father. Truth of the matter is, if he is a suspect based off the the way he looks, then I guess I'm a suspect too. No ones deserves to be hunted like a wild animal. Outnumbered, then murdered in cold blood. Racism is still very real. And it has killed more of us than any pandemic. It's time for us to find a cure. This has to stop! One word Justice. #irunwithahmaud," Instagram photo, May 7, 2020, https://www.instagram.com/jeezy/.

104. Snoop Dogg (@snoopdogg), "I was murdered by an armed father and son who hunted me down and shot me as I jogged in a Georgia neighborhood. Neither of my killers has been charged. My name is Ahmaud Arbery," *Instagram photo*, May 8, 2020, https://www.instagram.com/snoopdogg/.

105. Alexandria Neason, "Ahmaud Arbery, Breonna Taylor, and Covering Black Deaths," *Columbia Journal Review*, May 20, 2020, https://www.cjr.org/criticism/ahmaud-arbery-breonna-taylor.php, and Malachy Browne, Anjali Singhvi, Natalie Reneau and Drew Jordan, "How the Police Killed Breonna Taylor," *The New York Times*, December 28, 2020, https://www.nytimes.com/video/us/100000007348445/breonna-taylor-death-cops.html?action=click&gtype=vhs&version=vhs-heading&module=vhs&region=title-area&cview=true&t=4.

106. Michael Levenson, "Prosecutors to Drop Charges against Boyfriend of Breonna Taylor," *The New York Times*, May 22, 2020, https://www.nytimes.com/2020/05/22/us/Breonna-Taylor-Kenneth-Walker.html.

107. Christopher Brito, "Family Sues after 26-year-old EMT is Shot and Killed in Her Own Home," *CBS News*, May 15, 2020, https://www.cbsnews.com/news/breonna-taylor-family-sues-wrongful-death-killed-police-louisville/.

108. Neason, "Covering Black Deaths."

109. Ibid.

110. TI (@troubleman31), "There is no way in hell the officers responsible for murdering #breonnataylor can be allowed to walk free. Our brothers are already being killed daily, but murdering our sisters can not be tolerated! We've gone beyond the boiling point. Show up and join @attorneycrump @untilfreedom @ju.niya @colorofchange @blmlouisville to stand for sis! #fightforbreonna," Instagram photo, May 23, 2020, https://www.instagram.com/p/CAizvdYBhE8/?utm_source=ig_embed.

111. Public Enemy, "Fight the Power (Remix 2020)."

112. Aleia Woods, "Rappers Demand Justice for George Floyd, Who Was Killed by a Police Officer that Pinned Knee on Floyd's Neck," *XXL*, May 27, 2020, https://www.xxlmag.com/news/2020/05/rappers-justice-george-floyd-killed-police-officer/.

113. Cardi B (@iamcardib), "Enough is enough! What will it take? A civil war? A new president? Violent riots? It's tired! I'm tired! The country is tired! You don't put fear in people when you do this you just show how coward you are! And how America is really not the land of the free!," *Instagram photo*, May 27, 2020, https://www.instagram.com/p/CArHyduAZ_a/?utm_source=ig_embed.

114. TI (@troubleman31), "So fuckin sick of posting this shit Maaaaan . . . But then if we don't, it goes unnoticed. I'm ready when y'all is . . . IT WONT STOP UNTIL WE STOP IT!! ," *Instagram photo*, May 27, 2020, https://www.instagram.com/p/CAq0AMThMq9/?utm_source=ig_embed.

115. Tity Boi (2 Chainz) (@2chainz), "I can't post the video, I can still see the killer with his hands in his pocket and knee on the neck of a handcuffed black man rest in peace #georgefloyd and I hate him and all the cops that was there for it," Twitter, May 27, 2020, https://twitter.com/2chainz/status/1265629729861898241.

116. James Dinh, "Cardi B-Backed 'Justice for George Floyd' Petition Makes History, *The Breakfast Club*, May 29, 2020, https://thebreakfastclub.iheart.com/content/2020-05-29-cardi-b-backed-justice-for-george-floyd-petition-makes-history/?fbclid=IwAR2TEnvlwW9bKu-hTXU08ZNsE34vJcFBRshBsLBKXMFjD2_YLRyvVJJ4Rdc.

117. Ibid.

118. 15MOFERADIO, "LL COOL J DROPS BLACK LIVES MATTER FREESTYLE," YouTube Video, 2:37, May 31, 2020, https://www.youtube.com/watch?v=xjNTLSR4DGo.

119. Michael Collins, "Americans with Tax Issues Aren't Getting Their Coronavirus Stimulus Checks. They Suspect the IRS is Delaying Payment," *USA Today*, May 15, 2020, https://www.usatoday.com/story/news/politics/2020/05/15/coronavirus-irs-accused-delaying-stimulus-checks-over-tax-issues/3090114001/.

120. Ibid.

121. Ibid.

122. @thebryceisrightbih, "Minnesota riots are at another level. We need reform! We need justice! #georgefloyd #minnesota #copskillblackguy #xyzabc #fyp #protestors #riots," TikTok video, https://vm.tiktok.com/KmYPpM/, May 29, 2020, and Gambino, "This Is America." In addition, many recent TikTok videos have captured protestors of President Trump with YG's "FDT" playing in the background.

123. Fernandes, "'Obama Nation'," 91–2.

Chapter 4

"Look Around," "History Is Happening"

Heterogenous Topics in Lin-Manuel Miranda's Hamilton

The *Washington Post* critic Alexandra Petri wrote in September 2015: "I [just saw] *Hamilton*, the musical swallowing Broadway whole," followed by this parenthetical statement in all caps: "And whose cast recording is now available to stream online . . . This is like Broadway Christmas."[1] In its exuberance, Petri's comment was a cultural barometer for how well-received Lin-Manuel Miranda's eleven-Tony-award-winning *Hamilton* (2015) has been. To say that the musical has gained momentum since its premiere is an understatement. To paraphrase a line from the musical, *Hamilton* is "not a moment; it's a movement."[2] In a recent 2018 issue of *American Music* devoted entirely to the musical, Elizabeth Titrington Craft, Anne Searcy, Loren Kajikawa, and Justin Williams examine the political and sociological *tour de force* that the musical has become, including the powerful role of the digital world, especially Miranda's direct involvement with politics using YouTube, Twitter, Facebook, and Instagram as platforms.[3] Added to this is the tremendous reception of live performances and the use of particular vocal techniques, notably the innovation of including so much rap, along with the roles of choreography and engagement with the audience. Yet, the reception of the musical has changed since its premiere. As with many of the examples throughout this book, the 2016 election year and Trump's rise to power proved to be a transitional time for many artists. Similarly, *Hamilton* began to be interpreted by fans and critics alike for its role in political spheres and social movements. So, too, was the 2020 election year a transitional time, during which *Hamilton* became available for viewing on Disney Plus. I will first briefly review the musical and its reception. Then, in considering how *Hamilton* fits into the discourse of encoded symbols that is central in this book, I will analyze five topics—recognizable and repeated elements that resonate with marginalized groups of people and that simultaneously speak to the audience at large. My analysis in this chapter is based not on the recent Disney Plus release but upon my viewing of the original Broadway premiere in New York and a later performance in Atlanta, along with my repeated listenings to the album. The musical has become representative for highlighting chasms—in particular, differing perspectives on race, immigration, and the treatment of minorities—in America's current political landscape, another interpretation of what "This is America" could mean.

In its reception, either critiquing or praising *Hamilton* has become a way for many Americans to articulate their politics. These differences have been especially pronounced in the transition from the Obama administration to the Trump administration. Obama loved the musical and spoke to the cast about how it reflected American values of innovation and inclusion. He invited the cast to the White House and talked about the particular power of rap in this context, in a similar manner that Sujatha Fernandes described rap in the beginning of chapter 3. Obama stated that

> Rap is the language of revolution. Hip-hop is the backbeat. In each brilliantly crafted song, we hear the debates that shaped our nation, and we hear the debates that are still shaping our nation. We feel the fierce, youthful energy that animated the men and women of Hamilton's generation. And with a cast as diverse as America itself, including the outstandingly talented women, the show reminds us that this nation was built by more than just a few great men, and that it is an inheritance that belongs to all of us.[4]

In stark contrast, Trump tweeted that he heard that the musical was "overrated" and criticized it after cast members spoke about racial tolerance to former Vice President Mike Pence when he attended the show in November 2016.[5] Brandon Victor Dixon (b. 1981), who at the time played Aaron Burr, briefly addressed concerns to Pence:

> We, sir, are the diverse America who are alarmed and anxious that your new administration will not protect us, our planet, our children, our parents, or defend us and uphold our inalienable rights. We truly hope this show has inspired you to uphold our American values and work on behalf of all of us. All of us.[6]

After the incident, Trump angrily tweeted (and then deleted): "Very rude and insulting of Hamilton cast member to treat our great future V.P. Mike Pence to a theater lecture. Couldn't even memorize lines!"[7] He then unleashed a series of tweets against the musical, including one in which he proclaimed that "The Theater must always be a safe and special place. The cast of Hamilton was very rude last night to a very good man, Mike Pence. Apologize!"[8] Despite not having seen the musical, Trump's negative review included not only what he believed to be its overrated status but also the audacity of the cast itself. More specifically, his perception of the theater as "safe" implied that, in his opinion, the theater must be separated from real-world politics and that members inside a theater should not express political views. The cast's actions reflected what Trump believed to be an artistic infraction within a sacred space. The cast members that night made a statement—centuries in practice—that the theater was not insulated from ideology. These events in turn created a political rift.

Other negative reviews have critiqued Miranda's strategy of misaligning the race of historic figures with the perceived one of performers, arguing that *Hamilton* misses precious opportunities to address contemporary race issues or, worse, that it threatens to whitewash history by downplaying slavery. Black men and women represent characters who were not only Black but were also slaveholders. *Atlantic* reporter Spencer Kornhaber is puzzled that "*Hamilton* does not merely allow for some of the Founding Fathers to be non-White. It insists all of them be."[9] American historian Lyra Monteiro makes a compelling case for the inclusion of actual historical minorities in the cast of *Hamilton*, such as the slave Cato who worked with Hercules Mulligan as a spy against the British. Among her sources, she includes an inflammatory essay by Ishmael Reed entitled "Black Actors Dress Up Like Slave Traders . . . and It's Not Halloween."[10]

An essential element missing in such critiques of *Hamilton*—one that is rapidly changing in scholarship such as the 2018 *American Music* issue and that will surely continue to change given the recent digital video release of the Broadway performance—is a detailed discussion of the actual music that Miranda (b. 1980) uses to portray the characters. Monteiro reinforces this omission by repeatedly referring to *Hamilton* as a "play" rather than as a "musical" throughout her article. Her brief references to musical examples are missed opportunities to show that the music represents a multiracial and multiethnic cast of characters, both past and present. Monteiro bemoans that in *Hamilton* "there is only space for White heroes," forgetting in her continual reference to the work as a "play" that the "space" includes not only her analysis of words and skin color but also the very music that inhabits the space of such elements.[11]

My analytical approach in this chapter draws upon the methodology of the music theorist Horace J. Maxile, who suggests that the use of topics as a mode of analysis could help to address the "analysis/interpretation gap" for the music of minorities, in his recent research about the concert music of Black composers.[12] Maxile blends the approaches of Samuel Floyd, Jr.'s depictions of the Black experience, Kofi Agawu's interpretations of musical signs and semiotics, and Leonard Ratner's notion of topics as "subjects for musical discourse" in order to develop five African American "topics":

call-and-response, blues, spiritual/supernatural, jazz, and Signifyin(g).[13] In his work, Maxile expressed hope that his methodology could be applied to other genres and styles, noting that it might in turn result in "a set of 'American' topics . . . thus allow[ing] the scholar to rightly unite sounds deemed as American with their African-American roots."[14]

In *Hamilton*, it turns out that the analytical approach of exploring a wide range of topics helps to demonstrate profound and pan-American relationships between race and music. The topics that I explore include some overlaps with Maxile's. Further, the topics reflect the gestures and interaction with the audience that have been central themes in this book, especially the trope of the manner in which words are delivered and how the delivery can have a profound impact on language. The *Hamilton* topics are: (1) blue notes, (2) Miranda's so-called "island" rhythms in a long-long-short pattern, (3) rapping, (4) call-and-response, and (5) Signifyin(g) both in the use of musical borrowings and in the text of the libretto.[15] Like Maxile, I intend not for this to be an exhaustive list of topics but hope instead that it might continue the discussion for developing meaningful approaches to analysis in *Hamilton*. In relation to some of the other elements in this book that I have considered, such as body movement, vocal inflection, and audience engagement, the topics that I explore here most closely intersect with vocal inflection and audience engagement. The presence and overlap of musical markers within these topics in turn enhances the diversity that is built into the musical and is what has made it so politically relevant in today's America.

Before I explore the topics themselves in detail, I want to expound upon on the significance of the variety of African American topics in *Hamilton* as an example of Olly Wilson's "heterogeneous sound ideal." In his landmark 1981 essay "Black Music as An Art Form," Wilson described the "heterogeneous sound ideal tendency" as a "desirable musical sound texture . . . containing a combination of diverse timbres."[16] Within the instrument families—particularly the voice—Wilson also included a "range of timbres" that might include "moans, groans, yells, screams, shouts, [and] shifts in sonority" that can render a heterogenous effect.[17] According to Wilson, heterogeneity is ideal, because diverse timbres have the potential to keep the ear constantly engaged. As Wilson argues, "The desirable musical sound texture is one that contains a combination of diverse timbres. This fundamental bias for contrast of color—heterogeneity of sound rather than similarity of color or homogeneity of sound."[18]

In many cases, Miranda draws upon identifiably Black and African American musical traditions in *Hamilton*. But his incorporation of these traditions is often in the context of other stylistically contrasting and well-known genres that do not directly invoke African American traditions, such as the inclusion of the song "You'll Be Back" and the rest of the numbers that King

George sings that calls to mind the style of the Beatles.[19] In addition, the sung text in "You'll Be Back" follows "Farmer Refuted," a number that pits Samuel Seabury's sung lines with Baroque-style harpsichord accompaniment against Alexander Hamilton's rapped interjections. In these kinds of stylistic contrasts, ones that permeate the musical, Miranda broadens his base of appeal by including a heterogeneity of styles and not just sounds.[20] By using such a vast range of styles, Miranda increases the chances that at least one type of sound will appeal to at least one type of listener in addition to the listeners who already recognize and appreciate the overlap of styles, genres, and references. If the resulting mix of sounds and sights is heterogeneous, odds are that the resulting mix of listeners will be, too. In *Hamilton* there are so many elements contributing to the heterogeneous sound ideal that the effect is an infinitely recursive loop.

The heterogeneity is not merely sonically ideal. The variety of sounds becomes representative of a double-voiced narrative in which minorities appear as themselves, not as the way that they are perceived by majorities. As the artistic director of the Public Theater that produced *Hamilton's* off-Broadway premiere, Oskar Eustis (b. 1958) commented on this brand of inclusion: "By telling the story of the founding of the country through the eyes of a bastard, immigrant orphan, told entirely by people of color, [Miranda] is saying, 'This is our country. We get to lay claim to it.'"[21] Leslie Odom, Jr. (b. 1981) echoed this sentiment, saying that "It is quite literally taking the history that someone has tried to exclude us from and reclaiming it. We are saying we have the right to tell it too."[22] Comments such as these suggest that, for many, *Hamilton* has become representative of a critical reclamation of identity. A theme throughout this book has been the concept of gaze, who is watching whom, and being aware of how one is being watched, particularly as it relates to those who perceive themselves not to be in control interact with more powerful majorities that are in control. The topics that I analyze reveal a kind of being seen as a direct communication with minorities who would recognize and celebrate those traditions. The musical and visual elements directly incorporate the legacy of previously marginalized voices as the majority voice, as the history itself. Because minorities appear as themselves in the context of so much music that is traditionally associated with minority groups but that has been appropriated over and over again by Whites, the heterogeneity is also rhetorically ideal.

Turning now to the five musical topics that serve as the analytical basis of this chapter, I begin with the blues. As an enormously common feature in many traditions including not only musicals but also popular music and African American classical works, blue notes abound in *Hamilton* and as such can be easily identified as an African American topic. Notable examples in *Hamilton* include "Alexander Hamilton" with the words "in New York you can be a new man," featuring a flat scale degree five in B minor that becomes regularized throughout the rest of the opening number, highlighted by frequent shifts between F-sharp and F-natural, which also occurs in "The Schulyer Sisters," just before Aaron Burr joins the sisters onstage. In addition to the flattened scale degree in the diatonic D Major context, the additional blues custom of bending or scooping pitches punctuates shouts of "Hey!" a feature that also appears in the number "Helpless."[23] As another example of a conventional and recognizable blues element, after a brief introduction, "What'd I Miss" features a swing-tempo boogie-woogie accompaniment with characteristic blue notes for Thomas Jefferson.[24] And in all of his brief appearances on stage when King George muses to himself about whatever happened that he might have missed, he sings a line that humorously begins "Da da da da dat" to himself, and that line contains blue notes, a White performer performing a Black tradition.[25] That is nothing new, and the evocation of the Beatles style in his appearances also draws attention to the Black traditions used by the Beatles, but the ethnicity of King George as White on the *Hamilton* stage makes him the minority, another way that Miranda uses a topic such as the blues in order to effectively retell the story.

These examples are just a few instances of Miranda's frequent use of blue notes in *Hamilton*, drawing upon a familiar topic and relying on the audience's familiarity with the gesture given its pervasive presence in African American idioms, musicals and popular songs. Along with blues numbers in musicals such as *Show Boat* (Jerome Kern and Oscar Hammerstein, II, 1927), *Porgy and Bess* (George Gershwin, DuBose Heyward, and Ira Gershwin, 1935), and *West Side Story* (Leonard Bernstein and Stephen Sondheim, 1957) more recent instances of blues being incorporated into a Broadway musical include the revues *Bring in 'da Noise, Bring in 'da Funk* (Reg E. Gaines, George C. Wolfe, and Ann Duquesnay, 1995), *It Ain't Nothing but the Blues* (Charles Bevel, Lisa Gaithers, Randal Myler, Ron Taylor, and Dan Wheetman, 1999), and *The Scotsboro Boys* (David Thompson, John Kander, and Fred Ebb, 2010).[26] This presence of such a recognizable and common topic—again, Ratner's "subject for musical discourse"—appeals to the audience. Because the "subject" of the blues in this case is based upon African American traditions, it thus reflects one aspect of a celebration of Black identity, especially for the people onstage who are Black and whose ancestors created this genre. The cast's and the audience's understanding of the meaning of this incorporation changes the meaning of the story, knowing that Blacks and Latino performers are representing White political leaders of the past. That code reversal is the symbolic element contained in the blues topic.

The second category of topical analysis in *Hamilton* is the "island time" rhythm and its ability to conjure up a vast array of cultural landscapes. Musical depictions of these landscapes include pervasive rhythms of the

Caribbean, or the *habanera* long-long-short patterns that Miranda calls "island time" dancehall rhythms.[27] Such rhythms are common to many cultures and traditions, including the African *juba* and jazz *clave*. Loren Kajikawa elaborates on the multicultural origins of this 3+3+2 rhythm, noting that it "is common in the Jamaican dancehall, as well as in its Puerto Rican cousin reggaeton."[28] This is also a tremendously common rhythm in many popular songs across many genres.[29] The rhythmic pattern is regularized throughout *Hamilton*, such as in the opening of Aaron Burr's number "Wait for It," perhaps as a sonic foreshadowing of his final meeting with Alexander Hamilton, who was born in the Caribbean. It is also the ostinato throughout "Aaron Burr, Sir" and the showstopper Act I finale "Non-Stop"; it grounds layered entrances of five other motives from the musical, or what Miranda colorfully refers to as an "all-skate."[30] As the habanera rhythm begins, the other motives appear in the following order: (1) Eliza, singing "look around"; (2) Angelica calling out the "satisfied" motive; (3) Washington warning that "history has its eyes on you"; (4) Burr asking Hamilton "why do you assume you're the smartest in the room?"; and (5) the rest of the ensemble joining in with "non-stop." The resulting combination of such memorable motives alongside the cross-rhythmic results creates a formidable finale number for Act I. The variety of musical styles allows for the possibility for listeners of all different backgrounds to identify with the music in some way, building upon the notion that, as Kajikawa suggests, *Hamilton* "is claiming the United States for previously marginalized groups."[31] The island rhythm topic is one of the most multicultural of the five topics that I explore in this chapter. The possibility that rhythm could represent so many places and so many cultures depending on who performs the rhythm and how it is performed is an aspect of its potential to resonate with a broad audience.

The third Black topic in *Hamilton* is the frequency of rap in the musical. Of the musical's forty-six numbers, twenty-five—over half—incorporate rap in some manner.[32] Fifteen of those twenty-five numbers appear in the first act alone. Rap predominates in the first half to such a degree that, even though it is less present in the second half, it is the sound that many most associate with the musical. In addition, there is hardly any spoken dialogue as would be included in more traditional Broadway musicals; rap takes the place of such dialogue. In effect, Miranda is overturning cultural hierarchy and putting rap on top of the other styles that he uses results in turn for the other styles to take a secondary place in the course of this musical, just as Whiteness takes secondary place in the casting of people of color for people who were White in reality.[33] In his retelling of the story in such a way, Miranda demonstrates how rap can be rhetorically persuasive. Rap is used to change the narrative.

In addition, rapping—and the record-scratching that often accompanies it—is a heterogeneous topic in and of itself in that it contrasts to other more traditional musical numbers in *Hamilton* that do not feature rapping. In other words, in *Hamilton*, the act of rapping is a timbral contrast to the act of singing. The rhythmic delivery or flow of the rapped sections of *Hamilton* almost always features emphasis on unusual syllables in words, creating unexpected delights within the flow. The variety of rhythmic and timbral properties unique to a rapper's delivery is an example of one component of added heterogeneity. As Wilson explains, "a tendency to create musical events in which rhythmic clash or disagreement of accents is ideal" and is one "essence of the Black music tradition."[34] "Guns and Ships" is an example of Daveed Diggs (b. 1982) as the Marquis de Lafayette providing vocal shading (rapping with a French accent) and virtuosity (blisteringly rapid speed of delivery). In "Cabinet Battle no. 1" and "Cabinet Battle no. 2," bragging, boasting, and freestyle show the characters' knowledge and understanding not only of the political issues but also of the rap traditions that they represent. Rapping thus serves as a force for political debate and verbal dueling onstage. As Kajikawa notes, it also represents Hamilton's political prowess. In "My Shot," Kajikawa points out, "Hamilton delivers an onslaught of internal and multiple-word rhymes ('disadvantage,' 'learned to manage,' 'gun to brandish,' etc.) as well as enjambment, the poetic technique in which phrases cascade over the bar lines in effusive rhythm."[35] In addition, rapping represents kinship, such as in "Take a Break," during which Eliza—who otherwise sings—beatboxes while Philip raps. Rapping represents equality, such as in "The Schuyler Sisters," during which Angelica wants women to be included "in the sequel" to the Declaration of Independence.[36] Rapping is rooted in African American and Black traditions. Many characters in the musical participate in its gesturing, because it is the sonic centerpiece of *Hamilton*. The incorporation of so much rap represents a reclamation of culture by the subversive casting. In its strong presence, Miranda sonically and visually shows the audience who is owed the musical debts.

When Maxile described "a set of 'American' topics . . . thus allow[ing] the scholar to rightly unite sounds deemed as American with their African-American roots," he further noted that "such an inclusive and unifying position is both patriotic and political."[37] Rapping is one of the most salient political markers in *Hamilton* and has inspired a host of responses in the pendulum of American politics. One touching response came from Esteisy Seijas, a student at John Adams High School in Ozone Park, New York. Seijas was one of a number of high school students who got to attend a free live performance of *Hamilton* due to the partnership of the Public Theater Development Fund that has enabled tens of thousands of students to see live performances of plays and musicals in New York City. After the students had seen the show, Seijas's teacher Joe White gave the students an assignment: pair up, pick an issue to debate, and write a rap battle about it to be performed in front of the class. Seijas penned lyrics about marriage equality in which all kinds of love are equal, including this passage in the opening lines: "Everyone can be loved, including me. We live for the new, we live for the now."[38] Seijas's response is just one example of the potency of *Hamilton's* influence in American society today, and it shows how the topic of rapping has reverberated beyond its musical power onstage.

The fourth topic that I analyze is the dramatic effect of call-and-response throughout *Hamilton*. The musical is full of different types of call-and-response. To begin, *Hamilton* opens with the seeming rhetorical call of the question, "How does a bastard, orphan, son of a whore and a Scotsman dropped in the middle of a forgotten spot in the Caribbean by providence, impoverished, in squalor, grow up to be a hero and a father?"[39] Already, the seeming contrast of circumstances of birth, economies, cultures, landscapes, professions, and life moments invites the use of something like topics as a mode of inquiry, because there is a simultaneity and juxtaposition of events all captured in a single question. This is very similar to the simultaneity and juxtaposition of all of the different musical events highlighted in this chapter. The answer to the opening question is in the specificity of events in the musical that unfolds.

Throughout the musical, call-and-response serves as a topical reference in several numbers. In "My Shot," John Laurens interacts with the characters onstage, calling out "Ev'rybody sing," to which Hamilton, Lafayette, and Mulligan respond with "Whoa! Whoa! Whoa!" a line that is eventually also echoed by the company, and a response that is regularly featured in many other numbers.[40] In "Right Hand Man," for example, the "Whoa!" responses continue, as do ensemble responses of "Buck, buck, buck!" to Washington's call for a "right hand man."[41] There is also a lovely effect of a rhythmic response to the call of the lyrics in "My Shot" in the form of word painting. In all except the final iteration of "my shot," there is a beat of rest following the word "shot," so the shot is in effect saved for a moment and not thrown away. This effect also appears in Aaron Burr's number "Wait for It," in which an empty beat before the main chorus begins symbolizes waiting.[42] Following "My Shot," "The Story of Tonight" features Alexander Hamilton singing each line of the verse that is subsequently repeated by his comrades Lafayette, Mulligan, and Laurens.[43] Miranda worked closely with Hamilton biographer Ron Chernow (b. 1949), and both have commented on this scene, noting the historical impossibility of having all four men together at the same time. As Chernow described, that minor alteration made sense in the context of the plot of the musical. Even though the grouping of these figures is ahistorical, Chernow argued that it worked artistically, especially given its placement immediately after "My Shot."[44] It also creates a compelling scene of brotherhood, togetherness, and congeniality that is reinforced with the call-and-response topic. Strong sisterhood follows in the number "The Schuyler Sisters," in which a number of shouts, grunts, and exclamatory remarks punctuate and serve as responses—"Work!" "Unh!" Whoa!"—to the musical call of the lyrics.[45] King George sings to himself in call-and-response in "You'll Be Back," a number that recurs in variations throughout the musical, apparently amusing himself so much with his megalomaniacal thoughts that he can only respond in a delightfully ridiculous "Da da da da dat, da dat da da da ya da."[46] This response becomes so irresistible to him that he calls out for "Everybody!" to join, as the company responds in turn. Meanwhile, "Ten Duel Commandments" and the dueling in the cabinet battles have call-and-response built into the structure of the numbers.[47] In "Ten Duel Commandments," the number of the rule is called out as Burr, Hamilton, Laurens, and Lee take turns elucidating the rule. The back-and-forth rapping in the cabinet battles is itself call-and-response. And, reacting to "Washington on Your Side" as described in *Hamilton: The Revolution*, Miranda "was delighted when Busta Rhymes told him that he loved the old-school way that Burr, Jefferson, and Madison finished each other's sentences as they concocted a plan to destroy Hamilton."[48] In the same spirit, "Questlove called it a 'tug of war' song."[49] Whether characters are finishing sentences for each other or verbally playing tug-of-war, they are continually engaging in call-and-response.

There has even been an unintended call-and-response effect that one moment in the musical has created between the members of the cast and the members of the audience. Elizabeth Titrington Craft describes the effect:

> During the Battle of Yorktown scene, Hamilton and Lafayette greet one another confidently, saying, "Immigrants: We get the job done" and high-fiving. Even though the line comes early in the song—not at a natural climax [although the moment does stand out in that it is unaccompanied in the context of what surrounds it]—many early commentators noted that audiences broke into applause upon hearing it. Miranda himself said that they had to add bars to the song during the show's off-Broadway run because "it was getting such a reaction." . . . The audience responses demonstrate that *Hamilton* was perceived as speaking to contemporary political issues from the moment of its debut.[50]

Craft also discusses the relevance of such moments in contemporary movements, including #BlackLivesMatter. Regarding all of the resonances, Miranda himself said in an interview, "We're screaming 'Rise up,' and a lot of people are feeling that way."[51] So when audiences began to demonstrate their identification of the meaning of this moment by applauding at the utterance of "Immigrants: we get the job done"—a moment that is also a musical stopping point since it is unaccompanied, and the words are spoken in unison—it became a symbol of something much broader than the political moment onstage. For the audience members applauding, the moment symbolizes a reminder of the value of immigrants in this America, in today's America, during a time in which Trump wanted many of them out of America. The meaning of that statement changed based on the way in which it was performed. It has come to symbolize a current political topic, one that led to an engaged audience response.

The few examples that I have pointed out begin to demonstrate that call-and-response saturates *Hamilton* and adds to all of the emotions built into the plot, whether the emotions are delightful, endearing, shocking, or saddening. Yet some of the most heartfelt moments of the musical paradoxically occur where call-and-response is lacking in the music. For that matter, every time that call-and-response is musically missing, there is a physical formation of a ring in the staging of the characters. This occurs in addition to the very construction of the stage itself, which is designed to look like a record player, with the added possibility for the outside section of the circle to revolve in one direction and the inner circle to revolve in another. Thus, in the very construction of the stage, there is a visual echo of call-and-response—the circle formation that is central to such an activity—throughout the musical, whether or not call-and-response is occurring in the music itself. The ring formation is known as a "cypher" in the traditions including break dancing and the ring shout, visually calling to mind more African American references.

In one of many moving moments in *Hamilton*, the musical absence of call-and-response paired with the visual encircling of characters onstage adds to the emotional effect in Philip Hamilton's death scene "Stay Alive (Reprise)." Call-and-response in the form of repetition by rote learning ceases between Philip and Eliza as she tries to engage him in the singing games they played during his piano lessons as a child. The game first appears in the song "Take A Break."[52] Eliza sings and counts to nine in French using two melodic patterns, one ascending up through a minor sixth on diatonic notes of a major scale, and one descending in melodic inversion beginning an octave higher. Philip appears to answer in the form of exact repetition, with one critical alteration: he always sings the last three notes differently and in his own way, even after Eliza corrects him. In "Stay Alive (Reprise)," as Philip is struggling to breathe after having lost a duel to George Eaker, Eliza begins the counting and singing game in a desperate attempt to engage him.[53] She keeps repeating the last three notes that Philip always deliberately misses, but he is no longer able to answer. The ostinato rhythmic accompaniment simulating a heartbeat that has been present throughout this scene also stops at the moment of his death. Alexander and Eliza surround Philip. Despite the difficulties that Alexander and Eliza have faced in Alexander's previous misdeeds, the loss of their son is too tremendous for them to also lose each other. In the following song "It's Quiet Uptown," Eliza forgives Alexander after the unspeakable grief that they have endured, visually represented in the physical staging of the characters, standing in a circle and walking toward each other.[54]

In addition to the visual call-and-response of the characters responding to the notion of forgiveness, there is a metaphorical call-and-response to all of the questions asked by various characters throughout the musical. "Would that be enough?" asks Eliza. "What'd I miss?" says Jefferson.[55] The answer of forgiveness in "It's Quiet Uptown" is something ineffable in the music, paired with lyrics that match the sentiment: "There are moments that the words don't reach."[56] For all of the questions and uncertainties and tragedies in *Hamilton*, including at least two extramarital affairs, two deaths, and three on-stage duels, forgiveness is one answer that means more than words.

This section on the call-and-response topic began with the opening question of the musical. The closing question "Who lives, who dies, who tells your story?" is less specific than the opening one. As the events of the musical occur and the audience processes those events, this last question is more open-ended and directed at the audience. Significantly, Eliza lives a good long while after Alexander dies and is able to help tell his story.[57] But, as the question asks, this is not just "his" story. It is also Eliza's story. In fact, for the original Broadway actress Phillipa Soo (b. 1990) who played Eliza, she added a possible answer to the question. After the last iteration of the question, before the lights went dark, she added a gasp. Audience members have had widely varying interpretations of what that gasp meant, and she recently clarified how the meaning would change for her depending on the moment during the performance:

> Night to night [the meaning of the gasp] was different but it was a mixture of Eliza seeing that legacy, the orphanage (which is still standing), her kids telling her story. It's an exploration every day and you find new things every time. Sometimes, the [fourth] wall would break—it was looking out at all the beautiful audience faces and acknowledging the story that we had all just taken a ride to witness. The fact that we'd sat in the dark for two and a half hours, put ourselves in his shoes and told his story. So it was a culmination of all those things. We shot the film two weeks before my final show so a lot of what you're seeing is not just that performance, but also that year and moment in time—the hope and potential that lived in that moment.[58]

In the excerpted quote above, Soo referred to her final night performing with the original Broadway cast, which took place on July 9, 2016. Although she does not state so explicitly, her reference to "that year and moment in time" is most likely a reference to the 2016 presidential election and the potential sweeping change that could occur. In that interpretation of what the gasp meant, the answer to the question in the song became personal not only for the character she played onstage but also for her. In complex and changing ways, the question pertains to Hamilton, to Eliza, to the cast members, to the historical figures, and also, as the song's title states, the audience: the story is also yours.

The turn of focus to the second person at the end of the musical directly relates to the sense of urgency captured in all of the contemporary musical messages that I explore throughout this book. The specific answer is not named. But many people have symbolically suggested responses in several ways, including the cast's aforementioned message to Mike Pence in 2016. This occurred immediately after the musical had completed, so it can be read as one answer to the call of the question in the closing number. Former President Barack Obama offered another answer to this question almost one year prior to Pence's appearance. As Miranda explained in *Hamilton: The Revoultion*, "The Black first president exited; the first Black president appeared. On November 2, 2015, Chris Jackson and his castmates stood gaping offstage . . . as Barack Obama entered."[59] Fittingly relevant in this section on call-and-response, Obama waited for the applause to die down before asking "What'd I miss?" Although Obama had not actually seen the show that night—he had already attended a matinee in July 2015—he clearly knew and appreciated the material, noting that many musical moments in *Hamilton* tied to larger movements in America. In his speech, Obama expressed how *Hamilton* embodied that notion. He said that

> part of what's so powerful about this performance is it reminds us of the vital, crazy, kinetic energy that's at the heart of America. . . . Every single step of progress that we've made has been based on this notion that people can come together, and ideas can move like electricity through them, and a world can change.[60]

Who tells your story? In Obama's view, the power of simply sharing an idea—one version of telling a story—can unite people, create progress, and change the world.

A stirring response to how the story might be told occurred during the live performance of the Tony Awards on June 12, 2016. Early in the morning on the same day, twenty-nine-year-old [redacted] (1986–2016) killed forty-nine people and wounded fifty-three others at Pulse, a gay nightclub in Orlando, FL.[61] In the horrific act, the killer pledged allegiance to the terrorist group ISIS. In the performance of "The Battle of Yorktown" at the Tonys that evening, choreographer Andy Blankenbuehler (b. 1970) omitted the use of actual muskets as props, opting instead for pantomime. In doing so, he made a powerful statement about what "This is America" meant to him, highlighted in italics in the center of the quote:

> It's interesting, I think the most important moment for me in "Yorktown" ... I don't know if people have noticed this, but the ending of "The Battle of Yorktown" is the first time the American forces ever put guns in their hands, so to go through the whole show with no guns, and then the moment they win—they have guns in their hands, and they immediately put them down ... The moment of putting them down is actually one of my favorite moments in the show. *That's America to me. That's the American Revolution. That's our America today.* It's not taking up arms; it's wanting to put them down so that things can be right. I think that our decision to take out the guns today followed into that. I said to the cast, "When you put your not-gun gun to the floor today, that should be the *whole show*."[62]

In such an expressive act, Blankenbuehler offered another answer to the question "Who lives, who dies, who tells your story?" His choice to remove actual muskets in favor of pantomime in "The Battle of Yorktown" following a tragedy comments on gun culture as a national emergency. It reflects a broader belief that the theater is not a place for abstract commentary and isolated idealism; it is a place to start a conversation, to rise up, and to take action. Other possible responses to the metaphorical call of "Who lives, who dies, who tells your story" are playing out as we speak.

In the final section of this chapter, I will address the Signifyin(g) topic in *Hamilton*, whose very existence depends upon constantly fluctuating meaning and is dependent upon context, with its own brand of built-in symbolism. Musical borrowings comprise one component of Signifyin(g). Table 4.1 is a list of many musical borrowings in *Hamilton*.[63] In the column "type of borrowing," I use J. Peter Burkholder's "Elements of a Typology of Musical Borrowing" in *Oxford Music Online* not only to begin to distinguish between the various types of borrowing in *Hamilton* but also to suggest an enriched meaning that can result from the very act of borrowing, particularly through the ways in which Miranda is Signifyin(g).[64] In Signifyin(g), the way that the original material is reused is important. Henry Louis Gates, Jr. explains that Signifyin(g) entails "troping: the transformation of preexisting musical material by trifling with it, teasing it, or censuring it."[65] Gates's capitalization of the "S" means that the signification is figurative rather than literal. As the examples in table 4.1 demonstrate, Miranda's musical borrowings almost always "trifle with," "tease," or "censure" their original source material in Gates's conception of Signifyin(g).

Even though Miranda's and Jeremy McCarter's *Hamilton: The Revolution* book and libretto includes details about the musical inspirations for many of the

Table 4.1 Musical Borrowings in *Hamilton*

	Song Title	Source	Type of Borrowing	Timings
1	"Alexander Hamilton"	Leonard Bernstein and Stephen Sondheim, *West Side Story*, "Prologue"	Texture: snapping accompaniment (borrowing not mentioned in book, but allegiance to hip-hop + musicals is: "*Hamilton* is laced with these shout-outs to the traditions that birthed it, both hip-hop (DMX, Grandmaster Flash and the Furious Five) and musical theater (*South Pacific*, *The Last Five Years*). These serve, in part, as invitations, a signal to people from diverse backgrounds that the show is meant for them" *Hamilton: The Revolution* [HTR], 94. The snaps recur throughout *Hamilton*.	1:37 (*West Side Story* "Prologue"); opening (*Hamilton*)
2	"Aaron Burr, Sir"	Lauryn Hill, "Everything Is Everything"	Verse: "a-yo-yo-yo-yo" from John Laurens. Like the spelling out of a name referenced below, this is not unique to Lauryn Hill, but I include the reference here since Miranda specifically mentions her.	1:59 (Lauryn Hill, used as intro to her rap); 1:19, same function"
3	"My Shot"	2Pac, "Holla If Ya' Hear Me"	Homage; verse: "I gotta holler just to be heard."	opening (2Pac); 0:17 (*Hamilton*)
4	"My Shot"	Mobb Deep, "Shook Ones, Pt. II" (note: "Shook Ones" samples Quincy Jones and Herbie Hancock, who in turn borrowed, that is, Signifyin(g) tradition	Texture: "violins unleash a shrill, dissonant tone that slides higher as it goes" + literal quotation "I'm only nineteen" (HTR 94).	1:19 (Mobb Deep); 0:26 (*Hamilton*) (distorted violin is accompaniment at opening of "Shook Ones")
5	"My Shot"	Biggie Smalls, "Going Back to Cali"	Homage: spelling out of the name (of course, not only limited to Biggie. This is swagger hip-hop parlance.	1:48 (Biggie); 0:42 (*Hamilton*)

(*Continued*)

Table 4.1 Musical Borrowings in *Hamilton* (Continued)

	Song Title	Source	Type of Borrowing	Timings
6	"Right Hand Man"	Pharaohe Monch, "Simon Says"	Texture: "buck buck buck" for gunshot sound + effect of "a thousand guys in a basement."	0:27 (Pharaohe); 1:05–1:11 (*Hamilton*)
7	"Helpless"	Beyoncé and Jay-Z, "Crazy in Love" + Ja Rule	Allusion ("only alluded to, with a similar gesture, without itself being incorporated"): "Put 'Helpless' next to 'Crazy in Love': A sweet girl sings about the boy she loves, then the rough-around-the-edges boy pops up to rap his reply In both cases, he doesn't rap about her, he raps about himself." (HTR 69)	
8	"Helpless"	Ja Rule	Timbre, allusion: The Ja Rule reference is a growl at the end that started as a joke and then Lin kept it because it made Pippa laugh, so it becomes a timbre or quality of sound that is borrowed ("only alluded to, with a similar gesture, without itself being incorporated").	
9	"Ten Duel Commandments"	Biggie Smalls, "Ten Crack Commandments"	Homage: "The influence couldn't be more direct or profound . . . the rules of dueling slip neatly into spots originally occupied by the rules of selling crack. The enormous shadow of Biggie himself proved useful too, as his story helps to collapse the distance between the revolutionary era and our time." (HTR 95)	
10	"Meet Me Inside"	DMX "Party Up (Up in Here)"	Verse: ("Meet 'im inside! Meet 'im inside! Meet 'im inside, meet 'im meet 'im inside!") (specific borrowing of DMX).	DMX: "meet me outside, meet me meet me outside" 3:21; 0:24 (*Hamilton*)

"Look Around," "History Is Happening" 139

11	"Yorktown"	(no specific source/Busta Rhymes mentioned) + "The World Turned Upside Down"	Allusion, homage, verse: "Eliza's expecting me . . . Not only that, my Eliza's expecting" "This is the kind of thing that happens in hip-hop but not so much in musical theater: breaking the rhyme scheme to highlight a different meaning of the word." (HTR 121) "Part of the inspiration for the structure of 'Yorktown' is what I call the 'Busta Rhymes soft-loud-soft' technique. On countless songs, Busta will give you the smoothest, quietest delivery and then full-on scream the next verse." (HTR 122).	
12	"Cabinet Battle #1"	Grandmaster Flash & The Furious Five, "The Message"	Verse: Miranda doesn't mention the specific text relationship, although he does cite Grandmaster Flash as an inspiration. "The Message:" "It's like a jungle sometimes somehow it keeps me going under." // in *Hamilton* "such a blunder sometimes it makes me wonder why I even bring the thunder."	1:30 Grandmaster; 2:47 (*Hamilton*)
13	"Say No to This"	Jason Robert Brown, *The Last Five Years*, "Nobody Needs to Know"	Verse: "know"/"no" twist at end of song ("Nobody Needs to Know").	5:50–6:18 (*The Last Five Years*); 3:45 (*Hamilton*)
14	"The Room Where It Happens" (fake sample)	fake-out! 'deceptive borrowing?'	Timbre: trumpet sound that plays at beginning and between sections "is deliberately treated and processed to sound like an old jazz sample, but it's original." (HTR 187)	
15	"Cabinet Battle #2"	Biggie Smalls, "Juicy"	Verse: "and if you don't know, now you know, n***a" "Daveed, the first time he got the lyric: 'It's so hard not to say n**a at the end of this sentence. I'm fighting muscle memory!" (HTR 192)	1:08–1:11 (and other moments, "Juicy"); 0:59 (*Hamilton*)

(Continued)

Table 4.1 Musical Borrowings in *Hamilton* (Continued)

	Song Title	Source	Type of Borrowing	Timings
16	"Washington on Your Side"	D'Angelo (and Questlove), *Voodoo*	Homage: (the following is true for many examples of hip-hop and jazz, not just voodoo): "The kick drum and bass swing way, way back behind the beat, a feel that [Alex] Lacamoire loved hearing on D'Angelo's album *Voodoo*, which Questlove helped to mastermind." (HTR 198)	
17	"The Adams Administration"	Sherman Edwards and Peter Stone, *1776*	Verse: "Adams fires Hamilton. Privately calls him creole bastard in his taunts." (HTR 224)	
18	"We Know"	Lauryn Hill, "Lost Ones"?	Homage: Miranda originally wanted a Lauryn Hill quote, but she doesn't allow samples; example of homage without direct borrowing/"ya best g'wan run back where ya come from." (HTR 229)	0:54 (Hill); 0:39 (*Hamilton*)
19	"We Know"	"Cabinet Battle #2"; Biggie Smalls, "Juicy"	Verse, homage: see notes on Biggie above in column 9. (Miranda doesn't note this reference in HTR)	
20	"The Reynolds Pamphlet"	"No John Trumball" (deleted from *Hamilton Mixtape*)	Texture (rhythm): Miranda uses beat from "No John Trumball" for emotional effect and explains: "It's super contemporary and totally different from anything we've heard, and I love that the music that accompanies the nation's first sex scandal sounds so contemporary and crazy." (HTR 234).	2:00–end (*Hamilton*)
21	"Blow Us All Away"	Salt-N-Pepa, "Shoop"	Verse: "How 'bout when I get back, we all strip down to our socks?"/(Lin gets the lyrics wrong, but the spirit is there. "And he's coming this way Oooohhh!" but it's the same idea as the actual beginning of the song: "Oooo how you doin' baby? No, not you. You, the bow-legged one. Yeah, what's your name?"	"Shoop" opening; 0:43 (*Hamilton*)

numbers, table 4.1 has additional borrowings that are not mentioned in the book, such as the snapping accompaniment at the very beginning of *Hamilton* that evokes Leonard Bernstein's similar opening in *West Side Story* (1961).[66] Another borrowing not mentioned in the book is Grandmaster Flash & The Furious Five's "The Message" as a source for *Hamilton's* "Cabinet Battle #1" (as indicated in row 12 in table 4.1). The borrowing includes both the rhythm and syntactic rhyming of the words *and* of the laughing. The majority of the musical borrowings are from hip-hop, and Miranda often refers to specific songs. Table 4.1 also includes a column for a direct comparison of timings if the borrowing is a re-orchestrated sample. Other borrowings are more indirect, for instance, the Jay-Z and Beyoncé, Ja Rule (b. 1976 as Jeffrey Bruce Atkins), and Busta Rhymes references in rows 7, 8, and 11. Meanwhile, there are some artists, such as Lauryn Hill (b. 1975), who do not allow sampling. I have listed possible Hill sources in rows 2 and 18. The kaleidoscopic range of source material, sounds, and timbres in the musical borrowings in *Hamilton* is multicultural and continues to inspire new borrowings, such as *The Hamilton Mixtape* album released in 2016. Miranda's reuse of a variety of types of material powerfully signifies and adds meaning to the musical experience.

The act of borrowing or reusing by referencing previous material enriches the meaning of the original and is a central component of the process of Signifyin(g) itself. Consider, for instance, the reuse of The Notorious B.I.G.'s "Ten Crack Commandments" as the source material for "Ten Duel Commandments" (row 9 in table 4.1). I have already evaluated the role of rapping and call-and-response as African American topics in this number. That it is also a musical borrowing creates another interpretive angle. Miranda comments on how the biography of Biggie Smalls (another moniker for The Notorious B.I.G., born as Christopher Wallce (1972–1997)) makes the musical borrowing so trenchant:

> The influence couldn't be more direct or profound . . . the rules of dueling slip neatly into spots originally occupied by the rules of selling crack. The enormous shadow of Biggie himself proved useful, too, as his story helps to collapse the distance between the revolutionary era and our time.[67]

Just as Blankenbuehler noted that "That's America to me. That's the American Revolution. That's America today," lessening the historical distance between two such seemingly different eras, Miranda commented on how the practice of musical borrowing could also collapse this perceived distance. This historiographical perspective echoes Samuel Floyd, Jr.'s notion that "all African-American music making is driven by and permeated with the memory of things from the cultural past."[68] As such, he noted the following:

> In African-American music, musical figures signify by commenting on other musical figures, on themselves, on performances of other music, on performances of the same piece, and on completely new works of music.[69]

Miranda's statement about how a musical borrowing accomplishes the act of historically "collapsing the distance between the Revolutionary era and our time" parallels Floyd's description of Signifyin(g) in the reuse of material from the "cultural past." Both sentiments offer the performer and listener to recognize the source material, interpret it, reinterpret it, and then apply its relevance in some way.

This process represents a component of Signifyin(g) in that it uses an encoded narrative richly filled with multiple meanings and interpretations. The musicologist Robert Walser has commented on such a fluidity of meaning as it pertains to Signifyin(g), arguing that it

> works through reference, gesture, and dialogue to suggest multiple meanings through association. If signification assumes that meanings can be absolute, permanent, and objectively specified, signifyin' respects contingency, improvisation, relativity—the social production and negotiation of meanings.[70]

In the case of the musical borrowings in *Hamilton*, the "multiple meanings" through association happen in light of the relation of the borrowed material to the source material. Characters onstage sing or rap and in turn evoke past musical figures or numbers. But they also comment on their own position and make the material relevant to both the past and the present. The inferences that result reflect Maxile's belief that "the signifyin(g) process, then, is both dynamic (musical figures commenting on other musical figures) and intertextual (musical figures commenting on themselves)."[71] Because of this, he continues,

> Signifyin(g) is perhaps the most provocative and pervasive topic . . . many signifyin(g) factors, ranging from dueling and satire to gracious reverence, lie at the heart of countless eloquent and potent musical expressions of the African-American community.[72]

Whether through homage, timbre, allusion, or direct quotation, the musical borrowings in table 4.1 are one aspect of this brand of Signifyin(g).

In addition to Signifyin(g) in the music through incorporating borrowed material, Miranda also signifies in the combination of words and phrases that appear in the libretto. Frequently, Miranda uses sarcasm and humor as a means of Signifyin(g). This rhetorical gesturing is similar to Signifyin(g)'s function as a literary device as described by the cultural anthropologist Claudia Mitchell-Kernan, who argues that it "incorporates . . . a folk notion that dictionary entries for words are not always sufficient for interpreting meanings or messages, or that meaning goes beyond such interpretations," especially evident in "sarcasm, smart-alecky remarks, or compliments 'delivered in a left-handed fashion.'"[73] Mitchell-Kernan lists five ways that Signifyin(g) in such a way is possible, including (1) "what pretends to be informative may be persuasive"; (2) "being smart-alecky"; (3) "innuendo"; (4) the use of profanity, and, in particular, the term "motherfucker"; and (5) "changing in posture, speech rate, tone of voice, [or] facial expression."[74] In addition, I would add to Mitchell-Kernan's list a sixth category that Henry Gates, Jr. identifies, which is "talking about talking."[75] Table 4.2 is an annotated list of these six categories containing selected text examples of Signifyin(g) in *Hamilton*.

Signifyin(g) in the text thus adds another layer to the already multilayered Signifyin(g) existent in all of the musical borrowings in *Hamilton*. One begins to get a sense of how multifaceted the topic of Signifyin(g) is given the coexistence of musical borrowings and textual references. In turn, this coexistence increases the likelihood for multiple meanings and interpretations of the new material, since there are many intersections with preexisting material. These types of new meanings are built into the process of Signifyin(g). The musicologist Ayana Smith elaborates upon this point in an article exploring the role of Signifyin(g) in the blues, stating that

> The originality and ingenuity of the author, composer and performer is in his or her ability to create something new out of something pre-existing.... The creative artist must trope in a way that comments upon the original in a new interpretive context. Signifyin(g), therefore, creates a new subtext through the intersection of the original with the trope.[76]

In this spirit, in addition to the examples of textual Signifyin(g) in table 4.2, the musical borrowings in table 4.1 are examples of what Gates elegantly refers to as "embedded signification."[77] To make an analogy to the changed meaning of the word "Signifyin(g)" with the capitalization of the first letter and the parentheses around the last letter, "embedded signification" might be imagined as "Signifying(g)" with the "S" in bold font. The symbolic meaning of the word changes based upon how it is rendered, even in its typeface.

Finally, it is through the topic of Signifyin(g) that Miranda relies on our understanding that many of the Founding Fathers were White as a humorous, ironic, and ultimately sincere opportunity to embrace a variety of traditions. His visionary casting choices signify on the notion of race itself. Miranda, as with all of the artists discussed in this book, effectively represents a country bitterly at odds, something that Alexander Hamilton himself eerily foreshadowed would lead to a bloody civil conflict. Miranda's deliberate choices not only capture struggles in the nascent America but also suggest that race, alongside other contentious issues, is worth reexamining in the present day. Miranda's fellow cast members agree. Daveed Diggs said that the show

Table 4.2 Selected Examples of Signifyin(g) in *Hamilton*

(1) "what pretends to be informative may intend to be persuasive"

"The Schuyler Sisters": Angelica wants to compel Thomas Jefferson to "include women in the sequel" to the Declaration of Independence.

"Non-Stop": Alexander Hamilton tries to convince Aaron Burr to help him defend his "new client," the "U.S. Constitution" and tries to trick Burr into thinking it's a person, not a document, that he will defend.

(2) "being smart-alecky"

"The Story of Tonight" (reprise): "If the tomcat can get married, there's hope for our ass after all" and "Raise a glass to freedom . . . something you will never see again."

General New Jersey mockery ("The Farmer Refuted," 1:16 and "Blow Us All Away," 1:42)

(3) "innuendo . . . allud[ing] to and imply[ing] things which are never made explicit"

"The Schuyler Sisters": Angelica Schuyler/Burr: "Burr, you disgust me. "Ah, so you discuss me? I'm a trust fund baby you can trust me."

"Yorktown": "Eliza's expecting me . . . Not only that, my Eliza's expecting." Miranda: "This is the kind of thing that happens in hip-hop but not so much in musical theater: breaking the rhyme scheme to highlight a different meaning of the word." (HTR, 122)

"Satisfied": many meanings for satisfied, including: (a) Angelica's search for knowledge, looking for a mind as sharp as hers; (b) Alexander's similar state; (c) dueling; (d) double entendre for sexual satisfaction.

(4) "the use of mother fucker is a rather common term of address in . . . acts of verbal dueling"

"The Adams Administration" ("sit down, John, you fat mother fucker")

"Washington on Your Side" ("Southern mother-fucking Democratic Republicans")

(5) "Changing in posture, speech rate, tone of voice, facial expression, etc. may signal a change in meaning."

"My Shot": religious overtones in call-and-response with "my shot" and "rise up"

"Guns and Ships:" ("sir he knows what to do in a *trench, ingenuitive* and fluent in *French*")

(6) "talking about talking"

"My Shot": (Alexander, interrupting everything, including himself): "Oh, am I talkin' too loud? Sometimes I get overexcited, shoot off at the mouth."

"made me more American . . . [until *Hamilton*] I always felt at odds with this country."[78] Leslie Odom, Jr. remarked that

> Playing a Founding Father has made [me] feel newly invested in the country's origins, something that always seemed remote from [my] life as a Black man in America. The empathy that requires, the connections you make, the lines you draw between the things you want and the things they wanted, that you love and they loved, I never found all of that connective tissue before this show.[79]

Such "connective tissue" has affected millions of fans in a similar way. As former First Lady Michelle Obama (b. 1964) put it, simultaneously commenting on the diversity and inclusion built into *Hamilton* while also offering another response to "who tells your story,"

> *Hamilton* touched me because it reflected the kind of history I'd lived myself. It told a story about America that allowed the diversity in. I thought about this afterward: So many of us go through life with our stories hidden, feeling ashamed or afraid when our whole truth doesn't live up to some established ideal. We grow up with messages that tell us that there's only one way to be American—that if our skin is dark or our hips are wide, if we don't experience love in a particular way, if we speak another language or come from another country, then we don't belong. That is, until someone dares to start telling that story differently.[80]

In all of the responses, the music, the way that the music is performed, and who is represented in the performance have often clearly and meaningfully resonated with cast members and audience members alike. This has created a resonance that echoes the current state of a host of controversial topics in America, from gun laws to race relations to ongoing debates about the treatment of minorities.

Returning to the critics of the musical who accuse Miranda of whitewashing and ignoring the topic of slavery in his race-conscious casting, the analytical framework of African American topics helps to demonstrate that Miranda is being deliberately ironic in his choice to use minorities to represent White Founding Fathers. The topics reveal a way for minorities to be seen *and* heard. As critics such as Monteiro and Reed have argued, *Hamilton* does not pay enough, if any, attention to the American historical monstrosity of slavery, and Miranda's choice to draw attention to a minority cast representing slaveholders is not only shocking but also shameful. Is there any way to reconcile this historical monster in a way that would feel proper? What would be right? If a White woman played the role of Alexander Hamilton, for example, would critics have had as much of a problem with whatever kind of statement that casting choice makes? White women in Hamilton's time were not literally enslaved, but they had no vote. Black women were not only enslaved but denied women's suffrage in many Southern states on the first take of the 19th Amendment in 1920. The most blatant thing in our eyes and ears in this telling of *Hamilton* is that, with its multicultural cast and multiethnic music, minorities are overtaking the narrative. It is a hypothetical "what if." It forces us to deal with America's brutal treatment of African Americans at the outset, because it seems so far-fetched that minorities would represent historical figures that owned enslaved persons.

It is impossible to deal appropriately with the nuance of a Thomas Jefferson or Alexander Hamilton. In the retrospective of history, they are examples of slaveowners who wielded a tremendous amount of power as White men in society. In the context of the American Revolution, they are the subversive revolutionaries without power. They are demanding freedom from King George, the only character who is always White. Miranda is creating a visual of what the power structure was for the Founding Fathers, because in a larger geopolitical sense, they did not have power. The American Revolution was a fight for freedom that resulted in freedom for only a part of the population. Considering Miranda's very deliberate choice to divorce the history of racial impression from the promise of America, he confronts race through the casting in an incredibly complicated look at America. Seen from this perspective, one interpretation of his casting choices is that he is refighting the American Revolution with people of color in those roles, enacting the next steps of the Revolution. The musical ends not with Alexander Hamilton's death but rather by focusing on legacies. History is the telling of the past through the lens of the present. Now this musical is part of Alexander Hamliton's legacy. To enact this legacy in the bodies of people of color and the sound of people of color gets closer to what the revolutionaries were trying to do.

Thus, we must move past the criticisms of Monteiro and Reed. They miss Miranda's point. This musical is not about slavery, nor is it about the racial politics of the eighteenth century. It is about the history of a Founding Father. It represents the current politics of race in America in another telling of "This is America." It is told by minorities. This very fact embodies the Signifyin(g) tradition and celebrates, not denigrates, minorities. As a minority, Miranda is acutely aware of the issues surrounding his casting choices. For example, it is clear that Chris Jackson (b. 1975) does not look like George Washington. George Washington owned enslaved persons, the critics argue, so how on earth is it appropriate for Jackson to impersonate Washington? Miranda is able to divorce the history of racial impression from the promise of America today. Miranda is one of the most celebrated composers in America. Because of the casting choices and the variety of musical styles that he uses, Miranda offers not a Pollyanna, land-of-opportunity, melting-pot take on America, but rather an incredibly complicated look into race. Sonically, Miranda's inclusion of African American topics represents a reclamation of Black and African American culture. Politically, the American Revolution was a fight for freedom that only resulted in freedom for a certain portion of the population. Rhetorically, in refighting that fight with people of color in these roles, Miranda is enacting the next steps of the revolution. In the context of the American Revolution, the Founding Fathers are the subversive revolutionaries without power demanding freedom from King George III, who as I have noted is always represented as a White character in *Hamilton*. Miranda creates a visual of what the power structure was for the Founding Fathers. In the context of today, seeing a Black Alexander Hamilton is seeing into the soul of American race relations and of the legacy that could result.

In the concluding number, "Who Lives, Who Dies, Who Tells Your Story?" the focus is entirely on legacy. The musical ends not by focusing on Alexander Hamilton's death but rather on Eliza's legacy and implicitly also on *our* legacy. Everyone in the audience, onstage, online, and streaming has become part of this legacy. In understanding the musical in this light, along with the multiple layers of embedded signification in all of the African American topics, one finds an implicit communication between performer and audience. Rising up and raising their voices, minorities become a part of a history that once ignored—and that, in many ways, has continued to ignore—them. Being seen and being heard are the two most fundamental things that must be present for the art to represent something actionable in our current society, especially as it pertains to social justice.

These empathic inclusions in *Hamilton* are present not only in a story told by the Founding Fathers and Mothers of the United States but also by the Founding Fathers and Mothers of the multiplicity of topics that comprise this American musical. We can better understand and appreciate the complexity of such a heterogeneous synchrony of sights and sounds by beginning to evaluate *Hamilton's* musical content more deeply, in this case by evaluating a colorful variety of topics, including the blues, characteristic rhythms, rapping, call-and-response, and Signifyin(g). In *Hamilton*, Miranda is telling us, literally and figuratively, to "look around," to "rise up," that "history is happening," and most importantly, that "life does not discriminate."[81]

NOTES

1. Alexandra Petri, "'Hamilton' and the End of Irony," *Washington Post*, September 21, 2015, https://www.washingtonpost.com/blogs/compost/wp/2015/09/21/hamilton-and-the-end-of-irony/.

2. Lin-Manuel Miranda, "My Shot," track 3 on *Hamilton: An American Musical (Original Broadway Cast Recording)*, September 25, 2015, 2015 Hamilton Uptown, LLC under Exclusive License to Atlantic Recording Corporation for the United States and WEA International Inc. for the World outside of the United States, Apple Music.

3. *American Music* 36, no. 4 (Winter 2018).

4. The White House Office of the Press Secretary, "Remarks by the President at 'Hamilton at the White House'," March 14, 2016, https://obamawhitehouse.archives.gov/the-press-office/2016/03/14/remarks-president-hamilton-white-house.

5. Donald J. Trump, *Twitter post*, November 20, 2016, 6:22 a.m., https://twitter.com/realDonaldTrump/status/800298286204723200.

6. TOI Staff, "Trump Accuses 'Hamilton' Cast of Harassing Pence with Post-Show Plea," *The Times of Israel*, November 19, 2016, https://www.timesofisrael.com/trump-accuses-hamilton-cast-of-harassing-pence-with-post-show-plea/.

7. Eric Bradner, "'Hamilton': The Latest Feud Trump Won't Let Go," *CNN Politics*, November 21, 2016, https://www.cnn.com/2016/11/20/politics/donald-trump-hamilton-feud/index.html.

8. Donald J. Trump, *Twitter post*, November 19, 2016, 8:56 a.m., https://twitter.com/realDonaldTrump/status/799974635274194947.

9. Spencer Kornhaber, "*Hamilton*: Casting after Colorblindness," *The Atlantic*, March 31, 2016, http://www.theatlantic.com/entertainment/archive/2016/03/hamilton-casting/476247/.

10. Lyra Monteiro, "Race-Conscious Casting and the Erasure of the Black Past in Lin-Manuel Miranda's *Hamilton*," *The Public Historian* 38, no. 1 (February 2016): 89–98.

11. Ibid., 96.

12. Horace J. Maxile, Jr., "Signs, Symphonies, Signifyin(g): African-American Cultural Topics as Analytical Approach to the Music of Black Composers," *Black Music Research Journal* 28, no. 1 (Spring 2008): 123.

13. Ibid., 127.

14. Ibid., 136.

15. Lin-Manuel Miranda and Jeremy McCarter, *Hamilton: The Revolution* (New York: Grand Central Publishing, 2016), 137.

16. Olly Wilson, "Black Music as an Art Form," *Black Music Research Journal* 3 (1983): 3.

17. Olly Wilson, "The Heterogeneous Sound Ideal in African-American Music," in *Signifyin(g), Sanctifyin', and Slam Dunking: A Reader in African American Expressive Culture*, edited by Gena Dagel Caponi (Amherst: The University of Massachusetts Press, 1999), 160. For instance, a string quartet is timbrally homogeneous, whereas a "drum, metal bell and flute" are "timbrally heterogeneous" (160).

18. Ibid.

19. Lin-Manuel Miranda, "You'll Be Back," track 7 on *Hamilton: An American Musical (Original Broadway Recording)*, September 25, 2015, 2015 Hamilton Uptown, LLC under Exclusive License to Atlantic Recording Corporation for the United States and WEA International for the World outside of the United States, Apple Music.

20. Anne Danielson makes a similar argument for the instant-hit-status of Michael Jackson's song "Don't Stop 'Til You Get Enough," writing that "through the combination of a compelling micro-rhythmic design derived from previous Black dance music styles with a pop song format and production techniques that were mainstream friendly and not marked by race, Jackson and his producer, Quincy Jones, achieved a critical balance that transcended the segregation of the music market, neutralizing the cultural background and historical baggage of what otherwise would have been deemed 'Black' music." Anne Danielson, "The Sound of Crossover: Micro-Rhythm and Sonic Pleasure in Michael Jackson's 'Don't Stop' Til You Get Enough," *Popular Music & Society* 35, no. 2 (May 2012): 151.

21. Rebecca Mead, "All about the Hamiltons," *The New Yorker*, February 9, 2015, https://www.newyorker.com/magazine/2015/02/09/hamiltons.

22. Ibid.

23. "Alexander Hamilton," track 1; "The Schuyler Sisters," track 5; "Helpless," track 10; all on Lin-Manuel Miranda, *Hamilton: An American Musical*.

24. "What'd I Miss," track 1 (Act 2), on Ibid.

25. "You'll Be Back," track 7; "What Comes Next;" track 21, "I Know Him," track 10 (Act 2), on Ibid.

26. For a more comprehensive list of other musicals that incorporate black topics, see Erin E. Evans, "20 Black Musicals that Livened up Broadway," *The Root: Black News, Opinions, Politics, and Culture*, June 16, 2015, https://www.theroot.com/20-black-musicals-that-livened-up-broadway-1790860369. *The Scotsboro Boys* (2010) also featured minstrel tropes as social critiques, having a run of just two months on Broadway despite receiving twelve Tony nominations.

27. *Hamilton: The Revolution*, 137.

28. Loren Kajikawa, "'Young, Scrappy, and Hungry': *Hamilton*, Hip Hop, and Race," *American Music* 36, no. 4 (Winter 2018): 469.

29. Following is a list in chronological order of several popular songs that feature the 3+3+2 rhythm or a close derivation. The songs encompass many different styles and eras, revealing the popularity and multiculturalisms of the 3+3+2 rhythm (all album citations are Apple Music): Various Artists, "Havana," track 10 on *Guys and Dolls (Original Studio Cast) [First Complete Score Recording]*, June 18, 1996, 1996 JAY Productions Ltd.; Tom Waits, "Jockey Full of Bourbon," track 4 on *Rain Dogs*, January 1, 1985, 1985 The Island Def Jam Music Group; The Rolling Stones, "Sweethearts Together," track 10 on *Voodoo Lounge*, July 3, 1994, 2012 Promotone B.V., under Exclusive License to Universal International Music B.V.; Gilles Andrieux and Vincent Courtois, "Djanli, Partie 1," track 4 on *Touareg Volume IV*, January 1, 1997, 1997 Al Sur; Missy Elliott, "Get Ur Freak On," track 5 on *Miss E . . . So Addictive*, May 14, 2001, 2001 Elektra Entertainment Group Inc. for the United States and WEA International Inc. for the World outside of the United States; Prince, "Incense and Candles," track 5 on *3121*, March 21, 2006, 2006 NPG Records, Inc. Manufactured and Distributed by Legacy Recordings; Run the Jewels, "Blockbuster Night, Pt. 2 (feat. Despot & Wiki)," track 2 on *Run the Jewels 2*, October 24, 2014, 2014 Run the Jewels, under Exclusive License to Mass Appeal; Drake, "Controlla," track 11 on *Views*, April 29, 2016, 2016 Young Money Entertainment/Cash Money

Records; J. Balvin and Willy William, "Mi Gente (feat. Beyoncé)," Single, September 28, 2017, 2017 Scorpio Music, under Exclusive License to Universal Music Latin Entertainment / Republic (Columbia Records/Parkwood Ventures).

30. *Hamilton: The Revolution*, 143.

31. Kajikawa, "'Young, Scrappy, and Hungry'," 476.

32. In the first act, numbers featuring rap include (1) "Alexander Hamilton"; (2) "Aaron Burr, Sir"; (3) "My Shot"; (4) "The Schuyler Sisters"; (5) "Farmer Refuted"; (6) "Right Hand Man"; (7) "A Winter's Ball"; (8) "Helpless"; (9) "Satisfied"; (10) "Stay Alive"; (11) "Ten Duel Commandments"; (12) "Meet Me Inside"; (13) "Guns and Ships"; (14) "The Battle of Yorktown"; and (15) "Non-Stop." In the second act, numbers featuring rap include (16) "Cabinet Battle #1"; (17) "Schuyler Defeated"; (18) "Cabinet Battle #2"; (19) "Washington on Your Side"; (20) "The Adams Administration"; (21) "The Reynolds Pamphlet"; (22) "Blow Us All Away"; (23) "The Election of 1800"; (24) "Your Obedient Servant"; and (25) "The World Was Wide Enough." All track titles are from Lin-Manuel Miranda, *Hamilton: An American Musical*.

33. I thank Kristen Turner for bringing this point to my attention. She also reminded me of a recent Fresh Air interview during which Jonathan Groff talked about how his role as King George represents an excellent example of privilege. While the king is only on stage for nine minutes, he receives the same kind of recognition and attention the rest of the cast, notably, the leads who are on stage for almost the entire musical. Terry Gross, "'Mindhunter' Actor Jonathan Groff on His Most Life-Altering Roles," *Fresh Air*, podcast audio, October 31, 2017, https://www.npr.org/programs/fresh-air/2017/10/31/561116006/fresh-air-for-oct-31-2017-actor-jonathan-groff-on-mindhunter-and-hamilton.

34. Olly Wilson, "The Heterogeneous Sound Ideal in African American Music."

35. Kajikawa, "'Young, Scrappy, and Hungry'," 473.

36. Miranda, "The Schuyler Sisters."

37. Maxile, "Signs, Symphonies, Signifyin(g)," 136.

38. Esteisy Seijas, "A Rap Written for a Debate on Marriage Equality," cited in Miranda and McCarter, *Hamilton*, 158.

39. Lin-Manuel Miranda, "Alexander Hamilton," track 1 on *Hamilton: An American Musical*.

40. Lin-Manuel Miranda, "My Shot," track 3.

41. Lin-Manuel Miranda, "Right Hand Man," track 8 on Ibid.

42. Lin-Manuel Miranda, "Wait for It," track 13 on Ibid.

43. Lin-Manuel Miranda, "The Story of Tonight," track 4 on Ibid.

44. Miranda, *Hamilton: The Revolution*, 33.

45. Miranda, "The Schuyler Sisters," track 5 on *Hamilton: An American Revolution*.

46. (See endnote 25).

47. Lin-Manuel Miranda, "Ten Duel Commandments," track 15 on *Hamilton: An American Revolution*.

48. Miranda, *Hamilton: The Revolution*, 198.

49. Ibid.

50. Elizabeth Titrington Craft, "Headfirst into an Abyss: The Politics and Political Reception of *Hamilton*," *American Music* 36, no. 4 (Winter 2018): 432.

51. Mead, "All about the Hamiltons."

52. Lin-Manuel Miranda, "Take a Break," track 3 (Act 2) on *Hamilton: An American Revolution*.

53. Lin-Manuel Miranda, "Stay Alive (Reprise)," track 17 (Act 2) on Ibid.

54. Lin-Manuel Miranda, "It's Quiet Uptown," track 18 (Act 2) on Ibid.

55. Lin-Manuel Miranda, "That Would be Enough," track 17; and "What'd I Miss," track 1 (Act 2), both on Ibid.

56. Miranda, "It's Quiet Uptown."

57. Eliza Hamilton lived from 1757 to 1854; Alexander Hamilton lived from 1755 to 1804.

58. Alex Wood, "Phillipa Soo Explains What Eliza's Gasp Means at the end of *Hamilton*," *WhatsOnStage*, July 30, 2020, https://www.whatsonstage.com/london-theatre/news/phillipa-soo-hamilton-gasp-meaning_52089.html?fbclid=IwAR3S7i_rdNqqEbLCeYCaZA4jwrFuV4tpV-cWXYZsdOLBxj6R9AxB8J9Y4tc.

59. Miranda and McCarter, *Hamilton*, Epilogue.

60. Ibid.

61. A full list of the victims is available online at: Hannah Bloch, Rebecca Hersher, Camila Domonoske, Merrit Kennedy, and Colin Dwyer, "'They Were So Beautiful': Remembering Those Murdered in Orlando," *NPR*, June 13, 2016, https://www.npr.org/sections/thetwo-way/2016/06/12/481785763/heres-what-we-know-about-the-orlando-shooting-victims.

62. Ruthie Fierberg, "Updated: *Hamilton* Choreographer on Removing Muskets from Tonys Performance," *Playbill*, June 12, 2016, http://www.playbill.com/article/breaking-hamilton-amends-tony-performance-in-light-of-orlando-tragedy.

63. This is an ongoing list, as I continue to learn about additional borrowings. Sources mentioned in *Hamilton: The Revolution* are marked by [HTR], along with the corresponding page number.

64. J. Peter Burkholder, "Elements of a Typology of Musical Borrowing," *Grove Music Online*, http://www.oxfordmusiconline.com.

65. Henry Louis Gates, quoted in Maxile, "Signs, Symphonies, Signifyin(g)," 128.

66. Citations in Table 4.1 from *Hamilton: The Revolution* are labeled as [HTR] followed by the page number. The album and track timings correspond to specific recordings of the albums and tracks that are listed in the bibliography.

67. Miranda and Carter, *Hamilton: The Revolution*, 95.

68. Floyd 1995, quoted in Maxile, "Signs, Symphonies, Signifyin(g)," 125.

69. Ibid., 128.

70. Robert Walser, "Out of Notes: Signification, Interpretation, and the Problem of Miles Davis," *The Musical Quarterly* 77, no. 2 (Summer 1993): 346.

71. Maxile, "Signs, Symphonies, Signifyin(g)," 128.

72. Ibid., 135.

73. Claudia Mitchell-Kernan, "Signifying, Loud-Talking, and Marking," in *Signifyin(g), Sanctifyin', and Slam Dunking: A Reader in African American Expressive*

Culture, edited by Gena Dagel Caponi (Amherst: University of Massachusetts Press, 1999), 311.

74. Ibid., 311, 319, 322, 323.

75. Henry Louis Gates, Jr., *The Signifying Monkey: A Theory of African-American Literary Criticism*, 25th ed. (Oxford: Oxford University Press, 2014), xxii.

76. Ayana Smith, "Blues, Criticism, and the Signifying Trickster," *Popular Music* 24, no. 2 (May 2005): 184.

77. Gates, Jr., *The Signifying Monkey*, xxxi.

78. Miranda and McCarter, *Hamilton*, 149.

79. Ibid., 160.

80. Michelle Obama, *Becoming* (New York: Crown Publishing Group, 2018), 415.

81. All of the quotations come from snippets of lyrics in several songs in the musical (Lin-Manuel Miranda, *Hamilton: An American Musical*). "Look around" appears in several numbers and begins the song "That Would Be Enough" (track 17); "Rise up" is in "My Shot" (track 3); "History is happening" is in "The Schuyler Sisters" (track 5) and "Life doesn't discriminate" appears in "Wait for It" (track 13).

Conclusion

The particular nature of these works, the passion they have generated, the closeness with many Americans' desire for change, and the various types of digital proximities they exhibit give an artistic and a musical voice to what many people are thinking about when it comes to uttering the phrase "This is America." The meaning of the sentence is not merely factual. It does not mean something as simple as pointing to a map and identifying America, and it most certainly does not mean identifying with a national pride. In all of the encoded gestures that help to create the meaning of "This is America" in the way that Gambino performs it, and in the repetition of these gestures that I explore throughout the book, all of the artists make a statement that America is in a state of chaos driven by prejudices against disadvantaged groups. The examples call attention to the inequities of race, gender, class, religion, and politics in America in vividly engaging ways, using tropes of encoded resistance.

In turn, these calls to attention affect both listener and creator. They allow for the possibility of multivalent readings of the artistic and musical works. Viewing the pieces in this way, with the possibility of multivalence, suggests that there is profound cultural and sociological work to do if we are also going to be able to hear each other and listen to each other. Just as the works in consideration in this book are themselves a call to action, so, too, is this book a call to action for social justice. I have made an attempt to foreground some of the issues in our face that we would do well to discuss, debate, and consider, questions of who has power when such things as race, gender, class, and religion come into play when we are interacting with art and music. I have offered some examples of art and music throughout this text that show the injustices in today's America. These works symbolically fight for social justice. They also hold a mirror toward the audience, toward those who recognize the gestures and repeated tropes not only as symbols of distress and discord but also as calls to action. The subsequent steps to be taken must be actionable. What will we read to educate ourselves more about racism, misogyny, gender discrimination, sexism, and classism in America? What further steps will we take? What phone calls will we make? What marches will we join? What petitions will we sign? What votes will we cast? How will we lead our lives? As the African American studies scholar Carol Anderson has powerfully expressed, as more Americans are beginning to take these kinds of actions,

> As thousands take to the streets to march, as lawsuit after lawsuit rains down on the courts, as boycott after boycott sends the economic and cultural message of an empowered and unbowed people, and as honest, fact-based dialogues about race and racism converge with those on class, sexual orientation, and gender, they say "we are one."[1]

On top of these types of actions, if we can learn to evaluate on a deeper level the works such as those included in this book—and many others that I do not know about, hope to learn about, or have inadvertently left out—perhaps we can continue to learn to hear them in new and meaningful ways. And perhaps we can begin to hear each other more productively, too. Let us begin that conversation. This could be America.

NOTE

1. Carol Anderson, *White Rage: The Unspoken Truth of Our Racial Divide* (New York: Bloomsbury, 2017), 175.

Bibliography

Abdelmahmoud, Elamin. "Rewriting Country Music's Racist History." *Rolling Stone.* June 5, 2020. https://www.rollingstone.com/music/music-country/country-music-racist-history-1010052/?fbclid=IwAR2ZnjDB-RNMP5pl1KEwaLoTLN-JpaYbCL-T3ZSahh26mBTnLU9zgIe2FIw.

ACLU. "Guantánamo Bay Detention Camp." 2020 American Civil Liberties Union. https://www.aclu.org/issues/national-security/detention/guantanamo-bay-detention-camp.

Adetiba, Elizabeth. "Q&A Tarana Burke." *Nation* 305, no. 15 (December 2017): 5.

Akingbe, Niyi, and Paul Ayodele Onanuga. "'Voicing Protest': Performing Cross-Cultural Revolt in Gambino's 'This Is America' and Falz's 'This Is Nigeria.'" *Contemporary Music Review: Popular Music in Nigeria: Language, Context and Milieu* 39, no. 1 (January 2, 2020): 6–36. https://doi.org/10.1080/07494467.2020.1753473.

Alexander, Michelle. *The New Jim Crow: Mass Incarceration in the Age of Colorblindness.* 10th ed. New York: The New Press, 2020.

Alipour, Touba. http://www.toubaalipour.com. Interviewed by Katie Rios via telephone. April 2020.

Amoako, Aida. "Why the Dancing Makes 'This Is America' So Uncomfortable to Watch." *The Atlantic.* May 8, 2018. https://www.theatlantic.com/entertainment/archive/2018/05/this-is-america-childish-gambino-donald-glover-kinesthetic-empathy-dance/559928/.

Anderson, Carol. *White Rage: The Unspoken Truth of Our Racial Divide.* New York: Bloomsbury, 2017.

Anderson, Laurie. *All the Things I Lost in the Flood: Essays on Pictures, Language, and Code.* New York: Rizzoli Electa, 2018.

———. "From the Air." Track 1 on *Big Science.* April 19, 1982. 2007 Nonesuch Records, Inc. Apple Music.

———. *Heart of a Dog.* Directed by Laurie Anderson. Burbank: Nonesuch Records, 2015. Video.

———. "Transitory Life." Track 1 of *Homeland*. 2010 Nonesuch Records, Inc. Apple Music.

Anderson, Monica. "The Hashtag #BlackLivesMatter Emerges: Social Activism on Twitter." *Pew Research Center*. August 15, 2016. https://www.pewresearch.org/internet/2016/08/15/the-hashtag-blacklivesmatter-emerges-social-activism-on-twitter/#fn-16486-9.

Andrews, Travis M. "Beyoncé Controversially Sampled New Orleans Culture in 'Lemonade'. Now She's Being Sued for It." *The Washington Post*. February 8, 2017. https://www.washingtonpost.com/news/morning-mix/wp/2017/02/08/beyonce-controversially-sampled-new-orleans-culture-in-lemonade-now-shes-being-sued-for-it/.

Appleton, Michael. "Hurricane Katrina." *History*. August 9, 2019. https://www.history.com/topics/natural-disasters-and-environment/hurricane-katrina.

Austin, Joe. *Taking the Train: How Graffiti Art Became an Urban Crisis in New York City*. New York: Columbia University Press, 2001.

Baker, Peter Baker, Raymond Zhong, and Russell Goldman. "Twitter Places Warning on a Trump Tweet, Saying It Glorified Violence." *The New York Times*. May 29, 2020. https://www.nytimes.com/2020/05/29/technology/trump-twitter-minneapolis-george-floyd.html?action=click&module=Top%20Stories&pgtype=Homepage.

Bagshaw, Joanne L., and Soraya Chemaly. *The Feminist Handbook: Practical Tools to Resist Sexism and Dismantle the Patriarchy*. Oakland: New Harbinger Publications, 2019.

Baldwin, James. *The Fire Next Time*. Reprint. New York: Vintage International, 1993.

Balestrini, Nassim Winnie. "Intermedial On/Offstage Auto/Biography: Lin-Manuel Miranda's *Hamilton*, Hip Hop, and Historiography." In *Intermediality, Life Writing, and America Studies: Interdisciplinary Studies*, edited by Nassim Winnie Balestrini and Ina Bergmann. Berlin/Boston: Walter de Gruyter GmbH, 2018, 211–32.

Bernstein, Leonard and Stephen Soundheim. "Prologue." Track 2 of *West Side Story (New Broadway Cast Recording – 2009)*. May 28, 2009. 2009 Sony Music Entertainment.

Berry, Michael. *Listening to Rap: An Introduction*. New York: Routledge, 2018. Apple Music.

BET. "Hip Hop Community Demands Justice after Video of Ahmaud Arbery's Shooting Death Surfaces." *BET*. May 7, 2020. https://www.bet.com/music/2020/05/07/hip-hop-reacts-to-footage-of-ahmaud-arbeys-shooting-death.html.

BETNetworks. "Eminem Rips Donald Trump in BET Hip Hop Awards Freestyle Cypher." *YouTube Video*, 4:34. October 10, 2017. https://www.youtube.com/watch?v=LunHybOKIjU.

Beyoncé. Black Is King. Directed/performed by Beyoncé. Los Angeles and Burbank, Parkwood Entertainment and Walt Disney Pictures, 2020. Movie.

Beyoncé. "Black Parade." Track 17 on *The Lion King: The Gift [Deluxe Edition]*. Compilation (P) 2020 Parkwood Entertainment LLC, under Exclusive License to Columbia Records, A Division of Sony Music Entertainment. Apple Music.

———. "Crazy in Love (feat. Jay-Z)." Track 1 on *Dangerously in Love*. June 24, 2003. 2003 J Records, 2003 Sony Music Entertainment Inc. Apple Music.

———. "Formation." *YouTube Video*, 4:53. February 6, 2016. https://www.youtube.com/watch?time_continue=267&v=LrCHz1gwzTo&feature=emb_logo.

———. "Freedom." *YouTube Video*, 4:49. April 22, 2019. https://www.youtube.com/watch?v=7FWF9375hUA.

"Black Lives Matter." 2020. https://Blacklivesmatter.com/about.

"Black Lives Matter: Herstory." 2020. https://Blacklivesmatter.com/herstory.

Bloch, Hannah, Rebecca Hersher, Camila Domonoske, Merrit Kennedy, and Colin Dwyer. "'They Were So Beautiful': Remembering Those Murdered in Orlando." *NPR*. June 13, 2016, https://www.npr.org/sections/thetwo-way/2016/06/12/481785763/heres-what-we-know-about-the-orlando-shooting-victims.

Bradner, Eric. "'Hamilton': The Latest Feud Trump Won't Let Go." *CNN Politics*. November 21, 2016. https://www.cnn.com/2016/11/20/politics/donald-trump-hamilton-feud/index.html.

Breakfast Club Power 105.1 FM. "Breakfast Club Classic: Childish Gambino AKA Donald Glover on White Privilege & Twitter Activism." *YouTube Video*, 33:00. May 10, 2018. https://www.youtube.com/watch?v=28sTZge1Lyo.

Brito, Christopher. "Family Sues after 26-year-old EMT is Shot and Killed in Her Own Home." *CBS News*. May 15, 2020. https://www.cbsnews.com/news/breonna-taylor-family-sues-wrongful-death-killed-police-louisville/.

Brody, Richard. "The Worst Thing about 'Birth of a Nation' Is How Good It Is." *The New Yorker*. February 1, 2013. https://www.newyorker.com/culture/richard-brody/the-worst-thing-about-birth-of-a-nation-is-how-good-it-is.

Brooks, Kinitra D. and Kameelah L. Martin. *The Lemonade Reader: Beyoncé, Black Feminism, and Spirituality*. Milton: Routledge, 2019.

Brown, Jason Robert. "Nobody Needs to Know." Track 13 on *The Last Five Years (Original Cast Recording)*. April 1, 2002. 2005 Sh-K-Boom Records Inc. Apple Music.

Browne, Malachy, Anjali Singhvi, Natalie Reneau and Drew Jordan. "How the Police Killed Breonna Taylor." *The New York Times*. December 28, 2020. https://www.nytimes.com/video/us/100000007348445/breonna-taylor-death-cops.html?action=click&gtype=vhs&version=vhs-heading&module=vhs&region=title-area&cview=true&t=4.

Buckley, Cara. "Powerful Hollywood Women Unveil Anti-Harassment Action Plan." *The New York Times*. January 1, 2018. https://www.nytimes.com/2018/01/01/movies/times-up-hollywood-women-sexual-harassment.html.

Bun B. Interview with DJ Envy, Angela Yee, and Charlamagne tha God. *The Breakfast Club*. Podcast audio. September 22, 2020. https://podcasts.apple.com/ca/podcast/wedding-charge-rate/id1232428553?i=1000492131770.

Burkholder, J. Peter. "Elements of a Typology of Musical Borrowing." *Oxford Music Online*. https://www.oxfordmusiconline.com/grovemusic/view/10.1093/gmo/9781561592630.001.0001/omo-9781561592630-e-8000922757.

Cardi B (@iamcardib). 2020. "Enough is enough!" *Instagram*, May 27, 2020. https://www.instagram.com/p/CArHyduAZ_a/?utm_source=ig_embed.

Carmichael, Rodney. "With 'Eve,' Rapsody Wields the Legacies of Legendary Black Women, from Nina to Serena." *NPR Music*. August 9, 2019. https://www.npr.org/2019/08/09/749645215/with-eve-rapsody-wields-the-legacies-of-legendary-black-women-from-nina-to-seren.

Carroll, Rebecca. "The Birth of a Nation: How Nate Parker Failed to Remake History." *The Guardian*. October 10, 2016. https://www.theguardian.com/film/filmblog/2016/oct/10/the-birth-of-a-nation-problems-nate-parker.

Castleman, Craig. *Getting Up: Subway Graffiti in New York*. Cambridge: The Massachusetts Institute of Technology, 1982.

Chang, Jeff. *Can't Stop Won't Stop: A History of the Hip-Hop Generation*. New York: St. Martin's, 2005.

ChannelZERO. "Public Enemy – Fight the Power (2020 Remix) feat. Nas, Rapsody, Black Thought, Jahi, YG & Questlove." *YouTube Video*, 4:59. August 28, 2020. https://www.youtube.com/watch?v=nNUl8bAKdi4.

Chapelle, Dave. "Kendrick Lamar by Dave Chappelle." *Interview Magazine*. July 12, 2017. https://www.interviewmagazine.com/music/kendrick-lamar-cover#_.

Charity, Justin. "We Are Living in Eminem's White America." *The Ringer*. December 18, 2017. https://www.theringer.com/2017/12/18/16788430/eminem-revival-donald-trump-white-america.

Charleswell, Cherise. "Getting into Formation: Beyoncé, The Affirmation of Blackness, and Black Women's Agency over Their Bodies." *ProudFlesh: New Afrikan Journal of Culture, Politics and Consciousness* no. 13 (2016, online): https://www.africaknowledgeproject.org/index.php/proudflesh/article/view/3027.

Childs, Dennis. *Slaves of the State: Black Incarceration from the Chain Gang to the Penitentiary* Minneapolis: University of Minnesota Press, 2015.

Chutel, Lynsey. "The Choreographer Who Brought Africa to Childish Gambino's 'This Is America' Had a Clear Message." *Quartz Africa*. May 17, 2018. https://qz.com/africa/1280777/childish-gambinos-african-pop-dance-moves-were-created-by-this-rwandan-choreographer/.

Cinque, Toija, Christopher Moore, and Sean Redmond, Editors. *Enchanting David Bowie: Space/Time/Body/Memory*. 1st ed. New York: Bloomsbury Academic & Professional, 2015.

CNN. "Read Janelle Monáe's Empowering Grammy Speech." *CNN*. January 28, 2018. https://www.cnn.com/2018/01/28/entertainment/janelle-monae-grammy-speech/index.html.

CNN Transcript. "Anderson Cooper 360 Degrees." *CNN*. September 2, 2005. http://edition.cnn.com/TRANSCRIPTS/0509/02/acd.01.html.

Collins, Michael. "Americans with Tax Issues Aren't Getting Their Coronavirus Stimulus Checks. They Suspect the IRS is Delaying Payment." *USA Today*. May 15, 2020. https://www.usatoday.com/story/news/politics/2020/05/15/coronavirus-irs-accused-delaying-stimulus-checks-over-tax-issues/3090114001/.

Collins, Patricia Hill. *Black Feminist Thought: Knowledge, Consciousness, and the Politics of Empowerment*. 2nd ed. New York: Routledge Classics, 2009.

Cornish, Audie and Monika Evstatieva. "Donald Glover's 'This Is America' Holds Ugly Truths to Be Self-Evident." *NPR*. May 7, 2018. https://www.npr.org/2018/

05/07/609150167/donald-glovers-this-is-america-holds-ugly-truths-to-be-self-evid ent?fbclid=IwAR0lenULK-4-2sAcBrM9aUJn0wKDFHIXcKR-NULrRJ-kNFb eoZ1ieFMyc4g.

Craft, Elizabeth Titrington. "Headfirst into an Abyss: The Politics and Political Reception of *Hamilton*." *American Music* 36, no. 4 (Winter 2018): 429–47.

Crossley, Nick. *Connecting Sounds: The Social Life of Music*. Manchester: Manchester University Press, 2019.

Daileda, Colin. "Why Were 30 Black Students Kicked out of a Trump Rally in Georgia?" *Mashable*. March 1, 2016. https://mashable.com/2016/03/01/black-st udents-ejected-donald-trump-rally/.

D'Angelo. *Voodoo*. January 25, 2000. Virgin Records.

Danielson, Anne. "The Sound of Crossover: Micro-Rhythm and Sonic Pleasure in Michael Jackson's 'Don't Stop 'Til You Get Enough'." *Popular Music & Society* 35, no. 2 (May 2012): 151–68.

DeClue, Jennifer. "To Visualize the Queen Diva!: Toward Black Feminist Trans Inclusivity in Beyoncé's 'Formation'." *Transgender Studies Quarterly* 4, no. 2 (2017): 219–25.

Deitsch, Richard. "How the Super Bowl 50 Ratings Stack Up." *Sports Illustrated*. February 8, 2016. https://www.si.com/nfl/2016/02/09/super-bowl-50-tv-ratings-m edia-circus.

Dell'Antonio, Andrew. 2020. "I doubt there are many — any? — folks in the bubble of my FB feed who don't understand why it's important to assert that #BlackLivesMatter - but maybe some of you do, and I think this is a good explanation which points to the central role generational wealth plays in success in the US, and clarifies why Black folks have been structurally hampered by the systemic racism on which the USian nation was built, politically and economically, even after they ostensibly gained equal legal standing." . September 14, 2020. https ://www.facebook.com/andrew.dellantonio/posts/10116217303580500.

Demby, Gene and Shereen Marisol Meraji, "Is Trump Really That Racist?" *Code Switch*. Podcast audio. October 21, 2020. https://www.npr.org/transcripts/925385389.

Dinh, James. "Cardi B-Backed 'Justice for George Floyd' Petition Makes History. *The Breakfast Club*. May 29, 2020. https://thebreakfastclub.iheart.com/content/2 020-05-29-cardi-b-backed-justice-for-george-floyd-petition-makes-history/?fbclid =IwAR2TEnvlwW9bKu-hTXU08ZNsE34vJcFBRshBsLBKXMFjD2_YLRyv VJJ4Rdc.

DMX. "Party Up." Track 7 on . . . *And Then There Was X*. December 21, 1999. A Def Jams Release. 1999 UMG Recordings, Inc. Apple Music.

Driscoll, Christopher M., Monica R. Miller, and Anthony B. Pinn. *Kendrick Lamar and the Making of Black Meaning*. Routledge Studies in Hip Hop and Religion Series. Milton Park, UK: Taylor & Francis Group, 2019.

Du Bois, WEB. *The Souls of Black Folk; Essays and Sketches*. Chicago, AG McClurg, 1903, New York: Johnson Reprint Corp., 1968.

East of Underground. "I Love You." Track 8 on *Hell Below: East of Underground, The Black Seeds, & The Sound Trek*. August 28, 2007. 2011 Now Again Records. Apple Music.

Edwards, Sherman and Peter Stone. *1776 (Original Broadway Cast Recording).* March 1969. Originally Released 1969 Sony BMG Music Entertainment.

Eidsheim, Nina Sun. *The Race of Sound: Listening, Timbre & Vocality in African American Music.* Durham: Duke University Press, 2019.

Elam Jr., Harry J and Kennell Jackson. *Black Cultural Traffic: Crossroads in Global Performance and Popular Culture.* Ann Arbor: University of Michigan Press, 2005.

Eminem. "Framed." Track 12 on *Revival.* December 15, 2017. Aftermath/Shady/ Interscope Records. 2018 Apple Music.

———. "Like Home." Track 9 on *Revival.* December 15, 2017. Aftermath/Shady/ Interscope Records. 2017 Apple Music.

EminemMusic. "Eminem – Darkness (Official Video)." *YouTube Video*, 6:09. January 16, 2020. https://www.youtube.com/watch?v=RHQC4fAhcbU.

Evans, Erin E. "20 Black Musicals that Livened up Broadway." *The Root: Black News, Opinions, Politics, and Culture.* June 16, 2015. https://www.theroot.com/20-black-musicals-that-livened-up-broadway-1790860369.

Fear, David. "Run the Jewels Wish Their New Album Didn't Make So Much Sense Right Now." *Rolling Stone.* June 18, 2020. https://www.rollingstone.com/music/music-features/run-the-jewels-rtj-4-interview-el-p-killer-mike-1015466/.

"The Federation." https://www.facebook.com/WeFederation/.

———. *Pentagram.* https://www.pentagram.com/work/the-federation/story.

———. *State of the Arts NYC.* https://stateoftheartsnyc.net/2018/02/21/the-force-behind-the-federation.

———. *StoryCorps Archives.* https://archive.storycorps.org/communities/the-federation.

Feiner, Lauren. "Twitter Flagged Another Trump Tweet for Violating Its Policies." *CNBC.* June 23, 2020. https://www.cnbc.com/2020/06/23/twitter-labeled-another-trump-tweet-for-violating-its-policies.html.

Feliciano-Santos, Sherina. "Visibility and Agency: An Analysis of Media Responses to Childish Gambino's 'This Is America.'" *Anthropology Now* 10, no. 2 (May 4, 2018): 102–5. https://doi.org/10.1080/19428200.2018.1494460.

Ferris State University. "Jim Crow Museum of Racist Memorabilia." https://www.ferris.edu/jimcrow/.

Fierberg, Ruthie. "Updated: *Hamilton* Choreographer on Removing Muskets from Tonys Performance." *Playbill.* June 12, 2016. http://www.playbill.com/article/breaking-hamilton-amends-tony-performance-in-light-of-orlando-tragedy.

Foster, Tiffany. "'This Is America' Really IS America, and That's a Shame." *Black Girl in Maine Media.* May 17, 2018. https://blackgirlinmaine.com/current-events/this-is-america-really-is-america-and-thats-a-shame/.

Frances, Jane. "The Three Graces: Composition and Meaning in a Roman Context." *Greece & Rome* 49, no. 2 (October 2002): 180–98.

Gammage, Marquita. "Pop Culture without Culture: Examining the Public Backlash to Beyoncé's Super Bowl 50 Performance." *Journal of Black Studies* 48, no. 8 (2017): 715–31.

Garcia, Sandra. "Where Did BIPOC Come From?" *The New York Times*, June 17, 2020, https://www.nytimes.com/article/what-is-bipoc.html.

Garrett, Charles Hiroshi. "*Hamilton* Forum: Guest Editor's Introduction." *American Music* 36, no. 4 (Winter 2018): 407–11.

Gates, Jr., Henry Louis. *The Signifying Monkey: A Theory of African-American Literary Criticism*. 25th ed. Oxford: Oxford University Press, 2014.

Giddens, Rhiannon. "At the Purchaser's Option." *YouTube Video*, 4:16. January 13, 2017. https://www.youtube.com/watch?v=6vy9xTS0QxM.

———. Liner notes for *Songs of Our Native Daughters*. Smithsonian Folkways Recordings. SFW CD 40232, 2019. 1 compact disc.

———. 2016. "My work as a whole is about excavating and shining a light on pieces of history that not only need to be seen and heard, but that can also add to the conversation about what's going on now." *Facebook*, February 27, 2020. https://www.facebook.com/pg/RhiannonGiddensMusic/posts/?ref=page_internal.

Glover, Donald. "Childish Gambino – This Is America (Official Video)." *YouTubeVideo*, 4:04. May 5, 2018. https://www.youtube.com/watch?v=VYOjWnS4cMY.

Gomez, Alan and Kaila White. "Here Are All the Victims of the Las Vegas Shooting." *USA Today*. October 6, 2017. https://www.usatoday.com/story/news/nation/2017/10/06/here-all-victims-las-vegas-shooting/733236001/.

Gosa, Travis L. and Erik Nielson, eds. *The Hip Hop & Obama Reader*. Oxford: Oxford University Press, 2015.

Graham, David. "Making Art in the Age of Trump." *The Atlantic*. June 1, 2016. https://www.theatlantic.com/entertainment/archive/2016/06/laurie-anderson-qa-hamilton-trump-hillary/485054/.

Grandmaster Flash and The Furious Five. "The Message." Track 7 on *The Message*. October 1, 1982. 2004 Sugar Hill Records. Manufactured and Marketed by Warner Strategic Marketing. Apple Music.

Greene, Linda S., Lolita Buckner Inniss, and Bridget J. Crawford. "Talking about Black Lives Matter and #MeToo." *Wisconsin Journal of Law, Gender & Society* 34, no. 2 (2019): 109–77.

Grogan, Bailey E. "This Is America: Symbolism and Imagery in the Musical Work of Childish Gambino." MA Thesis. California State University, Long Beach, 2019.

Gross, Terry. "'Mindhunter' Actor Jonathan Groff on His Most Life-Altering Roles." *Fresh Air*. Podcast audio. October 31, 2017. https://www.npr.org/programs/fresh-air/2017/10/31/561116006/fresh-air-for-oct-31-2017-actor-jonathan-groff-on-mindhunter-and-hamilton.

GZA. "Liquid Swords." Track 1 on *Liquid Swords*. January 1, 1995. 2015 Geffen Records. Apple Music.

Harbert, Elissa. "*Hamilton* and History Musicals." *American Music* 36, no. 4 (Winter 2018): 412–28.

Hart, Benjamin and Chas Dunner. "3 Dead and Dozens Injured after Violent White-Nationalist Rally in Virginia." *New York Intelligencer*. August 13, 2017. https://nymag.com/intelligencer/2017/08/state-of-emergency-in-va-after-white-nationalist-rally.html

Hassan, Carma, Gregory Krieg and Melonyce McAfee. "Police Union Calls for Law Enforcement Labor to Boycott Beyoncé's World Tour." *CNN*. February 20, 2016. https://www.cnn.com/2016/02/19/us/beyonce-police-boycott/index.html.

Hawkins, Stan, Editor. *The Routledge Research Companion to Popular Music and Gender*. Abington: Routledge, 2017.

Herman, Steve. "Trump's Public Expletives Another Break with Presidential Decorum." *VOA News*. October 12, 2019. https://www.voanews.com/usa/us-politics/trumps-public-expletives-another-break-presidential-decorum.

Hernandez, Eugene. "Laurie Anderson & Special Guests." *Film at Lincoln Center*. Podcast Audio. December 6, 2017. https://soundcloud.com/filmlinc/159-laurie-anderson-special-guests.

Hight, Jewly. "'Songs of Our Native Daughters' Lays Out a Crucial, Updated Framework for Americana." February 14, 2019. https://www.npr.org/2019/02/14/693624881/first-listen-our-native-daughters-songs-of-our-native-daughters.

Hill, Lauryn. "Everything Is Everything." Track 13 on *The Miseducation of Lauryn Hill*. August 25, 1998. Ruffhouse Records and Columbia Records. Apple Music.

———. "Lost Ones." Track 2 on *The Miseducation of Lauryn Hill*. August 25, 1998. Ruffhouse Records and Columbia Records. Apple Music.

History.com Editors. "Black Panthers." *history.com*. June 6, 2019. https://www.history.com/topics/civil-rights-movement/Black-panthers.

Hogeland, William, ed. *Historians on Hamilton: How a Blockbuster Musical Is Restaging America's Past*. New Brunswick: Rutgers University Press, 2018.

Howard, Theresa Ruth. "A Dancer's Take on 'This Is America': Is the Dance a Distraction or Something Deeper?" *Dance Magazine*. May 10, 2018. https://www.dancemagazine.com/this-is-america-dance-2567663747.html.

"I May Destroy You." Spotify Playlist. 2020. https://open.spotify.com/playlist/37i9dQZF1DWUcT0QzTFbgH.

Izadi, Elahe Izadi. "'Rewriting the Black American Story': Hip-hop's Protest Anthems Respond to Police Shootings." *Washington Post*. September 23, 2016. https://www.washingtonpost.com/news/arts-and-entertainment/wp/2016/09/23/rewriting-the-black-american-story-hip-hops-protest-anthems-respond-to-police-shootings/.

Jacobs, Jennifer. "Black Students Ejected from Trump Rally in GA." *USA Today*. March 1, 2016. https://www.usatoday.com/story/news/politics/elections/2016/02/29/donald-trump-georgia-rally-valdosta/81129964/.

Jay Z. "Minority Report." Track 13 on *Kingdom Come*. November 21, 2006. Roc-A-Fella Records and Def Jam Recordings. Apple Music.

Jeezy (@jeezy). 2020. "My heart goes out to the family of Ahmaud Arbey. Instagram, May 7, 2020. https://www.instagram.com/jeezy/.

Jennings, Carly. "The Love Note That Launched a Movement." *ASA Footnotes: A Publication of the American Sociological Association* 48, no. 4 (July/August 2020): https://www.asanet.org/news-events/footnotes/jul-aug-2020/features/love-note-launched-movement.

Johnson, Kennedi. *Rage Fueled Rants of a Tired Black Girl Found Here*. https://kennediajohnson.com/blog-2/.

Jones, Trina and Kimberly Jade Norwood. "Aggressive Encounters and White Fragility: Deconstructing the Trope of the Angry Black Woman." *Iowa Law Review* 102, no. 5 (July 2017): 2017–69.

Joseph, Sayeed. "'We Gon' Be Alright': Mental Health and the Blues in Kendrick Lamar's *To Pimp a Butterfly*." *Ethnomusicology Review* (2017): https://ethnomusicologyreview.ucla.edu/journal/volume/21/piece/990.

Kajikawa, Loren. "Eminem's 'My Name Is': Signifying Whiteness, Rearticulating Race." *Journal of the Society for American Music* 3, no. 3 (August 2009): 341–56.

———. *Sounding Race in Rap Songs*. Oakland: University of California Press, 2015.

———. "'Young, Scrappy, and Hungry': *Hamilton*, Hip Hop, and Race." *American Music* 36, no. 4 (Winter 2018): 467–86.

Kalkandelen, Zulal. "Laurie Anderson Performing @ Moogfest." *YouTube Video*, 4:18, May 23, 2016, https://www.youtube.com/watch?v=uoxvAzmXwPQ&feature=emb_logo.

Kaplan, Ilana. *Childish Gambino "This Is America": All of the Hidden References in Hit Music Video*. *The Independent (Online)*. London: Independent Digital News & Media, 2018.

Katz, Mark. *Build: The Power of Hip Hop Diplomacy in a Divided World*. Oxford: Oxford University Press, 2020.

———. 2020. "Fellow white people." Facebook, May 27, 2020. https://www.facebook.com/mark.katz.3766/posts/10158636251895962.

Kaye, Ben. "21 Savage Gives Intimate Performance of 'A Lot' on Fallon: Watch." *Entertainment News*. January 29, 2019. https://consequenceofsound.net/2019/01/21-savage-performs-fallon/.

Kearse, Steven. "Childish Gambino: This Is America." *Pitchfork*. May 7, 2018. https://pitchfork.com/reviews/tracks/childish-gambino-this-is-america/.

Keneally, Meghan. "A Look back at Trump Comments Perceived by Some as Encouraging Violence." *abc News*. October 19, 2018. https://abcnews.go.com/Politics/back-trump-comments-perceived-encouraging-violence/story?id=48415766.

Kernodle, Tammy. "No More Tears and Prayers: Black Women, Black Music, and the Mythology of Post-Racial America." Paper presented at the annual meeting of the American Musicological Society, Boston, MA, 2019.

Keyes, Cheryl L. *Rap Music and Street Consciousness*. Urbana: University of Chicago Press, 2002.

Khan-Cullors, Patrisse and Asha Bandele. *When They Call You a Terrorist: A Black Lives Matter Memoir*. New York: St. Martin's Griffin, 2018.

Kornhaber, Spencer. "*Hamilton*: Casting after Colorblindness." *The Atlantic*. March 31, 2016. http://www.theatlantic.com/entertainment/archive/2016/03/hamilton-casting/476247/.

Kwun, Aileen. "Artists Mark Trump's Inauguration Anniversary with Day of Protest Art." *CNN Style*. January 9, 2018. https://www.cnn.com/style/article/trump-one-year-art-action-day/index.html.

Kynard, Carmen. *Vernacular Insurrections: Race, Black Protest, and the New Century in Composition-Literacies Studies*. Albany: State University of New York Press, 2013.

Lady Gaga. "Born This Way." Track 2 of *Born This Way (Special Edition)*. May 23, 2011. 2014 Interscope Records. Apple Music.

Lamar, Kendrick. "Mortal Man." Track 16 on *To Pimp a Butterfly*. March 16, 2015. 2015 Aftermath/Interscope (Top Dawg Entertainment). Apple Music.

Langone, Alix. "#MeToo and Time's Up Founders Explain the Difference between the 2 Movements—And How They're Alike." *TIME*. March 22, 2018. https://time.com/5189945/whats-the-difference-between-the-metoo-and-times-up-movements/.

The Laura Flanders Show. "Laurie Anderson & Mohammed el Gharini: Habeas Corpus." *YouTube Video*, 26:01. November 3, 2015. https://www.youtube.com/watch?v=WfuvAG_gXUM.

LeMesurier, Jennifer Lin. "Winking at Excess: Racist Kinesiologies in Childish Gambino's 'This Is America'." *Rhetoric Society Quarterly* 50, no. 2 (2020): 139–51.

Levenson, Michael. "Prosecutors to Drop Charges against Boyfriend of Breonna Taylor." *The New York Times*. May 22, 2020. https://www.nytimes.com/2020/05/22/us/Breonna-Taylor-Kenneth-Walker.html.

Levin, Bess. "Trump Uses Coronavirus Press Conference to Confirm He's an Actual Sociopath." *Vanity Fair*. March 20, 2020. https://www.vanityfair.com/news/2020/03/donald-trump-peter-alexander-coronavirus-press-conference.

Lindmark, Sarah. "'Hip Hop Causes Violence': Arguments and Analyses Concerning Childish Gambino's 'This Is America'." Paper presented at the annual meeting of the American Musicological Society. Boston, MA, November 2019.

———. "'Watching Their Souls Speak': Interpreting the New Music Videos of Childish Gambino, Kendrick Lamar, and Beyoncé Knowles-Carter." MA Thesis. University of California Irvine, 2019.

Louisiana Channel. "Laurie Anderson Interview: We Are in Constant Panic Mode." *YouTube Video*, 3:22. February 5, 2019. https://www.youtube.com/watch?v=hpec93exiHI&feature=emb_logo.

MacDowell. "Margaret Atwood & Laurie Anderson with Michael Chabon for 2019 Chairman's Evening." *YouTube Video*, 1:00:07. December 12, 2019. https://www.youtube.com/watch?v=ud9hjJ1b1zQ.

"Mama's Cryin' Long (feat. Rhiannon Giddens, Amythyst Kiah, and Allison Russell)." Track 7 on *Songs of Our Native Daughters*. February 22, 2019. Smithsonian Folkways Recordings. Apple Music.

Mamo, Heran. "Rapsody Captures Why This Election Gives Black Americans a 'Fighting Chance' in '12 Problems' Video: Watch." *Billboard*. October 30, 2020. https://www.billboard.com/articles/columns/hip-hop/9475390/rapsody-12-problems-video-interview.

Marrison, Matthew D. "Race, Blacksound, and the (Re)Making of Musicological Discourse." *Journal of the American Musicological Society* 72, no. 3 (Fall 2019): 781–823.

Maultsby, Portia K. and Mellonee V. Burnim, Editors. *African American Music: An Introduction*, 2d ed. New York: Routledge, 2014.

———. *Issues in African American Music: Power, Gender, Race, Representation*. New York: Routledge, 2017.

Maxile, Horace J. "Signs, Symphonies, Signifyin(g): African-American Cultural Topics as Analytical Approach to the Music of Black Composers." *Black Music Research Journal* 28, no. 1 (Spring 2008): 123–38.

McClary, Susan. *Feminine Endings: Music, Gender, and Sexuality.* Minneapolis: University of Minnesota Press, 1991.

McGlone, Peggy. "For the Third Year in a Row, Trump's Budget Plan Eliminates Arts, Public TV and Library Funding." *The Washington Post.* March 18, 2019. https://www.washingtonpost.com/lifestyle/style/for-third-year-in-a-row-trumps-budget-plan-eliminates-arts-public-tv-and-library-funding/2019/03/18/e946db9a-49a2-11e9-9663-00ac73f49662_story.html.

McKenzie, Jon. "Laurie Anderson for Dummies." *TDR: The Drama Review* 41, no. 2 (Summer 1997): 30–50.

Mead, Rebecca. "All about the Hamiltons." *The New Yorker.* February 9, 2015. https://www.newyorker.com/magazine/2015/02/09/hamiltons.

"me too." *2020 me too.* https://metoomvmt.org.

Milano, Alyssa (@Alyssa_Milano). 2017. "If you've been sexually assaulted write 'me too' as a reply to this tweet." *Twitter*, October 15, 2017, 4:21 p.m. https://twitter.com/Alyssa_Milano/status/919659438700670976.

Miller, Hayley. "Childish Gambino's 'This Is America' Video, Explained." *Huffpost.* May 7, 2018. https://www.huffpost.com/entry/childish-gambino-this-is-america_n_5af05c12e4b041fd2d28d8e9.

Miller, Stephen. "Black Workers Still Earn Less than Their White Counterparts." *Society for Human Resource Management.* June 11, 2020. https://www.shrm.org/resourcesandtools/hr-topics/compensation/pages/racial-wage-gaps-persistence-poses-challenge.aspx.

Miranda, Lin-Manuel. *Hamilton: An American Musical (Original Broadway Recording).* September 25, 2015. 2015 Hamilton Uptown, LLC under Exclusive License to Atlantic Recording Corporation for the United States and WEA International for the World outside of the United States.

Miranda, Lin-Manuel and Jeremy McCarter. *Hamilton: The Revolution.* New York: Grand Central Publishing, 2016.

Mitchell-Kernan, Claudia. "Signifying, Loud-Talking, and Marking." In *Signifyin(g), Sanctifyin', and Slam Dunking: A Reader in African American Expressive Culture*, edited by Gena Dagel Caponi. Amherst: The University of Massachusetts Press, 1999, 309–30.

Mobb Deep. "Shook Ones, Part II." Track 15 on *The Infamous.* April 25, 1995. 1995 RCA Records, a Division of Sony Music Entertainment. Apple Music.

Monáe, Janelle. "Dirty Computer." Track 1 on *Dirty Computer.* April 27, 2018. 2018 Bad Boy Records LLC for the United States and Wea International Inc. for the World outside of the United States. Apple Music.

Monteiro, Lyra. "Race-Conscious Casting and the Erasure of the Black Past in Lin-Manuel Miranda's *Hamilton*." *The Public Historian* 38, no. 1 (February 2016): 89–98.

"Moon Meets the Sun (feat. Rhiannon Giddens, Amythyst Kiah, and Allison Russell)." Track 2 on *Songs of Our Native Daughters.* February 22, 2019. Smithsonian Folkways Recordings. Apple Music.

Morrison, Matthew. "Race, Blacksound, and the (Re)Making of Musicological Discourse." *Journal of the American Musicological Society* 72, no. 3 (Fall 2019): 781–823.

Morton, Thomas. "Known Zones: The Noisey Guide to ATL's Trap Map." *Noisey*. February 9, 2015. https://www.vice.com/en_us/article/7b7yag/known-zones-0000575-v22n2.

MTV. "Kendrick Lamar Breaks down Tracks from 'To Pimp a Butterfly'." *YouTube Video*, 1:44. March 31, 2015. https://www.youtube.com/watch?v=AUEI_ep9iDs.

MTV News. "Donald Trump Says He Would Vote for Eminem at the Shady National Convention." *YouTube Video*, 2:04. October 11, 2017. https://www.youtube.com/watch?v=SuSkOQsv9fg.

Neason, Alexandria. "Ahmaud Arbery, Breonna Taylor, and Covering Black Deaths." *Columbia Journal Review*. May 20, 2020. https://www.cjr.org/criticism/ahmaud-arbery-breonna-taylor.php.

The New York Times Magazine. *The 1619 Project*. August 2019: 4–98.

NFL. " Beyoncé & Bruno Mars Crash the Pepsi Super Bowl 50 Halftime Show." *YouTube Video*, 4:37. February 11, 2016. https://www.youtube.com/watch?v=SDPITj1wlkg.

———. "Colin Kaepernick Explains Why He Sat During National Anthem." August 27, 2016. https://www.nfl.com/news/colin-kaepernick-explains-why-he-sat-during-national-anthem-0ap3000000691077.

Nielson, Erik. "'Can't C Me': Surveillance and Rap Music." *Journal of Black Studies* 40, no. 6 (July 2010): 1254–74.

The Notorious B.I.G. "Going back to Cali." Track 16 on *Life after Death (Remastered Version)*. March 25, 1997. 1997 Bad Boy Records, LLC. Apple Music.

———. "Juicy." Track 1 on *The Notorious B.I.G.: Greatest Hits*. March 25, 1997. 2007 Bad Boy Records and Atlantic Records. Apple Music.

———. "Ten Crack Commandments." Track 9 on *The Notorious B.I.G.: Greatest Hits*. March 25, 1997. 2007 Bad Boy Records and Atlantic Records. Apple Music.

Obama, Michelle. *Becoming*. New York: Crown Publishing Group, 2018.

Ono, Yoko (@yokoono). 2016. "Dear Friends, I would like to share this message with you as my response to @realDonaldTrump love, yoko." *Twitter*, November 11, 2016, 4:21 PM. https://twitter.com/yokoono/status/797187458505080834.

Orejuela, Fernando and Stephanie Shonekan, eds. *Black Lives Matter & Music: Protest, Intervention, Reflection*. Bloomington: Indiana University Press, 2018.

"Origin of the Black Panther Party Logo." Source Material from the H.K. Yuen Archive. http://www.docspopuli.org/articles/Yuen/BPP_logo.html.

Osman, Ladan. "Slaying New Black Notions: Childish Gambino's 'This Is America.'" *World Literature Today* 92, no. 4 (2018): 40–1. https://doi.org/10.7588/worllitetoda.92.4.0040.

Peterson, James Braxton. *In Media Res: Race, Identity, and Pop Culture in the Twenty-First Century*. Lewisburg: Bucknell University Press, 2015.

Petri, Alexandra. "*Hamilton* and the End of Irony." *Washingtonpost.com*, September 21, 2015. https://www.washingtonpost.com/blogs/compost/wp/2015/09/21/hamilton-and-the-end-of-irony/

Pharoahe Monch. "Simon Says." Track 1 on *Simon Says – EP*. October 19, 1999. 2019 Trescadecaphobia Music. Apple Music.

Public Enemy. "State of the Union: STFU." Track 3 on *What You Gonna Do When the Grid Goes Down?* September 25, 2020. 2020 Enemy Records, LLC, under Exclusive License to Def Jam Recordings, a Division of UMG Recordings, Inc. Apple Music.

Ramler, Mari E. "Beyoncé's Performance of Identification As a Diamond: Reclaiming Bodies and Voices in 'Formation.'" *constellations: a cultural rhetorics publishing space* 1 (May 2018): 1–20.

Raine, Sarah, and Catherine Strong, eds. *Towards Gender Equality in the Music Industry: Education, Practice, and Strategies for Change.* New York: Bloomsbury Academic, 2019.

Rao, Sonia. *"This Is America": Breaking down Childish Gambino's Powerful New Music Video: Donald Glover's Video, Released over the Weekend, Appears to Reference Minstrel Characters and Police Brutality. Washington Post–Blogs.* Washington: WP Company LLC d/b/a The Washington Post, 2018.

Rapsody. "Rapsody – Ibtihaj ft. D'Angelo, GZA." *YouTube Video*, 5:14. August 2, 2019. https://www.youtube.com/watch?time_continue=44&v=jhMk_wLm07E&feature=emb_logo.

———. "12 Problems" (Extended Version). *YouTube Video*, 6:18. October 30, 2020. https://www.youtube.com/watch?v=_mkhkaw84k8.

Rath, Aron. "Trump Inherits Guantanamo's Remaining Detainees." *NPR News.* January 19, 2017. https://www.npr.org/2017/01/19/510448989/trump-inherits-guantanamos-remaining-detainees.

Reid, Gail. "Black Marching Bands." *Black Renaissance/Renaissance Noire* 14, no. 2 (Fall 2014): 166–73.

Reilly, Katie. "President Trump Again Blames 'Both Sides' for Charlottesville Violence." *TIME.* August 15, 2017. https://time.com/4902129/president-donald-trump-both-sides-charlottesville/.

Remarks by the President at 'Hamilton at the White House.' March 14, 2016. https://obamawhitehouse.archives.gov/the-press-office/2016/03/14/remarks-president-hamilton-white-house.

Richards, Chris. "It's a Brave New World. Why Is Our Protest Music Stuck in the Past?" *Washington Post.* September 4, 2019. https://www.washingtonpost.com/lifestyle/style/its-a-brave-new-world-why-is-our-protest-music-stuck-in-the-past/2019/09/03/7d9c1056-ca97-11e9-a4f3-c081a126de70_story.html.

Richardson, Elaine B. *African American Literacies.* New York: Routledge, 2003.

Richardson, Elaine B. and Alice Ragland. "#StayWoke: The Language and Literacies of the #BlackLivesMatter Movement." *Community Literacy Journal* 12, no. 2 (2018): 27–56.

Roberts, John Storm. *Latin Jazz: The First of the Fusions, 1880s to Today.* New York: Schirmer Books, 1999.

Roberts, Tyah-Amoy. *What Childish Gambino Gets Right—and Wrong—About Youth Culture in "This Is America": Gambino Criticizes Our Fascination with the Latest Dance Crazes While Injustice Is Happening All Around Us, Almost as If We Cannot Be Multidimensional Beings and Recognize Both. Washington Post–Blogs.* Washington: WP Company LLC d/b/a The Washington Post, 2018.

Robinson, Fatima. "A Tribe Called Quest Performs at the Grammys 2017." *Vimeo Video*, 5:28, November 26, 2018, https://vimeo.com/302978618.

Romano, Renee C. and Claire Bond Potter, Editors. *Historians on Hamilton: How a Blockbuster Musical Is Restaging America's Past*. New Brunswick: Rutgers University Press, 2018.

Rose, Joel. "911 Tapes Raise Questions in Fla. Teen's Shooting." *NPR*. March 19, 2012. https://www.npr.org/2012/03/19/148902744/911-tapes-raise-questions-in-fla-teens-shooting-death.

Rose, Tricia. *Black Noise: Rap Music and Black Culture in Contemporary America*. Hanover, NH: University Press of New England, 1994.

———. *The Hip Hop Wars: What We Talk about When We Talk about Hip Hop—and Why It Matters*. New York: Basic Books, 2008.

Ross, Kihana Miraya. "Call It What It Is: Anti-Blackness." *The New York Times*. June 4, 2020. https://www.nytimes.com/2020/06/04/opinion/george-floyd-anti-blackness.html?action=click&module=Opinion&pgtype=Homepage.

Run the Jewels. *RTJ4*. June 3, 2020. 2020 Jewel Runners LLC under Exclusive License to BMG Rights Management (US) LLC. Apple Music.

Russell, Allison. "Allison Russell – Dream of America." *YouTube Video*, 9:38. October 30, 2020. https://www.youtube.com/watch?v=cgMj1hb1_c0&feature=emb_logo.

Salcedo, Andrea, Sanam Yar, and Gina Cherelus. "Coronavirus Travel Restrictions, Across the Globe." *The New York Times*. July 16, 2020. https://www.nytimes.com/article/coronavirus-travel-restrictions.html.

Salt-N-Pepa. "Shoop." Track 8 on *The Best of Salt-N-Pepa: 20th Century Masters: The Millenium Collection*. February 5, 2008. An Island Records Release; This Compilation 2008 UMG Recordings, Inc. Apple Music.

Sayej, Nadja. "language, politics, and performance with laurie anderson." *i-D*. March 7, 2017. https://i-d.vice.com/en_uk/article/gyvxg7/language-politics-and-performance-with-laurie-anderson.

Schartel Dunn, Stephanie, and Gwendelyn Nisbett. "If Childish Gambino Cares, I Care: Celebrity Endorsements and Psychological Reactance to Social Marketing Messages." *Social Marketing Quarterly* 26, no. 2 (June 2020): 80–92. https://doi.org/10.1177/1524500420917180.

Schwartz, Matthew S. "Rapper 21 Savage Arrested by ICE for Allegedly Overstaying Visa." *NPR Music News*. https://www.npr.org/2019/02/04/691210275/atlanta-rapper-21-savage-arrested-by-ice-for-allegedly-overstaying-visa.

Schwindt, Oriana. "Grammy 2017 Ratings Rise from the Last Two Years." *Variety*. February 13, 2017. https://variety.com/2017/tv/news/tv-ratings-grammy-ratings-2017-1201986602/.

Searcy, Anne. "Bringing Dance back to the Center in *Hamilton*." *American Music* 36, no. 4 (Winter 2018): 448–66.

Selvaratnam, Tanya. "Art Is Essential to Democracy." *Howlround Theatre Commons*. January 18, 2018, https://howlround.com/art-essential-democracy.

SFJAZZ. "Laurie Anderson – Songs for Women [Excerpt] (Live at SFJAZZ)." *YouTube Video*, 3:39. December 31, 2019. https://www.youtube.com/watch?v=W5sOpqoDLKE&feature=emb_logo.

Silver, Sherrie. "This Is America (Official Dance Tutorial Pt 1) by Choreographer Sherrie Silver." *YouTube Video*, 6:50. May 14, 2018. https://www.youtube.com/watch?v=9wBiZtW77AE.

———. "This Is America (Official Dance Tutorial Pt 2) by Choreographer Sherrie Silver." Sherrie Silver. *YouTube Video*, 7:48. May 30, 2018. https://www.youtube.com/watch?v=suRvNYrwaAY.

Simmons, Kimberly Eison. "Race and Racialized Experiences in Childish Gambino's 'This Is America.'" *Anthropology Now* 10, no. 2 (May 4, 2018): 112–15. https://doi.org/10.1080/19428200.2018.1494462.

Simon & Garfunkel. "The Sound of Silence." Track 1 on *Sounds of Silence*. January 17, 1966. All Rights Reserved by Columbia Records, a Division of Sony Music Entertainment. Apple Music.

Slate. "The Black Lives Matter Movement Started with Hurricane Katrina." *Ebony*. August 24, 2015. https://www.ebony.com/news/the-Black-lives-matter-movement-started-with-hurricane-katrina-981/.

Smith, Ayana. "Blues, Criticism, and the Signifying Trickster." *Popular Music* 24, no. 2 (May 2005): 179–91.

Smitherman, Geneva. *Talkin and Testifyin: The Language of Black America*. Detroit: Wayne State University Press, 1977.

Smithsonian Folkways. "The Making of 'Mama's Cryin' Long' from 'Songs of Our Native Daughters'." *YouTube Video*, 7:47. December 13, 2018. https://www.youtube.com/watch?time_continue=25&v=M7PvWw97Cq0&feature=emb_logo.

Snoop Dogg (@snoopdogg). 2020. "I was murdered by an armed father and son who hunted me down and shot me as I jogged in a Georgia neighborhood." *Instagram*, May 8, 2020. https://www.instagram.com/snoopdogg/.

Spanos, Brittany. "'This Is America' Actor Talks Donald Glover, Easter Eggs, and Trayvon Martin's Dad." *Rolling Stone*. May 10, 2018. https://www.rollingstone.com/music/music-features/this-is-america-actor-talks-donald-glover-easter-eggs-and-trayvon-martins-dad-628222/.

Stice, Joel. "10 Symbols You Missed in Childish Gambino's 'This Is America,' Explained." *Buzzworthy*. 2018. https://www.buzzworthy.com/references-from-childish-gambino-this-is-america/.

Swanson, Carl. "Laurie Anderson and Marilyn Minter Want Us All to Scream Bloody Murder on the Anniversary of Trump's Election." *New York Vulture*. November 2, 2017. https://www.vulture.com/2017/11/laurie-anderson-marilyn-minter-scream-about-2016-election.html.

The Founder of #MeToo Doesn't Want Us to Forget Victims of Color. Films On Demand, 2017. https://fod.infobase.com/PortalPlaylists.aspx?wID=237067&xtid=145897.

The Late Show with Stephen Colbert. "Janelle Monáe Performs 'Americans'." *YouTube Video*, 4:23. July 21, 2018. https://www.youtube.com/watch?v=9ivqFkLYxp8.

The New York Times. "Ahmaud Arbery Shooting: A Timeline of the Case." *The New York Times*. May 21, 2020. https://www.nytimes.com/article/ahmaud-arbery-timeline.html.

"This Is America." Spotify Playlist. 2020. https://open.spotify.com/playlist/38rkXZt2CMSiC82S7RWumw.

TI (@troubleman31). 2020. "So fuckin sick of posting this shit Maaaaan..." *Instagram*. May 27, 2020. https://www.instagram.com/p/CAq0AMThMq9/?utm_source=ig_embed.

———. 2020. "There is no way in hell the officers responsible for murdering #breonnataylor can be allowed to walk free." *Instagram*. May 23, 2020. https://www.instagram.com/p/CAizvdYBhE8/?utm_source=ig_embed.

"Time's Up." *2020 Time's Up Now*. https://timesupnow.org.

Tinsley, Omise'eke Natasha. *Beyoncé in Formation: Remixing Black Feminism*. Austin: University of Texas Press, 2018.

Tity Boi (2 Chainz) (@2chainz). 2020. "I can't post the video, I can still see the killer with his hands in his pocket and knee on the neck of a handcuffed black man rest in peace #georgefloyd and I hate him and all the cops that was there for it." *Twitter*. May 27, 2020. https://twitter.com/2chainz/status/1265629729861898241.

TOI Staff. "Trump Accuses 'Hamilton' Cast of Harassing Pence with Post-Show Plea." *The Times of Israel*. November 19, 2016. https://www.timesofisrael.com/trump-accuses-hamilton-cast-of-harassing-pence-with-post-show-plea/.

Tretin, Joel. http://www.joeltretinphotography.com. Interviewed by Katie Rios via telephone. December 2019.

A Tribe Called Quest. "Award Tour." Track 3 on *Midnight Marauders*. November 9, 1993. 1993 Zomba Recording LLC. Apple Music.

———. "Can I Kick It?." Track 4 on *The Anthology*. October 26, 1999. 1999 Zomba Recording LLC. Apple Music.

———. "Movin Backwards." Track 5 on *We Got It from Here . . . Thank You 4 Your Service*. November 11, 2016. 2016 Epic Records, a Division of Sony Music Entertainment. Apple Music.

Trier-Bieniek, Adrienne, ed. *The Beyoncé Effect: Essays on Sexuality, Race, and Feminism*. Jefferson, NC: McFarland, 2016.

Trump Accuses *Hamilton* Cast of Harassing Pence with Post-Show Plea. *The Times of Israel*. November 19, 2016. https://www.timesofisrael.com/trump-accuses-hamilton-cast-of-harassing-pence-with-post-show-plea/.

Trump, Donald J. 2020. "I finally saw @HamiltonMusical last night." *Twitter*, November 20, 2016, 6:22 a.m. https://twitter.com/realDonaldTrump/status/800298286204723200.

Turner, Richard Brent. *Jazz Religion, the Second Line, and Black New Orleans after Hurricane Katrina*. Bloomington: Indiana University Press, 2017.

Updated: *Hamilton* Choreographer on Removing Muskets from Tonys Performance. June 12, 2016. http://www.playbill.com/article/breaking-hamilton-amends-tony-performance-in-light-of-orlando-tragedy.

UPROXX Video. "Talib Kweli & Rapsody Talk Rap Influences, Being Pro Black, Kendrick, Jay Z, Eve | People's Party." *YouTube Video*, 1:14:15. March 2, 2020. https://www.youtube.com/watch?v=HDL9fx9fBX0.

Victor, Daniel. "Janelle Monáe Brings a 'Time's Up' Message to the Grammy Awards." *The New York Times*. January 28, 2018. https://www.nytimes.com/2018

/01/28/arts/music/janelle-monae-kesha-grammy-awards-metoo.html?login=email&auth=login-email.

Vox. "Ibtihaj Muhammad Was the First US Olympian to Wear a Hijab." *YouTube Video*, 3:58. February 10, 2017. https://www.youtube.com/watch?v=mr5j-Lkk7rw.

Walser, Robert. "Out of Notes: Signification, Interpretation, and the Problem of Miles Davis." *The Musical Quarterly* 77, no. 2 (Summer 1993): 343–65.

Watkins, S. Craig. *Hip Hop Matters: Politics, Pop Culture, and the Struggle for the Soul of a Movement*. Boston, MA: Beacon Press, 2005.

Weinstock, Matt. "Six Artists Revisit Their Works from the Early '80s." *New York Times*. April 26, 2018. https://www.nytimes.com/2018/04/26/t-magazine/larry-clark-laurie-anderson-bill-t-jones-80s-work.html?fbclid=IwAR0F0zodTA3Ym1wZhjzDINBi9_pq_5q03ykb0Jo8EGMmpHxRLOFknT5hpHs.

Weiser, Benjamin and William K. Rashbaum. "In Steve Bannon Case, Prosecutors Have 'Voluminous' Emails." *The New York Times*. August 31, 2020. https://www.nytimes.com/2020/08/31/nyregion/steve-bannon-build-the-wall-fraud.html.

White, Miles. *From Jim Crow to Jay-Z: Race, Rap, and the Performance of Masculinity*. Champaign: University of Illinois Press, 2011.

The White House Office of the Press Secretary. "Remarks by the President at 'Hamilton at the White House'." March 14, 2016. https://obamawhitehouse.archives.gov/the-press-office/2016/03/14/remarks-president-hamilton-white-house.

Whitely, Sheila, and Jedediah Sklower, editors. *Countercultures and Popular Music*. Burlington, VT: Ashgate, 2014.

Wilkerson, Isabel. *Caste: The Origins of Our Discontents*. New York: Random House, 2020.

Williams, Justin A. "'We Get the Job Done': Immigrant Discourse and Mixtape Authenticity in *The Hamilton Mixtape*." *American Music* 36, no. 4 (Winter 2018): 487–506.

Willson, Olly. "Black Music as an Art Form." *Black Music Research Journal* 3 (1983): 1–22.

———. "The Heterogeneous Sound Ideal in African-American Music." In *Signifyin(g), Sanctifyin', and Slam Dunking: A Reader in African American Expressive Culture*, edited by Gena Dagel Caponi. Amherst: The University of Massachusetts Press, 1999, 157–71.

Wonder, Stevie. "Can't Put It in the Hands of Fate." Single. 2020 UMG Recordings Inc.

Wood, Alex. "Phillipa Soo Explains What Eliza's Gasp Means at the end of Hamilton." *WhatsOnStage*. July 30, 2020. https://www.whatsonstage.com/london-theatre/news/phillipa-soo-hamilton-gasp-meaning_52089.html?fbclid=IwAR3S7i_rdNqqEbLCeYCaZA4jwrFuV4tpV-cWXYZsdOLBxj6R9AxB8J9Y4tc.

Woods, Aleia. "Rappers Demand Justice for George Floyd, Who Was Killed by a Police Officer that Pinned Knee on Floyd's Neck." *XXL*. May 27, 2020. https://www.xxlmag.com/news/2020/05/rappers-justice-george-floyd-killed-police-officer/.

WORLDSTARHIPHOP. "YG & Nipsey Hussle 'FDT (Fuck Donald Trump)' (WSHH Exclusive – Official Music Video). YouTube Video, 4:57. April 18, 2016. https://www.youtube.com/watch?v=WkZ5e94QnWk.

Yancy, George. *Backlash: What Happens When We Talk Honestly about Racism in America*. Lanham, MD: Rowman & Littlefield, 2018.

Zapotsky Matt, Josh Dawsey, Rosalind S. Helderman, and Shayna Jacobs. "Steve Bannon Charged with Defrauding Donors in Private Effort to Raise Money for Trump's Border Wall." *The Washington Post*. August 20, 2020. https://www.washingtonpost.com/national-security/stephen-bannon-arrested-charged/2020/08/20/6d46847c-e2ea-11ea-b69b-64f7b0477ed4_story.html.

Zaynab. "Childish Gambino's 'This Is America' Criticized as 'House Slave' Trauma Porn." *Hot New Hip Hop*, February 12, 2019, https://www.hotnewhiphop.com/childish-gambinos-this-is-america-criticized-as-house-slave-trauma-porn-news.71790.html.

2Pac. "Holler if Ya Hear Me." Track 1 on *Strictly 4 My N.[*.*.*.*.].Z.* January 1, 1993. 1993 Interscope Records. Apple Music.

15MOFERADIO, "LL COOL J DROPS BLACK LIVES MATTER FREESTYLE." *YouTube Video*, 2:37. May 31, 2020. https://www.youtube.com/watch?v=xjNTLSR4DGo.

21 Savage. "a lot." Track 1 on *i am > i was*. December 21, 2018. 2018 Slaughter Gang, LLC under Exclusive License to Epic Records, a Division of Sony Music Entertainment. Apple Music.

———. "Monster." Track 13 on *i am > i was*. December 21, 2018. 2018 Slaughter Gang, LLC under Exclusive License to Epic Records, a Division of Sony Music Entertainment. Apple Music.

———. "21 Savage – A Lot Ft. J. Cole." *YouTube Video*, 6:31. February 1, 2019. https://www.youtube.com/watch?time_continue=260&v=DmWWqogr_r8&feature=emb_logo.

@thebryceisrightbih. 2020. "Minnesota riots are at another level. We need reform! We need justice! #georgefloyd #minnesota #copskillblackguy #xyzabc #fyp #protestors #riots." *TikTok Video*, May 29, 2020. https://vm.tiktok.com/KmYPpM/.

Index

Aamer, Shaker, 37
"Aaron Burr, Sir" (*Hamilton*), 129
Abdullah, Melina, 58
Abraham-Joseph, Shéyaa Bin. *See* 21 Savage
Adichi, Chimamda Ngozi, 17
African American Language (AAL), 84–85
Agawu, Kofi, 125
Alexander, Peter, 31–32
Ali, Wajahat, 17
Alipour, Touba, 19, 20, 24–28, 51, 89–90. *See also* "America" (Alipour's sculpture)
All Things Considered, 6
"a lot" (21 Savage's performance), 97–99
al-Qaeda, 101
"Alright," 10
Ambré, 104
"America" (Alipour's sculpture), 24–28, 90
American Civil Liberties Union (ACLU), 18, 36
American Music, 123, 125
American Revolution, 147
"Americans" (Monáe), 45, 70–73; kneeling as protest, 72; marching, 71–72; Richards on, 72–73; "snatch," 71
Anderson, Laurie, 8–9, 51, 67, 107; *The Art of Falling*, 16; ERST, 29–30; "From the Air," 25–26; *Habeas Corpus*, 16, 35–38; *Landfall*, 29–30; language and, 28–32; *The Language of the Future*, 34–35; "O Superman," 16; scream and, 32–34. *See also* One Year of Resistance (exhibit)
Anderson .Paak, 90
animation, 64–65
anti-Blackness, 109
Anzaldúa, Gloria, 17–18
Arbery, Ahmaud, 110–11
Aristophanes, *The Birds*, 16, 34–35
"Art Action Day," 16–19. *See also* One Year of Resistance (exhibit)
artists, 2–3; audience engagement, 3, 7–8; dress and fashion, 7–8; encoded resistance, 2–3; gestures, 3–4; props and accessories, 8
The Art of Falling (Anderson's performance), 16
Asghedom, Ermias Joseph. *See* Nipsey Hussle
Atlanta, 95
Atlantic, 2, 125

"At the Purchaser's Option," 45, 63–65, 69
Atwood, Margaret, 17, 34
audience engagement, 7

Baker, Peter, 31
Baldwin, James, 18, 45, 65
Bandele, Asha, 14n26, 50
Bannon, Steve, 20–21
"Bannon's First Snowman." *See* "Donald Trump's First Snowman" (Tretin's photograph)
Barré, Anthony. *See* Messy Mya
Barthes, Roland, 7
"The Battle of Yorktown" (*Hamilton*), 135–36
Bell, Sean, 113
berets, 59
Bernstein, Leonard, 141
Beyoncé, 9, 11, 38, 45; *Black Is King*, 45, 57; *Lemonade*, 52, 53, 55, 57. *See also* "Formation" (Beyoncé's Super Bowl performance and video)
Big Freedia, 54
BIPOC communities, 11
The Birds (Aristophanes), 16, 34–35
The Birth of a Nation, 67–69
Bishop, Henry, 95
"Black Actors Dress Up Like Slave Traders. . . and It's Not Halloween" (Reed), 125
"Black Girl in Maine" (Foster), 10
#BlackGirlsMatter, 45
Black Is King (Beyoncé), 45, 57
Black Lives Matter (#BlackLivsmatter), 9, 45, 50–52, 81, 132; cofounders, 51; foundation, 51; Hurricane Katrina and, 53; inclusivity, 51
"The Black Lives Matter Movement Started with Hurricane Katrina," 53
"Black Music as An Art Form" (Wilson), 126
Black Muslim American, 101
Black Panther Party, 59–60
Black Panther Party for Self Defense, 60
Black women, 45; marginalization of, 45
#BlackWomenMatter, 45
Blankenbuehler, Andy, 135–36, 141
Bloods (gang), 88
body movement of raised arms and hands, 56–57
Borderlands/La Frontera: The New Mestiza (Anzaldúa), 18
Bowie, David, 8
The Breakfast Club (podcast), 81
Breitbart News, 20–21, 30
Bring in 'da Noise, Bring in 'da Funk, 128
Broadus, Calvin Cordozar, Jr. *See* Snoop Dogg
Brooks, Rayshard, 100
Brown, Michael, 57, 84
Brown, Shelina, 32
Buckley, Cara, 48
Build: The Power of Hip Hop Diplomacy in a Divided World (Katz), 81–82
Bun B (Bernard James Freeman), 81
Burke, Tarana, 47–48, 50
Burkholder, J. Peter, 136
Bush, George W., 35
Busta Rhymes, 91, 92, 101, 132, 141

"Cabinet Battle #1" (*Hamilton*), 130, 141
"Cabinet Battle #2" (*Hamilton*), 130
Calvin the Second, 1–2
"Can't Put It in the Hands of Fate," 100
Cardi B (Belcalis Almánzar), 112
Carmichael, Rodney, 6, 100–101
Carmichael, Stokely, 60–61
Carr, Greg, 10
Carroll, Rebecca, 68
Carter, Dwayne Michael. *See* Lil Wayne
Carter, Jimmy, 16

chain gang, 83
Change.org, 112–13
Chapelle, Dave, 83
Charity, Justin, 107–8
Charleswell, Cherise, 58
Chernow, Ron, 131
Childress, Brian, 87
Childs, Dennis, 83
choreographed movements, 8
Cinque, Toija, 7–8
Civil War, 22
clave, 129
clothing, 7
Cole, Jermaine Lamarr. *See* J. Cole
Coleman-Singleton, Sharonda, 22
Collins, Patricia Hill, 46
Consequence (Dexter Raimond Mills Jr., rapper), 90, 91
Cook, Alicia Augello. *See* Keys, Alicia
Cooper, Anderson, 53
Cornish, Audie, 6
coronavirus pandemic. *See* COVID-19 pandemic
COVID-19 pandemic, 11–12, 25, 111
Craft, Elizabeth Titrington, 123, 132
#CREATEYOURFUTURE campaign, 104
Crips (blue), 88
Crossley, Nick, 3–5, 7, 34
Curry, Alaina, 112–13

DAMN (Lamar's album), 83
"Darkness" (Eminem's music video), 106–9; perspective, 106; reenactment of a mass shooting, 106; screens with news headlines, 107
Davis, Jordan William. *See* Q-Tip (Kamaal Ibn John Fareed)
Declaration of Independence, 6, 130
DeClue, Jennifer, 54–55
Diggs, Daveed, 130, 143, 145
digital media, 7
Dirty Computer (Monáe's album), 70
divisive politics, 45
Dixon, Brandon Victor, 124

"Donald Glover's 'This Is America' Holds Ugly Truths to Be Self-Evident" (Cornish and Evstatieva), 6
"Donald Trump's First Snowman" (Tretin's photograph), 20–21, 94
"Don't Let Go," 104
double consciousness, 96
Douthit, Patrick Denard. *See* 9th Wonder
Drayton, William Jonathan. *See* Flavor Flav
Driscoll, Christopher, 82–83
Du Bois, W. E. B., 96
Duke, David, 88

Ebony, 53
"Elements of a Typology of Musical Borrowing" (Burkholder), 136
el Gharani, Mohammed, 36–38
Elliott, Philip, 20
Emanuel African Methodist Episcopal Church, Charleston, South Carolina, 6, 22, 96
Eminem: anti-Trump sentiment, 93–95; "Darkness," 106–9; *The Eminem Show*, 107; *Encore*, 108; freestyle rap video, 93–94; "Framed," 93; Kajikawa on, 108; "Like Home" featuring Alicia Keys, 94–95; *Music to Be Murdered By*, 106; *Revival*, 93; Secret Service, 93; White on, 108
The Eminem Show (Eminem's album), 107
Encore (Eminem's album), 108
Epps, Tauheed K. *See* 2 Chainz
ERST (Electronic Representation of Spoken Text), 29–30
Eustis, Oskar, 127
Evans, Marlana. *See* Rapsody
Eve (Rapsody's album), 100–101
Evstatieva, Monika, 6

"Farmer Refuted" (*Hamilton*), 127
fashion, 7
"FDT" (YG's video release), 86–89

The Federation, 18
female hip-hop artists, 100
Fernandes, Sujatha, 114, 124
50 Cent (Curtis James Jackson), 82
"Fight the Power," 100
"Fight the Power: Remix 2020," 100
The Fire Next Time (Baldwin), 18
Flanders, Laura, 36–37
Flavor Flav, 13n26
Fleetwood, Nicole, 7
Floyd, George, 100, 112–14
Floyd, Samuel, Jr., 125, 141–42
"Formation" (Beyoncé's Super Bowl performance and video), 11, 45, 52–63, 101; attire, accessories and appearance, 59; backlash/negative reception, 58–59; Black femininity, 55; Black Panther Party references, 59–60; call-and-response, 63; duality of joy and sorrow, 57; Kai on, 52; marching, 61–63; political statement, 62–63; symbolic gestures, 52, 56–57; timing of performance, 60; transformation, 57; vocal sample/sonic dissonance, 54–55
Foster, Tiffany, 10
Francis, Jane, 56
Freeman, Bernard James. *See* Bun B
"From the Air," 25–26

Gambino, Childish, 1. *See also* "This Is America" (Gambino)
Gammage, Marquita, 58–59
gangs, 88
Garner, Eric, 112, 113
Garza, Alicia, 50
Gates, Henry Louis, Jr., 136, 143
gaze, 127
gender politics of hip-hop, 100
gestures of resistance, 3–4
Giddens, Rhiannon, 38, 45, 63–70, 100; "At the Purchaser's Option," 45, 63–65, 69; country music, 64; Facebook post, 63–64; on folk festivals, 64. *See also Songs of Our Native Daughters* (Giddens)
Gladney, Brooke, 87
Glasco, Yvette, 104, 105
Glover, Donald. *See* Gambino, Childish
Goldman, Russell, 31
Grammy performance of A Tribe Called Quest (2017), 89–93; dressing and appearance, 90; immigration bans, 89–90; movement versus absence of movement, 91, 92; symbolic changes at background, 91; visual markers, 91, 92
Grammy performance of Lamar (2016), 82–86; "Alright," 84–86; appearance and dressing, 83–84; "The Blacker the Berry," 84, 86; blank map of Africa, 86; body movement, 84; "Untitled 3," 85–86
Grandmaster Flash & The Furious Five, 141
Guan, Frank, 95–96
Guantánamo Bay detention camp, 35–38
gun laws, 106
guns, 23
"Guns and Ships" (*Hamilton*), 130

habanera rhythm, 129
habeas corpus, 36
Habeas Corpus (Anderson's performance), 16, 35–38
Hall, Tammy, 33–34
Hamilton (Miranda's musical), 11, 114, 123–47; African American musical traditions, 126–27; blues/blue notes, 127–28; call-and-response, 131–36; eighteenth-century ideals, 11; heterogeneity, 126–27; "island time" rhythm, 128–29; musical borrowings, 136–43, *137–40*; Obama, Barack on, 124, 135; Obama, Michelle on, 145; rap/rapping, 114, 129–31; reception, 123–25; Signifyin(g), 136–45, *144*; Trump, Donald on, 9, 124–25

Hamilton: The Revolution (Miranda and McCarter), 132, 136, 141
The Hamilton Mixtape (album), 141
The Handmaid's Tale (Atwood), 34
"Hands up, don't shoot," 57
Harris, Clifford Joseph, Jr. *See* TI (hip-hop artist)
Harris, Robin, 105
Haubegger, Christy, 50
"Helpless" (*Hamilton*), 128
Hernandez, Peter Gene. *See* Mars, Bruno
Heyer, Heather, 22
Hight, Jewly, 65–66
hijab, 101, 102
Hill, Lauryn, 100, 141
The Hip Hop and Obama Reader, 81
hip-hop as resistance to Trump administration, 81–114; "a lot" (21 Savage's performance), 97–99; Eminem's work, 93–95, 106–9; "FDT" (YG's video release), 86–89; Grammy performance of A Tribe Called Quest (2017), 89–93; Grammy performance of Lamar (2016), 82–86; Rapsody's work, 99–105; responses to police and civilian brutality, 109–14; rhetorical power, 82; solidarity, 81–82; "This Is America" (Gambino), 95–97, 114
Historically Black Colleges and Universities, 61
Hitchcock, Alfred, 107
Homecoming, 45, 61
"Home Sweet Home," 95
Howard, Theresa Ruth, 97
Hurd, Cynthia, 22
Hurricane Katrina, 53, 54, 57
Hurricane Sandy, 30

"Ibtihaj" (Rapsody's song), 101–3
Ice Cube (O'Shea Jackson), 82
immigrants, 132–33
Immigrations and Customs Enforcement (ICE), 98
improvisational movements, 8
Instagram, 111–12
It Ain't Nothing but the Blues, 128
"It's Quiet Uptown" (*Hamilton*), 134
Izadi, Elahe, 109–10

J. Cole, 98
Jackson, Curtis James. *See* 50 Cent
Jackson, Jesse, 53
Jackson, Keenon Dequan Ray. *See* YG ("Young Gangster")
Jackson, Michael, 59
Jackson, O'Shea. *See* Ice Cube
Jackson, Susie, 22
Jay-Z (Shawn Corey Carter), 53–54
Jeezy, 110
Jenkins, Jay Wayne. *See* Jeezy
Jim Crow, 1–2, 5, 10, 14n26, 96, 97
Joseph, Sayeed, 86
juba, 129

Kaepernick, Colin, 72, 94, 100
Kai, Maiysha, 52, 58
Kajikawa, Loren, 108, 123, 129, 130
Kamaal Ibn John Fareed. *See* Q-Tip (Kamaal Ibn John Fareed, born Jonathan William Davis)
Katz, Mark, 81–82
Kennedy, John, 35
Kernodle, Tammy, 100
Kesha, 70
Keys, Alicia, 94
Khan-Cullors, Patrisse, 14n26, 50
Kiah, Amythyst, 65
King, Martin Luther, Jr., 72
King, Peter, 59
Knowles-Carter, Beyoncé Giselle. *See* Beyoncé
Kornhaber, Spencer, 125
Ku Klux Klan (KKK), 20, 21, 67, 87–88, 94
Kuti, Fela, 5
Kweli, Talib, 101
Kwun, Aileen, 18

Lake Borgne, New Orleans, 57
Lake Pontchartrain, New Orleans, 57
Lamar, Kendrick, 10, 82–86. *See also* Grammy performance of Lamar (2016)
Lance, Ethel Lee, 22
Landfall, 29–30
Langone, Alix, 50
The Language of the Future (Anderson's performance), 34–35
La Opinion, 48
Lapolt, Dina, 98
Larese, James, 106
The Late Show with Stephen Colbert, 45, 70
LeMesurier, Jennifer Lin, 97
Lemonade (Beyoncé), 52, 53, 55, 57
leotards, 59
Lil Wayne (Dwayne Michael Carter), 82
Lincoln, Patrick, 104
Lindmark, Sarah, 28, 59
"Liquid Swords," 101
LL Cool J, 113–14
Lowndes County Freedom Organization, 60. *See also* Black Panther Party

Malcom X, 59–60
"Mama's Cryin' Long" (*Songs of Our Native Daughters*), 68–70
Mamo, Heran, 104
Mardi Gras Indians, 62
marginalization of women, 9
marginalized groups, 15
Markman, Rob, 86
Mars, Bruno, 62–63
Martin, Trayvon, 50–51, 85
Mathers, Marshall. *See* Eminem
Matsoukas, Melina, 54
Maxile, Horace J., 125–26, 130
McCalla, Leyla, 65
"The Message" (Grandmaster Flash & The Furious Five), 141
Messy Mya, 54
#MeToo movement, 9, 45, 47–50
Michalchyshyn, Laura, 18, 67

Middleton-Doctor, DePayne, 22
Milano, Alyssa, 47. *See also* #MeToo movement
Miller, Monica, 82–83
Miller, Zeke J., 20
Mills, Dexter Raymond, Jr. *See* Consequence (rapper)
"Minority Report" (Jay-Z), 53–54
Minter, Marilyn, 32
Miranda, Lin-Manuel, 11, 123; *Hamilton* (musical), 11, 114, 123–47; *The Hamilton Mixtape* (album), 141; *Hamilton: The Revolution* (with Jeremy McCarter), 132, 136, 141; involvement with politics, 123
Mitchell-Kernan, Claudia, 142–43
Monáe, Janelle, 9, 38, 45, 46, 70–73, 100; "Americans," 70–73; *Dirty Computer*, 70; Grammy speech, 70
Monteiro, Lyra, 125
"Moon Meets the Sun" (*Songs of Our Native Daughters*), 73
Moore, Christopher, 8
Morrison, Matthew D., 11
Muhammad, Ali Shaheed, 91
Muhammad, Ibtihaj, 101
Murai, Hiro, 10, 95
Music to Be Murdered By (Eminem's album), 106
Muslim Americans, 101
My Resistance Movement (Ali), 17
"My Shot" (*Hamilton*), 130, 131

National Endowment for the Arts, 17
National Endowment for the Humanities, 17
Neason, Alexandria, 111
Nelson, Prince Rogers. *See* Prince
The New Grove Dictionary of Music and Musicians, 136
New Orleans, 53, 54, 56
Newton, Huey, 60
The New Yorker, 67
The New York Times, 48, 110
Nielsen, Erik, 89

9th Wonder (Patrick Denard Douthit), 101–2
Nipsey Hussle, 86, 88. *See also* "FDT" (YG's video release)
"Non-Stop" (*Hamilton*), 129
Notes of a Native Son (Baldwin), 45, 67
Notorious B.I.G., 84, 141

Obama, Barack, 35; on *Hamilton* (Miranda's musical), 124, 135
Obama, Michelle, 145
Odom, Leslie, Jr., 127, 145
Olympic games, 101
One Year of Resistance (exhibit), 18–28; "America" (Alipour's sculpture), 24–28; "Donald Trump's First Snowman" (Tretin's photograph), 20–21; "Selling Guns Like Gumballs" (Tretin's photograph), 23. *See also* "Art Action Day"
Ono, Yoko, 32, 33
"O Superman," 16

pantomime, 135–36
Payne, John Howard, 95
Peer, Ralph, 64
Pence, Mike, 9, 124, 135
Petri, Alexandra, 123
Phife Dawg, 90, 92
Pinckney, Clementa, 22
Pinn, Anthony, 82–83
"Pop Culture without Culture: Examining the Public Backlash to Beyoncé's Super Bowl 50 Performance" (Gammage), 58–59
popular music, 4
Porgy and Bess (musical), 128
The Power of Hip Hop Diplomacy in a Divided World (Katz), 81–82
"Praying" (Kesha), 70
Prince, 73
Public Enemy, 13n26, 100; "State of the Union: STFU," 13n26
Public Theater, 127

Q-Tip (Kamaal Ibn John Fareed born Jonathan William Davis), 90–92

"Race, Blacksound, and the (Re) Making of Musicological Discourse" (Morrison), 11
Ragland, Alice, 45–46, 57, 84–85
Rapsody, 99–105; *Eve*, 100–101; "Ibtihaj," 101–3; "12 Problems," 103–5
Ratner, Leonard, 125–26
Redmond, Sean, 8
Reed, Ishmael, 125
Reid, Gail, 62
Revival (Eminem's album), 93
"Revolution," 104
Rice, Tamir, 113
Richards, Chris, 9–11, 72–73
Richardson, Elaine, 45–46, 57, 84–85
"Right Hand Man" (*Hamilton*), 131
Rimes, Shonda, 49
Roberts, John Storm, 62
Rolling Stone, 12, 64
Ross, Kihana Miraya, 109
RTJ4 (album by Run the Jewels), 12
Run the Jewels, 12, 14n30
"Run the Jewels Wish Their New Album Didn't Make So Much Sense Right Now," 12
Russell, Allison, 65–67

Sanders, Tywanza, 22
#SayHerName, 45
"The Schulyer Sisters" (*Hamilton*), 128, 130, 132
Scorsese, Jay, 102
The Scotsboro Boys, 128
scream, 32–34
Seale, Bobby, 60
Searcy, Anne, 123
Sebert, Kesha Rose. *See* Kesha
Second Lines, 62
Section 80 (Lamar's album), 83
Seijas, Esteisy, 130–31

"Selling Guns Like Gumballs" (Tretin's photograph), 23
Selvaratnam, Taynya, 18, 19, 67
September 11, 2001, terrorist attacks, 101
sexual assault/harassment/violence, 47–50. *See also* #MeToo movement; #TimesUp
"Shady National Convention," 93
Shady, Slim. *See* Eminem
Show Boat (musical), 128
Signifyin(g), Gates's conception of, 136
Silver, Sherrie, 95
Simmons, Daniel, 22
Simon and Garfunkel, 106, 107
slaves/slavery, 4, 83
Smalls, Biggie. *See* Notorious B.I.G.
Smith, Ayana, 143
Smith, James Todd. *See* LL Cool J
Smith, Trevor George, Jr. *See* Busta Rhymes
Snoop Dogg (Calvin Cordozar Broadus Jr.), 110
social injustices, 45
social justice movements, 9
social media platforms, 7
Songs of Our Native Daughters (Giddens), 45, 63–70; behind-the-scenes process, 68–69; collaboration, 65–66; "daughters" reference, 65; liner notes, 66–68; "Mama's Cryin' Long," 68–70; message of inclusivity, 66; "Moon Meets the Sun," 73
Soo, Phillipa, 134
The Sound of Silence (Simon & Garfunkel's album), 106
Sreenivasan, Hari, 47–48
"State of the Union: STFU," 13n26
"Stay Alive (Reprise)" (*Hamilton*), 133
Stice, Joel, 6
Still Brazy, 86
"The Story of Tonight" (*Hamilton*), 131
styles of art and music, 5

"Take A Break" (*Hamilton*), 130, 133
Taylor, Breonna, 100, 111–14
Taylor, Malik Izaak. *See* Phife Dawg
"Ten Crack Commandments" (Notorious BIG), 141
"Ten Duel Commandments" (*Hamilton*), 132, 141
The Testaments (Atwood), 34
Thank You 4 Your Service, 91
"That Would Be Enough" (*Hamilton*), 134
Thirteenth Amendment, 83
"This Is America" (Gambino), 1–2, 56, 95–97, 114; dances, 95; encoded gestures, 5–7; inclusion of gospel choir, 6, 22, 96; Jim Crow reference, 1–2, 5, 10, 96, 97; lyrics, 23; musical message, 1; reception, 9–11; TikTok videos, 114; violence, 6, 8, 95–97; who is watching whom, 2, 96; YouTube videos, 2
Thompson, Myra, 22
T.I. (Clifford Joseph Harris Jr.), 111–12
TikTok videos, 114
Time, 20
#TimesUp, 9, 45, 49–50
Tinsley, Omise-eke, 55–56
Tometi, Opal, 50
The Tonight Show Starring Jimmy Fallon, 97–99
Tony Awards, 135–36
To Pimp a Butterfly (Lamar's album), 82
Tretin, Joel, 19–23, 94; "Donald Trump's First Snowman," 20–21, 94; "Selling Guns Like Gumballs," 23
A Tribe Called Quest, 9, 89–93. *See also* Grammy performance of A Tribe Called Quest (2017)
Trump, Donald, 11; Alipour on, 26–28; anger at press conferences, 31–32; being racist, 22; on *Hamilton* (Miranda's musical), 9, 124–25; immigration bans, 17, 89–90; language and rhetoric, 30–32; Ono's scream as protest, 32; Twitter and tweets, 22, 31. *See also* Anderson, Laurie; "Art Action

Day"; hip-hop as resistance to Trump administration; *One Year of Resistance* (exhibit)
Turner, Nat, 67
"12 Problems," 103–5
21 Savage (Shéyaa Bin Abraham-Joseph), 97–99
2 Chainz (Tauheed K. Epps), 112

Unite the Right rally, 21–22
Untitled Space, 18. *See also One Year of Resistance*
untitled unmastered (Lamar's album), 82
"Uptown Funk" (Bruno Mars), 62, 63

"Wait for It" (*Hamilton*), 129, 131
Walker, Alice, 101
Walker, Kenneth, 111
Walker's 911, 114
Walser, Robert, 142
"War on Terror," 35, 101
Washington, Kamasi, 84
"Washington on Your Side" (*Hamilton*), 132
water, 57
"We Are Living in Eminem's White America" (Charity), 107–8
Weinstein, Harvey, 47
"We Shall Overcome," 10, 66
We Should All Be Feminists (Adichi), 17
West, Kanye, 54, 82
West Side Story (musical), 128, 141
"We the People," 11, 90

"What'd I Miss?" (*Hamilton*), 128, 134
When They Call You a Terrorist: A Black Lives Matter Memoir (Khan-Cullors and Bandele), 50
White, Joe, 130–31
White, Miles, 108
White/Whiteness/White supremacists, 10, 21–22
"Who Lives, Who Dies, Who Tells Your Story?" (*Hamilton*), 147
"Who Shot Ya?" (Notorious B.I.G.'s rap), 84
Williams, Justin, 123
Wilson, Brian, 70
Wilson, Olly, 126
Winbush, Calvin. *See* Calvin the Second
Wittgenstein, Ludwig, 29
The Wizard of, 95
Women's March in Nashville, 66
Woods, Aleia, 112
workplace, sexual assault/harassment at, 48–49. *See also* #TimesUp

Yancy, George, 10, 22
YG ("Young Gangster," Keenon Dequan Ray Jackson) 86–89. *See also* "FDT" (YG's video release)
"You'll Be Back" (*Hamilton*), 126–27, 132
Young, Damon, 58

Zhhong, Raymond, 31
Zip Coon, 5, 97

About the Author

Katie Rios is an associate professor of music history at the Townsend School of Music at Mercer University in Macon, GA. Before teaching at Mercer University, she taught at the University of North Carolina at Pembroke and the Jacobs School of Music at Indiana University, where she completed her doctorate in musicology. In her first year of teaching at Mercer University, she received the Townsend School of Music Outstanding Teacher Award. She lives in Woodstock, Georgia.

www.ingramcontent.com/pod-product-compliance
Lightning Source LLC
Chambersburg PA
CBHW061715300426
44115CB00014B/2699